DAVID RABY

MEXICO
IN TRANSFORMATION
from AMLO to CLAUDIA

PRAXIS PRESS 2025

THIS PAGE INTENTIONALLY BLANK

DAVID RABY

MEXICO IN TRANSFORMATION

from AMLO to CLAUDIA

COVER PICTURE CREDIT: Jesús Ramírez Cuevas

Print edition: 978-1-899155-21-7
Digital edition: 978-1-899155-22-4

Published by Praxis Press 2025
Email: praxispress@me.com
Website: www.redletterspp.com

Praxis Press
c/o 26 Alder Road
Glasgow, G43 2UU
Scotland, Great Britain

ADVANCE COMMENTS ON MEXICO IN TRANSFORMATION

Francisco Domínguez, retired academic and indefatigable solidarity activist in London

> Raby offers a captivating historical context of Mexico's ongoing 4T transformation, tracing the nation's journey from the 1517 Chakan-putún naval battle to pivotal moments in the struggles for justice and self-determination, led by figures like Guerrero, Hidalgo, Juárez, Villa, Zapata, Cárdenas, and others, up to AMLO and Sheinbaum. Combining sharp journalism, solid historiography, sociological insights, and keen political analysis, this is a must-read.

Julie Lamin, author, Chair, NSCAG, NEU observer at Mexico elections 2018

> As the voices of Trump and the far-right grow louder, David Raby's book brings hope to all with a social conscience. In the words of Andrés Manuel López Obrador, (AMLO) Mexican president from 2018 to 2024: "Hope is a veryå powerful force." Combining his expert knowledge and interviews with Mexicans, Raby conveys in clear prose and fascinating detail the far-reaching social changes of Mexico's 'quiet revolution', based on the principle For the Good of All, but First, the Poor. The governments of AMLO and his successor, Claudia Sheinbaum, prove that actions bringing lasting benefits speak the loudest.

Tony Burke, former Assistant General Secretary, Unite the Union

> Having worked alongside Mexico's democratic and independent trade unions for many years, the history of the transformation of Mexico by AMLO and Claudia Sheinbaum, and the struggle to end pro-employer 'contract unions', anti-workers legislation, corrupt and right-wing politicians and governments, David Raby's book tells the full story of that long struggle and how Mexico is now building a progressive future.

Jesús Ramírez Cuevas, AMLO´s press secretary, now presidential advisor to Claudia Sheinbaum

> David Raby's book provides the Anglo-Saxon public with a privileged vision of the progressive political change taking place in Mexico...His journalistic work is enriched with historical references, interviews with protagonists and documented political observations. [The book] is a stimulating journey through the democratic efforts of a people to build a more just, free, egalitarian and humane society.

Renata Turrent, Director of Mexican public TV channel 11

> [Raby's book portrays as a Revolutionary Transformation] the profound political and social regime shift taking place in Mexico. Unique to the world, it stands out as a transformation accomplished through democratic and peaceful means, making possible the unimaginable: a revolution without breaking a single window.

William A Booth, Lecturer in Latin American History, University College Låondon

> This is a most welcome and timely book which offers a closer view of AMLO, his rise to power, his relationship with the Mexican Revolution, and some of his most impactful policies. Raby is an engaging and provocative writer, without resorting to jargon or tub-thumping. Most importantly the book is written with enormous affection for Mexico, a country and society which deserves not just more attention, but more respect.

Napoleón Gómez Urrutia, leader of Los Mineros Union, *New York Times* best-selling author and Mexican Congress member

> In a world where dominant narratives often seek to perpetuate inequality and obscure historical struggles, David Raby's book emerges as an essential tool to understand the roots, challenges and achievements of Mexico's Fourth transformation. With a profound and well-documented perspective, the author maps the resistance and hope embodied by AMLO, Morena and the Mexican people in

> pursuing social justice and sovereignty. I celebrate this work for its rigour and because it inspires us to continue building a more dignified, united and humane Mexico. Undoubtedly, it is indispensable for those who believe in change and transformation.

Derek Wall, successful author, independent eco-socialist campaigner

> David Raby's fascinating account of Mexico's rapid progress towards a socially just and participatory future, could not be more timely or more important. The country's 'Fourth Transformation' inevitably generates a clash with Trump's atavistic rule, nonetheless while challenged by a resurgent Monroe doctrine, this book suggests that under Claudia Sheinbaum hope might defeat despair.

Étienne von Bertrab, Lecturer in Development Planning, University College London

> An extraordinary period of Mexico related by a curious and attentive historian with acute understanding of Latin America. With investigative rigour and enthusiasm in equal measure, David Raby explores key aspects of the Fourth Transformation (4T) project initiated by AMLO and continued by Mexico's first female president, Claudia Sheinbaum. Through an impressive collection of facts and explanations together with fascinating first-hand accounts, David sheds light on the significance of the 4T. In a sea of prejudices and disinformation, the book is an essential read for anyone trying to understand contemporary Mexico and why AMLO's project and legacy offer hope and lessons for a world in trouble.

Pablo Navarrete, founder and co-editor, Alborada (www.alborada.net)

> David Raby combines his scholarly expertise and commitment to social justice to offer a sweeping yet accessible account of the historic achievements and challenges that Mexico has experienced under the left-wing governments of AMLO and now Claudia Sheinbaum. Essential reading.

CONTENTS

PREFACE by Jeremy Corbyn, MP — ix

FOREWORD and Acknowledgements — xi

INTRODUCTION A Revolutionary Transformation — xiii

1	Revolution, reform and repression	1
2	Crisis and popular resurgence, 1988-2018	11
3	'Civic austerity' and fighting corruption	23
4	Creating a welfare state in the context of a pandemic	31
5	Universal health care becomes a reality	41
6	'Sowing life': rural communities as a priority	47
7	Public Works: the Tren Maya	53
8	Justice for the native people	63
9	Dealing with the Colossus of The North	75
10	Reviving Mexico's Latin American Identity	89
11	Resource sovereignty: oil, gas, electricity and lithium	103
12	Crime, the military and public order	113
13	Labour, women and Mexican humanism	129

CONTENTS

14	Campeche: transformation despite problems	141
15	Acapulco: much more than disaster relief	153
16	The 2024 elections	159
17	The Transition: Claudia Presidenta	171
18	Claudia in office: the transformation continues	179
19	Conclusion	187
20	Bibliographical Note	193

Foreword

The day before AMLO was inaugurated in 2018 we had a long conversation about the future of Mexico. Amongst other things he told me he most admired the principal of the National Health Service and would love Mexico to achieve a similar style of welfare state. We also talked of economic transformation and environmental sustainability.

AMLO and Claudia walk in the footsteps of all the struggles of Mexican independence, the civil war and the 1917 constitution.

Mexico's radical strength is its history, people, understanding and respect for its ancient past. A respect empowered by love and respect for art, music and literature.

As Mexico now navigates a future where the problematic relationships with the USA have become even more complicated, its role in the leadership of Latin America and its place in the world as a voice for justice, peace and understanding is ever more important.

The huge social problems and inequality have to be tackled, the horrendous levels of historic corruption and drug related violence have to be tackled too.

David Raby's work is a great and realistic account of the way AMLO and now Claudia have managed to address the issues of inequality and poverty by investment in infrastructure, health and education. Above all an investment and empowerment of people.

A long developed and huge social movement propelled AMLO into office at the third attempt and then firmly voted for Claudia Sheinbaum.

In this complicated and violent century we need Mexico's non-alignment, and above all, a sense of hope.

Jeremy Corbyn, MP
Islington North, London

THIS PAGE INTENTIONALLY BLANK

Preface and Acknowledgements

Although I have an academic background, this is not an academic book. It is a committed book intended for a broad audience, above all in Britain and the English-speaking world. It is based on the conviction that Mexico's Fourth Transformation is a revolutionary process of global importance, whose significance has not yet been generally appreciated; it is informed by my academic training in history, thoroughly researched and referenced, but presented (I hope) in an accessible style.

Among those who have provided support and encouragement are my partner Luisa, whose love for Mexico and identification with its Transformation have since 2019 become if anything even greater than mine; Francisco Domínguez, Chilean exile and academic with indefatigable commitment to Latin American solidarity; Étienne von Bertrab, Mexican academic at University College London working on sustainable development and critical support for the Transformation of his homeland; and Tony Burke, trade union and solidarity activist. Much of the material in this volume was previously published in articles in the *Morning Star* newspaper and the Labour Outlook and Public Reading Rooms UK websites, and the support of their staff should be recognised. Then there is the critical moral support of Jeremy Corbyn MP and his partner Laura Álvarez, both committed to Mexico and its transformation. Recognition is also due to the Mexican Ambassador in London, Josefa González Blanco, whose infectious enthusiasm is a constant inspiration for those interested in her country. Other Mexicans and friends of Mexico in the UK who deserve a mention are Manuel Ruiz-Adame, Enrique Sáenz de Sicilia, María Pérez Ramos and William A Booth of University College London.

MEXICO IN TRANSFORMATION

In Mexico thanks are due to Napoleón Gómez Urrutia, leader of the Mining and Metallurgical åWorkers' Union Los Mineros and Morena Congress member; to Clara Brugada, Mayor of Iztapalapa and now Metro Mayor of the capital; Jesús Ramírez Cuevas, AMLO's media secretary and now Coordinator of Presidential Advisors; Violeta Vázquez Rojas, journalist and linguist at El Colegio de México; the satirical team of Los Chamucos ("The Devils"), in particular Pepe Hernández; Governor Layda Sansores of Campeche and her team, especially Elvira Nájera Danieli, Institutional Coordinator, Walther Patrón, Communications Secretary, and Esteban Hinojosa, Culture Secretary; Dra Alejandra Maza of the Mexico City Health Department; Eduardo Carmona, formerly of the Mexico City administration and now at INECC, the National Institute of Ecology and Climate Change; Renata Turrent, former Morena Congress member & now head of Channel 11 public TV; Gonzalo Ballesteros, civil servant; Hans Salazar, journalist; Meme Yamel, journalist; and John Ackerman, journalist and academic.

Finally a word of recognition to author Carlos Martínez and to my publisher, Kenny Coyle of Praxis Press, without whom this book would not have seen the light of day.

David L Raby
Norwich, UK

Introduction

A Revolutionary Transformation

For decades Mexico seemed unchanging, locked in a corrupt one-party state under the PRI (*Partido Revolucionario Institucional*, Institutional Revolutionary Party) which maintained a relatively progressive foreign policy and a tradition of asylum for those fleeing persecution elsewhere with corruption and repression at home. It remained apart from the dramatic struggles unfolding elsewhere in Latin America.

A serious electoral challenge from the left was defeated in 1988 by blatant fraud, and PRI policy turned further to the right with accelerated neoliberal privatisations and even greater corruption under Carlos Salinas de Gortari (1988-94). The only episode to hit the international headlines was the 1994 Zapatista uprising, heroic but largely frustrated: mostly limited to one of 32 states of this vast country, it ultimately had more international impact than in Mexico itself. The struggle for democracy and social justice would continue by more conventional means.

When the PRI was finally defeated in 2000 it was by the right-wing PAN (*Partido de Acción Nacional*, National Action Party) which offered more of the same, but worse. For three more six-year presidential terms PAN and PRI alike imposed unbridled neoliberal policies with greatly increased inequality and corruption.

AMLO's historic victory

But in July 2018 came dramatic change with the victory of Andrés Manuel López Obrador (known by his initials as AMLO) and his Morena party (*Movimiento de Regeneración Nacional*, Movement of National Regeneration). Coming from the left of the traditional establishment, AMLO ran for the presidency twice before and was defeated, almost certainly by fraud. But this time he won dramatically with 53%å of the vote in a three-way race, something quite unprecedented. Not only this, but his party won at all levels of government: both houses of Congress, several state governors and assemblies and many local governments.

This came about because over decades AMLO had shown enormous dedication and persistence in uniting the popular opposition, travelling the length and breadth of the country, and he ran a campaign concentrating on a few basic themes: real democracy, fighting corruption, ending impunity and providing benefits for the poor.

Mexico's importance is obvious: it has the second largest population in Latin America (130 million, following Brazil's 215 million), the third largest territory (after Brazil and Argentina), and a crucial situation bordering the USA, in some ways a curse but also of enormous geopolitical significance.

Conservatives have predictably condemned AMLO as a "populist", and many leftists have dismissed him as a timid reformist or worse. This book will argue that the critics are profoundly mistaken, and that (1) AMLO is in fact a radical leader whose long-term impact is potentially revolutionary; (2) that he and Morena represent the 21st-century resurgence of Mexico's revolutionary tradition going back at least to the great 1910-21 upheaval; and (3) that Mexico has since 2018 played the leading role in Latin America's second so-called "Pink Tide", and now with Claudia Sheinbaum its importance is greater than ever.

AMLO is not Hugo Chávez, and Mexico is not Venezuela. AMLO's style was very different: calm, measured, polite (although direct and at times rich in irony). He was quite clear that he was proposing a programme of radical change: the "Fourth Transformation" in Mexico's history (the first three being the independence struggle against Spain from 1810 to 1821, the liberal Reform movement under indigenous President Benito Juárez in the 1850s and 1860s, and the epic Revolution from 1910 to 1921). The first three all achieved fundamental changes, but at the cost of great conflict and violence. The Fourth Transformation (4T) is peaceful and democratic.

With the 4T AMLO was clearly proclaiming revolutionary intent, despite the fact that at the time of his victory the hemispheric outlook seemed overwhelmingly negative, with Trump in power in the US and right-wing presidents in Brazil, Colombia, Argentina and Chile.

'Civic Austerity': leading by example

From day one AMLO led by example, slashing his own presidential salary by 60% and calling on all high public officials, whether elected or appointed, to do the same. He refused to live in the traditional presidential mansion which has been turned into a museum and public meeting hall. Luxury spending by public officials was banned: no expense-account meals, no five-star hotels, no first-class travel, nor private cars or aircraft at public expense. AMLO announced he would sell the presidential airliner, and he flew economy class on ordinary commercial flights.

This is the meaning of his much-misunderstood plan of *"Austeridad Republicana"*, Civic Austerity: austerity for public officials, not for working people. "There cannot be a rich government with a poor people". A crucial component of this, with much wider political implications, was his abolition of the 8,000-strong Presidential Guard which was not only extremely expensive but had also served as a repressive praetorian force.

Another key element of the 4T Transformation is direct and constant communication with the people: AMLO held morning press conferences (*mañaneras*) every working day, from Monday to Friday at 7am, where he and his ministers presented policy and fielded questions from all and sundry. These sessions typically lasted two hours or more, and were attended by journalists from all types of conventional and social media, both mainstream and alternative. The President listened and responded to all with remarkable patience and openness, and now Claudia Sheinbaum is doing the same.

AMLO insisted on dialogue, constantly criticising the conservative opposition but always recognising their right to their opinions, insisting that he would never impose censorship of any kind: they could question him, attack him, insult him, and he would exercise his right of reply but allow total freedom of expression. Time and again he quoted Benito Juárez, "Nothing by Force, Everything by Reason". Also with his ministers and staff he travelled all round the country, typically at weekends, supervising public works, talking and listening to people in local communities. He really worked a seven-day week and encouraged his team to do likewise.

In economic and fiscal policy AMLO did not conform to leftist conventions: "civic austerity" was accompanied by a pledge not to raise taxes, when Mexican tax rates are far from excessive. But what the President did was to insist that all must pay their taxes, without exception: he greatly strengthened the tax collection department of the Finance Ministry, outlawing tax holidays and exemptions whether for wealthy individuals or corporations. He also repeatedly declared that corruption was Mexico's greatest problem, and while no-one would be persecuted on the basis of rumours, all documented allegations of corruption would be investigated and pursued in the courts.

Although with difficulty – corruption was pervasive, especially in the judicial system – significant progress was quickly apparent and real tax receipts rose substantially. By not raising tax rates and avoiding borrowing, the government gained credit in financial markets, and contrary to establishment predictions the peso stabilised and then began to appreciate against the dollar. Recognising that Civic Austerity, slashing luxury spending and avoiding waste, was for real, and that the anti-corruption campaign was more than just rhetoric, many corporations increased investment and showed a willingness to negotiate over tax payments: Walmart agreed to pay $350 million in back taxes. While the most conservative (and corrupt) business sectors remained hostile, several prominent magnates (the most notable being Carlos Slim) began to cooperate with AMLO.

For the Good of All, but First, the Poor

The result was that public investment and social spending could now increase substantially without inflation. The President's slogan "For the Good of All, but First, the Poor" soon began to produce results with the first truly universal public pension for senior citizens; incapacity benefits, at first limited to certain age groups but then extended to become universal; scholarships (grants) for all students from deprived families in public education; apprenticeships for young people in neither education or employment; and other welfare schemes. One of the most important programmes was *Sembrando Vida*, "Sowing Life", an agroforestry scheme providing grants to small peasant farmers, combining traditional agriculture with reforestation and ecological practices.

A key element of the welfare schemes was that all benefits were to be paid directly from the national treasury (*Hacienda*) to beneficiaries, eliminating corrupt intermediaries. This took time to implement, but was gradually made effective with the creation of a public Welfare Bank (*Banco del Bienestar*) which by 2024 would have over 2,700 branches, making it the most complete banking network in the country and eliminating the reliance of the poor on the exploitative practices of commercial banks.

Another essential goal was to overcome the chronic deficiencies of Mexico's health system, which had provided free coverage to public-sector workers but not to the majority of those in the informal economy, and even in the public sector had deteriorated with neoliberal privatisation. The Covid pandemic complicated matters, but unwavering commitment would lead to creation of something approaching a real Mexican NHS by the end of AMLO's term.

While working astutely to maintain market confidence, AMLO also made it clear from the start that he wanted to restore the capacity of the public sector to invest in strategic areas, ending neoliberal asset-stripping. PEMEX, the national oil and gas enterprise inherited from the landmark 1938 expropriation of foreign companies by President Lázaro Cárdenas but reduced to an empty shell by privatising measures culminating in Peña Nieto's 2013 "Energy Reform", was to be restored to primacy in hydrocarbon production. Similarly in electric power generation and distribution, the public CFE (*Comisión Federal de Electricidad*, Federal Electricity Commission), also marginalised by neoliberal privatisations, was to become once again the prime mover.

Again, with remarkable tactical astuteness AMLO reasserted public sector energy primacy not by headline-grabbing nationalisations but by anti-corruption measures, demonstrating that privatising contracts with companies like Spain's Iberdrola had been plagued by graft on an enormous scale. This was of course easy to demonstrate and was used as a legal basis to annul the contracts.

Astute relations with the US and solidarity with Latin America

But where AMLO revealed a political capacity bordering on genius was in his handling of relations with the Colossus of the North, the United States. While campaigning he had, quite rightly, been scathing in his denunciation of President Donald Trump's racist attacks on Mexican migrants, his plan to build a border wall and his threat of a 25% tariff on Mexican imports. Once in office, AMLO prioritised negotiation, sending his very capable Foreign Secretary Marcelo Ebrard to engage in talks and persuading Trump to drop the tariff proposal in return for new arrangements on migration.

Also, where Trump had threatened to abandon the Free Trade Treaty – a measure which would have been bad for the US and catastrophic for Mexico – AMLO surprised observers by achieving a far-reaching renegotiation in which the Energy Sector was excluded, recognising Mexican energy sovereignty; labour rights on both sides of the border were recognised for the first time; and small and medium businesses were explicitly included in the benefits of free trade. Early in July 2020 AMLO flew to Washington with Marcelo Ebrard and other key members of his Cabinet, and in a remarkable series of meetings and public ceremonies, the new USMCA (US-Mexico-Canada Agreement) was signed.[1]

Leftist critics predictably condemned this as capitulation to Trump, but they could not be more mistaken. Given the reality of a 3,150 km common border, the presence in the US of nearly 40 million first- and second-generation Mexican immigrants, and the existing level of economic integration, cooperation was essential, and what AMLO and his team achieved was extraordinary.

The new trade agreement was the most visible manifestation of a reassertion of Mexico's long tradition (abandoned by preceding neoliberal administrations) of non-intervention and respect for the sovereignty and self-determination of all nations, beginning with Mexico itself. Confrontation was to be avoided, and Mexico would seek good relations with its great northern neighbour regardless of ideology, but on a basis of mutual respect.

This reassertion of sovereignty was also manifest in the revival of Mexico's Latin American identity, assuming an active role in CELAC (the Community of Latin American and Caribbean States) and good relations with Cuba and Venezuela among others. The most dramatic example of this came with the coup against Evo Morales in Bolivia in November 2019, with AMLO's immediate action in sending a Mexican Air Force plane with both military and diplomatic staff on board to rescue the deposed Bolivian

President[2]. They saved Evo's life, and Bolivian revolutionaries have not forgotten.

Mexico also played a key role in the progressive Puebla Group of Latin American politicians, intellectuals and diplomats, founded in the Mexican city in July 2019, and gave significant support to the reforming government of Argentina under Alberto Fernández from December 2019 onwards. Mexico exercised the rotating presidency of CELAC for two years (2019-21) and did much to revive the organisation which had been in decline, leading the way in promoting new institutional activities and financing for the regional organisation.

Finally, Mexico under AMLO took a remarkably strong stance in support of Cuba, repeatedly condemning the US blockade, not just in words but in actions, providing much-needed supplies delivered by Mexican naval vessels when the US tightened restrictions. This is another remarkable example of how AMLO has succeeded in maintaining good relations with Washington while openly defying its Latin American policies, an approach which is continuing under Claudia Sheinbaum.

Infrastructure and the military

Another area in which AMLO has confounded the critics is infrastructural investment: roads, railways, ports, airports, irrigation works. Recovery of PEMEX required investment in restoring oil refineries and building a new one at Dos Bocas, Tabasco, not to increase oil production but to ensure that what is produced is refined in Mexico for domestic use, rather than the neoliberal policy of exporting crude oil while importing refined products. Similarly, as the Mexico City airport was heavily overburdened, both PAN and PRI were planning a vast new airport in the Lake Texcoco area, at enormous expense and doing immense ecological damage to a sensitive wetland area. AMLO campaigned against this and won a popular vote on the subject, cancelling the existing plan and building an alternative airport at the Santa Lucía airbase north of the capital, for less than half the cost and much less environmentally damaging.

Then came railways, above all, the Mayan Railway (*Tren Maya*), over 1,500 km in the southeast region, looping round the Yucatán peninsula. In part it restored the old Southeastern Railway initiated by Lázaro Cárdenas in 1937 and completed in 1950, which had provided both passenger and goods services for some four decades before being abandoned in the neoliberal era.

The *Tren Maya* represents the biggest public investment in the neglected and impoverished southeast in living memory, indeed probably the biggest ever. It has been the object of sustained and vitriolic criticism on ecological grounds, criticisms which are absurd in that existing development in the region was based on uncontrolled speculative tourist development of Cancún and the "Mayan Riviera" with no consideration of the environment, and many of the critics are linked to the corrupt tourist operators. The new railway serves Mayan archaeological sites and historic colonial cities as well as beach resorts, with good long-term employment of local people, promoting local produce and culture, with environmentally sensitive design and subsidised fares for local inhabitants. It has been built in record time by a combination of public and private investors, much of it was already functioning as of May 2024, and it is extremely popular with local people. AMLO made it clear that this was intended to be the beginning of a long-term plan to restore rail passenger services throughout the country, and Claudia Sheinbaum has been even more categorical on this, insisting that she will restore passenger trains on more than 3,000 km of track.

This and other infrastructural projects will be examined in detail later; what is striking is the efficiency of design and execution of these ambitious projects. All too often progressive governments fail through inefficient execution of ambitious projects; AMLO confounded the critics by efficient and cost-effective public investment far superior to the corruption-plagued efforts of his predecessors.

Infrastructural investment was directly linked to what for many was AMLO's most controversial policy, his alliance with the military and reliance on them in many areas. He has argued that civilian politicians and civil servants were often more corrupt than the military, and that in repressive actions and human rights abuses it was the politicians who were mainly responsible, with the military just obeying orders. He also stressed the revolutionary origins of the Mexican military and their identification with national identity and traditions, as "the people in uniform", a concept typical of radical regimes elsewhere (Cuba, Venezuela, Nicaragua). The commitment of the military to the 4T Transformation is complete, and now they have surprised many by their acceptance – indeed enthusiastic support – of Claudia Sheinbaum as the first female Commander-in-Chief.

It should be apparent from this brief summary that there is a powerful case for viewing AMLO as not just progressive but revolutionary, and those who dismiss him are much mistaken. The fact that he ended his term with exceptional popularity ratings, and handed over to an equally popular woman committed to continuation of the 4T Transformation, is confirmation of his historic stature. He described his philosophy of government as "Mexican Humanism", a concept which has been accepted now by Claudia Sheinbaum.

Claudia's first two months in office have been remarkably successful and she has proved to be every bit as capable and committed to the Fourth Transformation as was AMLO, and very firm and direct in her public statements. The prospects for Mexico were looking very good until 8 November 2024 and the comprehensive victory of Donald Trump in the US elections. Given Trump's hostile declarations and the inclusion in his cabinet of right-wing extremist Marco Rubio (leader of the most anti-

Communist Cuban-American mafia), the prospects are alarming. However, Mexico could not be better prepared to resist than with Claudia Sheinbaum and a highly motivated population in the Morena party and its allies.

NOTES

1 D L Raby, "AMLO in the Lion's Den", https://prruk.org/amlo-in-the-lions-den/, published 14 July 2020.
2 Andrés Manuel López Obrador, *A la Mitad del Camino*, México 2021: Planeta, pp 138-174.å

AMLO (above) and Sheinbaum (left) have won dramatic victories for social progress.

1

Revolution, reform and repression

The great Mexican revolution that began in 1910 is known to most people only through folklore and Hollywood stereotypes. Many will have a romantic image of peasant leader Emiliano Zapata (although possibly now only through the neo-Zapatistas of recent decades who borrowed his name), and possibly also of Francisco (Pancho) Villa, regarded primarily as a bandit.

Those with at least a passing knowledge of Mexican history may be aware that these two popular revolutionaries appeared briefly to have triumphed in 1914, only to be defeated subsequently by more bourgeois leaders who outmanoeuvred them over the next three to four years.

For most socialists, whether reformist or revolutionary, the Mexican revolution was then overshadowed by the Bolshevik revolution in Russia and by other socialist movements in Europe and Asia; regarded as lacking a structured political party or clear ideology, it is dismissed as an heroic failure.

This negative vision is seriously misleading: although partially neutralised, the revolutionary impetus did not disappear, and the Constitutionalist movement which triumphed from 1916 onwards was profoundly influenced by anarcho-syndicalist and Marxist intellectuals and insurgents who inspired a radical vision and praxis with no parallel in the Western hemisphere at the time.

They produced a Constitution in February 1917 which confirmed the separation of Church and State, promised universal secular education, declared land and subsoil rights (minerals) to be the eminent domain of the Nation, recognised peasants' right to land, and promised labour rights including the right to strike and to organise.

Mass insurgency had completely destroyed the old federal army of the dictatorship, and the new Mexican army institutionalised from 1917 onwards had revolutionary roots.

Origins and character of Mexico's great revolution

To understand the revolution it is necessary to realise that it was a reaction against three and a half decades of dictatorship under Porfirio Díaz, himself a former liberal insurgent; and that Díaz's rule was the Mexican manifestation of the global capitalist and imperialist boom which prevailed from roughly 1870 to the First World War.

The first industrial revolution in Britain had reached its apogee by the 1860s, and as the USA emerged strengthened from its Civil War, German and Italian unification and the Meiji restoration in Japan paved the way for industrialisation in those countries. The colonial carve-up of Africa and Oceania reflected an unprecedented rush for mineral and agricultural resources and cheap labour.

Latin American countries, most of them already independent, now underwent the first great experience of neocolonialism. Mexico in particular, having lost slightly more than half its original territory to the US in the war of 1846-48, had also just suffered a major French invasion.

This had already produced a radical reaction in Mexico with the Liberal Reform movement led by the great indigenous president Benito Juárez (described by AMLO as the country's greatest leader). Despite all the setbacks, this established the principle of secularism, separation of Church and State, which would never be abandoned and in which Mexico was far ahead of other Latin American countries. Civil registration of births, deaths and marriages and the right to divorce were also adopted well in advance of other countries in the region.

Porfirio Díaz, backed by global capital, would preside over a boom of mining, commercial agriculture, building of railways and ports and early industrialisation, but at the expense of extreme inequality, looting of resources and expropriation of indigenous and peasant lands far exceeding what had occurred in 300 years of Spanish colonial rule.

Resistance was brutally repressed, with the crushing of the Mayan Indian revolt in the Yucatán and the Yaquis in Sonora. Thousands of Yaquis were deported to the Yucatán (4,000 km away at the opposite end of the country) to work as virtual slaves (debt peons) on henequén (sisal hemp) plantations alongside the local Mayans.

Labour rights were non-existent and strikes were suppressed by force, in the mines, on the railways and in textile factories. Great symbolic and practical importance pertains to the June 1906 strike at the Greene Consolidated Copper Co. in Cananea, Sonora, repressed by Mexican state and federal forces assisted by hundreds of US filibusters;[1] and to the January

1907 textile strike in Rio Blanco, Veracruz, where over 200 workers and members of their families were shot point-blank by troops[2].

Such brutality inevitably led to political radicalisation, for example with the formation of the Mexican Liberal Party led by Ricardo Flores Magón, of anarcho-syndicalist ideology and linked to the Industrial Workers of the World across the US border (indeed this Party already existed before the strikes, and *Magonistas* were involved in the protests).

It is no accident that today AMLO refers to the neoliberal period from 1983 to 2018 as "Neo-Porfirismo", a contemporary expression of the same imperialist, exploitative and repressive tendencies as the Porfirio Díaz era. While the massive upsurge in imperialist exploitation in the Díaz period led to partially successful reform movements in several Latin American countries, particularly those that experienced large-scale European immigration (Argentina, Uruguay, Brazil, Chile), it was only in Mexico that it produced a mass popular revolution. This was clearly a result of the country's peculiar experience of large-scale invasion by the US and France combined with the existence of an extensive communal and indigenous peasantry and an emerging working class exposed to global ideological influences.

The sequence of events leading to the initial revolutionary upheaval was also exceptional. In 1910, the centenary of the independence revolt against Spain, with Díaz turning 80 and hinting that he might retire, he reneged on this decision and arranged to be "re-elected" yet again. With unrest spreading, a most unlikely figure, Francisco I Madero – scion of one of Mexico's wealthiest families, but having studied in France and California and acquired surprisingly democratic ideals – stood as opposition candidate and campaigned all over the country. Arrested and jailed, he escaped and crossed the border into Texas, issuing a call (his "Plan of San Luís Potosí") for the people to rise up in revolution on 20 November 1910.

Madero had recruited a number of followers and many others knew of his Plan and sympathised. On 20 November several small groups did take up arms, and over the next two months revolt spread, leading to extensive conflict. By May, Díaz's federal army (which had not faced serious combat in 40 years) was falling apart; the dictator left for Europe and in June Madero entered Mexico City in triumph.[3]

With scrupulous respect for constitutional protocol, Madero allowed a caretaker provisional President to take charge and waited for free elections to be held (the first truly democratic elections in Mexico), and became President in November 1911. But he swiftly discovered that the conservative opposition – great landlords and capitalists, both Mexican and foreign – were not willing to accept significant reforms.

Madero's problems were not limited to the oligarchy and foreign interests. The mass revolt that had brought him to power consisted not just of liberal-minded merchants and reforming entrepreneurs like himself, but of tens of thousands of peasant farmers, cowboys, mineworkers, labourers in factories and on railways, marginalised intellectuals and indigenous communities.

They backed Madero because he had offered effective leadership, and because he showed at least minimal awareness of their greatest concern: land. His Plan included one clause referring to restoration of lands to peasant communities that had been unjustly deprived of it under Díaz.

This was a crucial element in the initial support for Madero from peasant and working-class revolutionary leaders like Emiliano Zapata and Francisco Villa.

Zapata was the bilingual (Spanish and Nahuatl) leader of a peasant community in Morelos State, not far south of the capital, who tried by legal means and then with arms to reclaim community lands seized by a neighbouring *hacienda* (estate) for commercial sugar production. He rapidly became leader of a broad peasant movement in Morelos and neighbouring states of the Centre-South.

When Madero failed to take effective action to restore lands, Zapata issued his own revolutionary Plan of Ayala and led the *Ejército Revolucionario del Sur* (Revolutionary Army of the South) in revolt.

As for Pancho Villa, he was one of many self-made leaders who backed Madero in the vast northern regions of Mexico, very different from the more densely-populated and indigenous Centre-South which was Zapata's homeland.

The North, much of it desert or semi-desert with arid plains and mountain ranges stretching to the US border, had an economy based on mining and extensive cattle ranching interspersed with fertile valleys and irrigation agriculture.

From the mid-19th century large-scale investment in mining, export agriculture and ranching was accompanied by railway construction. Isolated agricultural and commercial settlements coexisted with a highly mobile population of cowboys, mineworkers, itinerant traders, railway and industrial labourers and bandits.

Much of the population had access to horses and guns, and as discontent grew at the corruption and repression of the Díaz regime and the oligarchy it favoured, local revolts could very quickly generate formidable insurgent cavalry units. Villa was one of several revolutionary leaders to emerge in this way in the 1910-13 period, becoming for a while the most powerful insurgent commander in the country.

As a young man Villa had worked as a debt peon on a hacienda, and left to escape exploitation, joining a group of outlaws in the mountains. He later worked in a variety of trades and was respected by many in the region, and when in late 1910 groups of insurgent horsemen in Chihuahua gathered in response to Madero's call to arms, they unanimously chose Villa as their leader.

The coup against Madero and the second phase of the revolution

These were the popular forces which Madero had helped to unleash, and which would ensure that his overthrow would not lead to an oligarchic restoration. The coup, when it came, was a melodramatic tragedy with few, if any, parallels. The "Tragic Ten Days" (really lasting about a fortnight, from 9 to 22 February 1913) was a military and civilian seizure of power organised by the most reactionary and oligarchic elites with the open support of US Ambassador Henry Lane Wilson. They subjected the central Zócalo square and surrounding areas to indiscriminate machine-gun fire and shelling, causing hundreds, if not thousands, of deaths. Madero, his brother and his Vice-President were murdered, and cynical negotiations involving Félix Díaz (the dictator's nephew), the treacherous General Victoriano Huerta and the Ambassador (among others) led to Huerta's appointment as President.[4]

Mexicans have not forgotten this brutal coup and the role of the United States, and AMLO has insisted that people today should see it as an object lesson: democracy will only triumph if political leaders identify with the common people and their material needs, and if the people mobilise to support their leaders.

Huerta would rule as dictator for 18 months; his coup radicalised the revolution which entered a dramatic second phase. Villa, Zapata and other insurgent leaders immediately denounced the coup, and significantly, one State Governor, Venustiano Carranza of Coahuila, launched a "Constitutionalist" movement to defend legality and democracy.

Over the next 18 months intense warfare spread across the country until Huerta's regime collapsed and revolution triumphed once again in August 1914. There were great celebrations as the peasant or plebeian leaders Villa and Zapata occupied the National Palace, and a photograph which has become iconic shows Villa on the presidential throne and Zapata beside him.

But the process was not so simple: Carranza's Constitutionalist movement had also played a major role in the overthrow of Huerta, and in the previous few months had split with both Villa and Zapata. By the end of 1914 there was open conflict between these contending factions.

During 1915-16 there was renewed large-scale warfare between the Constitutionalists whose main military commander was Álvaro Obregón, and the forces of Zapata and (above all) Villa. By late 1916 both Zapata and Villa were reduced to a marginal position, holding out in their respective home territories but nothing more.

The Constitutionalists were more bourgeois in their leadership and outlook; Carranza, Obregón and their associates appealed to a more middle-class following. But they were not reactionaries and also had significant worker and peasant support, and in November 1916 they convened a Constitutional Convention in the colonial city of Querétaro, not far north of Mexico City. The delegates to the Convention represented the insurgent forces, including some former zapatistas and villistas. Merchants and entrepreneurs mingled with farmers, workers and intellectuals to debate all aspects of the nation's future.

In February 1917 – so coinciding with the initial revolutionary upheaval in Russia, but several months before the Bolshevik victory – a new Constitution was adopted in Mexico, which (with many amendments) is still the law of the land today. Several of the delegates were influenced by socialist ideas, whether utopian or Marxist, or by anarchism, and it was they who inserted the key clauses already mentioned, to maintain separation of Church and State, for public secular education, land for the landless, workers' rights and public ownership of subsoil rights.

Lázaro Cárdenas and the revolution in power

Political tensions and contradictions limited the scope of implementation of the progressive clauses until the presidency of Lázaro Cárdenas (1934-40) who greatly increased agrarian reform, promoted workers' rights and organisation, implemented socialist education, nationalised railways and petroleum, pioneered indigenous peoples' rights (the first Latin American leader to do so), assisted the Spanish Republic against Franco and granted asylum to Spanish Republicans, and also to Leon Trotsky.

Cárdenas is one of AMLO's role models: the historic Mexican presidents he most admires are Benito Juárez, Francisco I Madero and Lázaro Cárdenas. Clearly Cárdenas was able to take such bold progressive measures because the popular movement expressed in the armed revolution was still a force in the post-revolutionary state, and in the global depression of the 1930s it found expression through his leadership. He was also favoured by the international context of a progressive president, Franklin Delano Roosevelt, in the US, and the threat of fascism which persuaded Washington to accept the Mexican oil expropriation. It should also be mentioned that the two historic US presidents admired by AMLO are Abraham Lincoln and Franklin Delano Roosevelt.

Towards the end of his term many Mexicans wanted Cárdenas to continue, but he adhered strictly to Madero's principle of "No Re-election" which has been maintained ever since. Moreover, from late 1938 onwards the issue of the presidential succession became critical: the left gathered around Francisco J Múgica, a close associate of Cárdenas from the same State of Michoacán, well known for his socialist tendencies and his intention to accelerate the agrarian reform and nationalise further key sectors such as mining and banking.

Here the struggle intensified dramatically, clearly along class lines: conservative forces including landlord interests, major Mexican industrialists centred in the northeastern city of Monterrey, and the Catholic Church, instigated the fear of communism and threatened armed rebellion. They organised both inside the official party (PRM, *Partido de la Revolución Mexicana* or Party of the Mexican Revolution) and outside, led by a prominent General, Juan Andreu Almazán. A new conservative party, the PAN (*Partido de Acción Nacional*, National Action Party) was formed in 1939, rejecting everything the revolution had achieved under Cárdenas.

It was in these circumstances that Múgica was obliged to withdraw his candidacy in July 1939: Cárdenas himself recognised that armed rebellion and civil war was a real danger, and accepted the arguments of many of his allies in the labour and peasant movements, that a compromise solution must be found. Hence the promotion of the centrist candidacy of General Manuel Ávila Camacho, Cárdenas' Secretary of Defence who had a reputation as a moderate.

Revolutionary transformation interrupted

1940 was undoubtedly the turning-point where the post-revolutionary regime stabilised as a national capitalist and developmentalist project. The popular achievements of the revolution were not abandoned: peasant communities (*ejidos*) retained the land they had been granted, organised labour retained union rights and benefits (although on a limited, sectoral basis), public secular education continued to predominate and the state played a major role in development through the national oil company PEMEX and a complex of public enterprises including a National Development Bank (*Nacional Financiera*). The conservative PAN remained marginal and the most reactionary forces represented by Almazán were also marginalised; but this was only achieved by accepting the presence of powerful bourgeois interests within the system and in the official party, renamed in 1946 as the PRI (*Partido Revolucionario Institucional*, Institutional Revolutionary Party). The path of development was clearly capitalist, a compromise with both national and foreign capital.

The left and the popular movement remained significant within the PRI and the government until the early 1960s. The early years of the presidency of Adolfo López Mateos (1958-64) witnessed renewed acceleration of the agrarian reform, nationalisation of electric power in September 1960, the launching of a universal free school textbook scheme (which was denounced as "communist" by the PAN), and Mexico's decision to maintain relations with revolutionary Cuba when it was expelled from the Organisation of American States at Washington's behest in January 1962.

Indeed, López Mateos had declared in July 1960 that his government was "on the extreme left within the Constitution"[5] and he had to confront serious tensions with the business elite at home and with the United States. But contradictory tendencies were manifest, with suppression of independent trade unionists on the railways and in the teachers' movement, and a brutal state-sponsored execution of the independent peasant leader Rubén Jaramillo in May 1962.

Bourgeois hegemony and decay

López Mateos' successor was the conservative authoritarian Gustavo Díaz Ordaz, and it was on his watch that a decisive repressive episode occurred: the Tlatelolco massacre of 2 October 1968. The student protest movement had been growing for over three months, with increasing support from the wider population; but with the Olympic Games (a major symbolic event for the regime) due to start on 12 October, the government was determined to stop the protests. Rather than negotiate, they sent in the military to crush a huge rally which took place on 2 October in the central Plaza of the Three Cultures. A peaceful mass rally turned into a massacre when apparently indiscriminate shooting broke out. Over 300 people (indeed, probably more than 500) were killed, and the PRI never really recovered from this stain on its record. As a young doctoral student from the University of Warwick in Britain, I was in the city at the time but fortunately not at the site of the massacre; it nevertheless had a traumatic impact on my view of Mexico.

Over the next twenty years some sections of the regime manoeuvred to try to maintain its legitimacy, but further episodes of brutal repression accompanied the emergence of revolutionary guerrilla movements, particularly in the southern state of Guerrero. Then in the 1980s Mexico's adoption of the neoliberal policies prevailing throughout the Western world destroyed what remained of PRI developmental strategy and led to profound crisis.

There are two crucial elements to bear in mind in analysis of the growing corruption and repression of the PRI in the decade leading up to Tlatelolco: evidence of CIA penetration at the highest level, and the rise of the Presidential Guard as a praetorian force of 8,000 men independent in practice from the regular army. There is evidence that members of the Presidential Guard acted as provocateurs to precipitate the 1968 massacre when the regular military command wanted to exercise restraint: Díaz Ordaz' long-retired Defence Secretary, General Marcelino García Barragán, made these accusations, with documentation, in an interview in his last years in the 1980s.[6] He also alleges that Díaz Ordaz shared direct responsibility, and hints (no more) that the CIA was involved. This is very relevant in understanding how fundamental AMLO's commitment to change has been: one of his first actions as President was to dissolve the Presidential Guard.[7]

In the early 1980s several groups both inside and outside the PRI began organising for a left challenge in the elections. In 1987 a number of groups came together in the National Democratic Front and launched the presidential candidacy of Cuauhtémoc Cárdenas, son of the great Lázaro Cárdenas.

As the July 1988 elections approached, for the first time ever there was popular expectation of an opposition victory. When the count began on the night of 6-7 July, early reports indicated a slight lead for Cuauhtémoc over the PRI candidate Carlos Salinas de Gortari. Then it was reported that there was a sudden failure of the computer system, and when the count resumed a couple of hours later, Salinas surprisingly took the lead and was declared the victor with just over 50% of the vote to 31% for Cuauhtémoc and 17% for Manuel Clouthier of the PAN.

Everything pointed to blatant electoral fraud, and widespread protests followed. But Cuauhtémoc Cárdenas did not take decisive action, and the PRI succeeded in imposing Salinas as President and maintaining control for the time being. It can be stated without a doubt that from this time on, the entire political system was in crisis.

NOTES

1. William Weber Johnson, *Heroic Mexico: The Narrative History of a Twentieth-Century Revolution,* New York: Doubleday & Co, 1968, pp.30-31.
2. Johnson, pp. 31-32.
3. Pedro Salmerón Sanginés, *La División del Norte: la tierra, los hombres y la historia de un ejército del pueblo,* México: Planeta, 2018, p. 230.
4. Johnson, *Heroic Mexico,* pp 93-128 provides a detailed account of the coup.
5. Instituto Nacional de Estudios Políticos, *Memoria Política de México. Biografía: Adolfo López Mateos.* Autora: Doralicia Carmona Dávila. www.memoriapoliticademexico.org/Biografias/LMA09.html. Consulted 1 May 2024.
6. Julio Scherer y Carlos Monsiváis, *Parte de Guerra: Tlatelolco 1968.* México: Nuevo Siglo-Aguilar, 1999. This explosive book had virtually disappeared from circulation when it was circulated again in 2023 by Pedro Salmerón Sanginés, and quoted by AMLO.
7. Andrés Manuel López Obrador, *Hacia una Economía Moral,* México 2019: Planeta, p. 77.

2

Crisis and popular resurgence, 1988-2018

Electoral fraud was institutionalised in Mexico long before 1988; neoliberal policies were already being implemented from 1983 onwards; and corruption was already commonplace. But Carlos Salinas de Gortari became President through the most blatant fraud yet; he accelerated neoliberal privatisations exponentially; and corruption exploded on his watch. He is with good reason regarded as the godfather of the country's descent into a mafia-like regime.

Salinas began by arresting several union leaders, privatising the telephone company and the banks, the steel industry and in fact hundreds of public enterprises. In November 1991 he got Congress to pass a fundamental agrarian counter-reform, destroying the crucial constitutional guarantee of Article 27 which declared all land, water and subsoil rights to be the eminent domain of the nation and gave rural communities the right to receive land in communal units known as *ejidos*. Individual members of ejidos were now for the first time allowed to rent, mortgage or sell their plots, and corporations were allowed to buy ejido land.[1]

All of this was followed by the signing in 1993 of NAFTA, the North American Free Trade Agreement with the US and Canada, which opened up Mexico more than ever before to US and Canadian trade and investment, leading to a sell-off of industries and natural resources and a race to the bottom in terms of real wages and labour rights in all three countries. It was this which sparked the revolt of the neo-Zapatistas, the EZLN (*Ejército Zapatista de Liberación Nacional*, Zapatista Army of National Liberation) in Chiapas, symbolically beginning on 1st January 1994 when NAFTA came into effect.

The EZLN had a dramatic impact, initially arousing much public sympathy in Mexico and internationally. As a fighting force they were severely limited and were more than willing to accept a truce after 12 days. Their identification with the indigenous people (many of them indeed being indigenous), with the agrarian cause and with popular democracy, and their denunciation of the sellout free trade treaty, all attracted sympathy and revived revolutionary memories. The authorities could not contemplate insurgent gains on any scale, but Salinas was in the last year of his term and desperately needed a smooth transition of power.

Further abuses by the authorities led to repeated armed incidents until the signing of the San Andrés accords in February 1996, which addressed several insurgent demands in the Zapatista heartlands of the Chiapas highlands (*Los Altos*) and the Sierra Norte of Chiapas. But continued abuses, including the use of repressive paramilitaries, culminated in the Acteal massacre of December 1997 in which 45 indigenous people were killed by paramilitaries (and it was only in 2020 under AMLO that the federal authorities accepted responsibility).

Such brutal tactics confirmed the corrupt and repressive character of the Mexican state, which the reforms of Salinas and his PRI successor Ernesto Zedillo had done nothing to improve. But the Zapatistas lacked not only the military resources to expand their territory, but also the political capacity to become an effective national force. Despite isolated actions and demonstrations in Guerrero, Morelos, the Federal District and elsewhere, they remained marginal.

Unbridled neoliberalism and mafia rule

In the meantime, the regime's crisis deepened with uncontrolled speculative financial flows induced by Salinas' deregulation and the international overconfidence associated with neoliberalism. Doubts in financial markets about the real strength of the Mexican economy were compounded by political upheaval.[2]

The years 1993-94 witnessed not only the Zapatista uprising, but also a series of political assassinations which reflected the mafia-like characteristics of the disintegrating PRI. In fact the first suspicious assassination occurred on 24 May 1993: Cardinal Juan Jesús Posadas Ocampo, Bishop of Guadalajara, was gunned down at the city's airport. It was said that this was due to confusion, that members of a drug cartel confused him with their rival *El Chapo* Guzmán, head of the Sinaloa cartel, who was also at the airport and using a similar car. But others maintain that the Cardinal had information which he was about to reveal on cartel links to prominent politicians.

Then on 23 March 1994 Luis Donaldo Colosio, designated four months earlier as the official candidate for the presidential succession, was assassinated at a public rally in Tijuana. Colosio had the public backing of Salinas, but there were indications that he had in fact lost the favour of the outgoing president because of reformist statements he had made in the meantime.

The official version has it that Colosio was shot by a lone gunman who was arrested and condemned, but many reports suggested that there was a second assassin. Further evidence has recently come to light suggesting that that the second gunman was linked to the CISEN (National Intelligence Centre), confirming suspicions that it was a state crime ordered at the highest level. AMLO has recently declared that the Colosio case must be thoroughly investigated once again to clarify responsibility.

Six months later, on 28 September 1994, another leading politician, José Francisco Ruiz Massieu, was shot dead in Mexico City. Ruiz Massieu was Secretary-General of the PRI and former brother-in-law of President Salinas. Again, the material assassin was arrested, tried and condemned, but many details remained unclear, and among those apparently implicated was Raúl Salinas, the President's brother (who would be arrested in February 1995 but released ten years later and absolved of all charges).

It should be pointed out that while episodes of violent repression had long characterised the rule of the PRI, there had been no high-level assassinations since 1928 (a year before the official party, originally called the PNR, even existed), and this succession of such events indicated that infighting at the highest level was now prevalent. While the PRI succeeded in imposing another candidate, Ernesto Zedillo, in place of Colosio for the December 1994 – November 2000 presidential term, it was clearly losing control.

The chaotic events of 1994 also precipitated the long overdue financial crisis. On 20 December 1994 Zedillo's Finance Minister announced "greater flexibility in the flotation of the peso", devaluation by any other name, and in a matter of days the currency fell by 50%, several banks collapsed, and thousands of people lost their jobs and savings.

Capital flight brought the danger of a suspension of Mexico's international payments, and only an emergency US credit of $20 billion bailed out the country's Treasury. Subsequently Zedillo rescued the banks with the creation of FOBAPROA, the Banking Fund for the Protection of Savings, which was a massive conversion of private into public debt. As AMLO has declared, "the crisis of December 1994 paled against the massive debt that FOBAPROA had assumed", which in September 2016 was estimated at US $46.1 billion, or 4.46% of GDP, and would take at least 70 years to pay off.[3]

In the neoliberal era such public bailouts of private banks and other companies are the norm in many countries, but the scale on which they occurred in Mexico in this period is remarkable. There is much evidence of corruption on a huge scale, and the fact that Raúl Salinas (for example) was absolved of all charges after 2005 should not be taken at face value, given the notorious corruption of the judicial system. AMLO quotes a 1998 report by the US Government Accountability Office titled "Raúl Salinas,

Citibank, and Money Laundering Allegations" to the effect that in 1992-94 he transferred US $100 million through various international Citibank accounts using front men and false names.[4]

The practice of the "revolving door" between public office and private financial interests also became prevalent in this period: Ernesto Zedillo later became a member of the board of Citibank, no doubt in recognition of his bailing out of the banks. It was also Zedillo who privatised Mexico's railways (and the privatised companies then ended passenger trains); on leaving the presidency he became a member of the board of Union Pacific Railroad. Adrian Lajous, Director of PEMEX under Zedillo, later became an advisor to the oil multinational Schlumberger.[5] These are only a few of dozens of such cases.

It would be impossible to understand the catastrophic impact of Carlos Salinas' and Ernesto Zedillo's policies without addressing the nature of neoliberalism and corruption (which go hand in hand). Thus Salinas began with a package of social measures called "Solidarity" or *Pronasol*, which on the face of it sounded quite positive.[6]

Pronasol targeted significant funds to relatively deprived areas of the country for investment in roads, other public works, schools, clinics and cultural activities, with community participation. It was intended to counter the negative effects of neoliberalism. But it was used in a clientelistic manner to bolster support for the PRI, and was insufficient to counter cutbacks in the regular budgets for health, education and social spending, above all with rising inflation and stagnating wages. It was also beset by corruption from the beginning.

When Carlos Salinas became President, there was one Mexican on the Forbes world billionaires list; when he left, there were 24. Salinas would no doubt view this as an index of success, but when you realise that it coincided with a corresponding increase in the number of Mexicans living in poverty, the real impact of his policies becomes clear.

The opposition in crisis

This chaotic scenario was what the democratic movement faced as it challenged the established power of both PRI and PAN. After the 1988 fraud, those who had backed Cuauhtémoc Cárdenas came together to form the PRD (*Partido de la Revolución Democrática*, Party of the Democratic Revolution). Its founders included Cárdenas, Porfirio Muñoz Ledo, Ifigenia Martínez and AMLO; it was also supported by the Mexican Communist Party, the Unified Socialist Party, the Workers' Party (PT) and the Socialist Party.

The PRD rapidly became the main opposition party and fielded candidates in elections at all levels, but brutal repression and ineffective campaigning limited its progress. It was in these circumstances that the right-wing PAN began to gain ground.

The PRD did achieve a significant success in 1997 with the victory of Cuauhtémoc Cárdenas in the elections for Head of Government (Metro Mayor) of Mexico City, reflecting the party's strength in the capital. It was the first time that this important position was open to popular vote. The PRD also won a majority in the local assembly of the capital.

The year 2000 brought what on the face of it was a major change, with the victory in the presidential election of Vicente Fox of the PAN, the first time in 71 years that the official party (PRI, known previously as PNR or PRM) had been defeated. But the fact that the victory was for the right-wing opposition and not the PRD showed that the popular movement was in crisis. The party's lack of progress with Cuauhtémoc Cárdenas as its figurehead accentuated internal rivalries and left the field open to the right.

AMLO's emergence

It was in this context that Andrés Manuel López Obrador emerged as by far the most successful politician in the PRD. AMLO had emerged as a grassroots activist in his home State of Tabasco, first in the PRI and then in the Democratic Current and from 1989 in the PRD.

Running twice for Governor of Tabasco, in 1988 and 1994, AMLO was tirelessly active in organising and leading local popular protests, and gained national support so that he was elected president of the PRD in 1996 (until 1999). His success in increasing the party's electoral presence laid the basis for his victory in elections for Head of Government of the Federal District in 2000, for what was now a six-year term. His impact in this position would make him unquestioned leader of the party and the popular movement.

What distinguished AMLO from the beginning was his unceasing, tireless campaigning: whether in elections or in leading popular protests over specific issues (such as the Tabasco peasants in 1994 demanding compensation for pollution caused by PEMEX), he never abandoned the struggle (although always relying on peaceful means).

What also became apparent from the year 2000 onwards was AMLO's creativity and efficiency in government. Despite vigorous opposition he succeeded in building an elevated viaduct (the *segundo piso*) of the capital's peripheral motorway, a project approved by citizens in a referendum. He also inaugurated the first express *Metrobus* line, 19.5km from north to south. He introduced a universal old-age pension for residents, the first such programme in the country, welfare schemes for the disabled, grants for farmers in rural areas of the Federal District, grants for small businesses, and free medical care for those without social security.

In education he created 16 new Pre-University Preparatory Schools and a new public University. He held daily press conferences to communicate with the people. AMLO's rule was also an economic and financial success, with public debt being kept under control through a reduction in luxury spending. All of these aspects of his administration prefigured the approach he would adopt as President from 2018 onwards.⁷

AMLO's success and popularity (at times reaching approval ratings of 85%) made him an obvious candidate for the presidency in the 2006 elections. President Vicente Fox of the PAN criticised his policies as "populist", and starting in May 2004 the federal Attorney General's office used a minor dispute over expropriation of a small plot of land for road construction to request AMLO's *desafuero*, a kind of impeachment. In April 2005 this measure was passed by the Congress, but subsequent legal disputes, backed above all by massive public rallies in support of AMLO, led to abandonment of the impeachment.

As a result AMLO was after all able to run in 2006, in fact his "precampaign" began in August 2005. As was already his established practice, he campaigned intensively all over the country and set forth a detailed political programme of 50 specific promises. His impact was such that his rivals, above all Felipe Calderón, candidate of the governing PAN, began an alarmist campaign of negative propaganda (above all in TV spots) with the slogan "López Obrador, a danger for Mexico". They compared him to Venezuelan President Hugo Chávez, at that time a bogeyman for the conservative establishment throughout Latin America.

Despite complaints by AMLO´s team the Electoral Institute allowed such tendentious propaganda, and also allowed paid political ads by right-wing business groups such as the *Consejo Coordinador Empresarial* (Entrepreneurs Coordinating Council) and several big corporations such as Pepsi and Jumex. These were clear violations of electoral law, but nothing was done.

As the vote on 2 July 2006 approached, the polls showed AMLO and Calderón neck-and-neck at around 34 to 36% each, with PRI candidate Roberto Madrazo on about 27%. The first official results gave victory to Calderón by a tiny margin, 250,000 votes or 0.62%. AMLO and his coalition called for a complete recount, but the authorities only granted a recount in a limited number of polling stations and the result remained essentially unchanged. There is in fact abundant evidence to confirm that the result was fraudulent, but the reality of power allowed Calderón to take office.

AMLO and his team denounced this blatant fraud⁸ and protested for months with rallies and a mass sit-in blocking the main Paseo de la Reforma avenue. They proclaimed AMLO as "legitimate President", but could not prevent Calderón's official inauguration on 1 December 2006.

These protest tactics were not successful, and sectors of the PRD including prominent figures like Cuauhtémoc Cárdenas went their own way. Over the next three years division plagued the democratic movement, despite the corrupt and repressive actions of President Calderón.

Calderón's War on Drugs

Calderón, who was President only through a very manipulative campaign with blatant interference by outgoing President Vicente Fox and a fraudulent rigging of the vote, took desperate action immediately after his inauguration to impose his authority and arouse popular support. In December 2006, just after taking office, he made a dramatic declaration of a "War on Drugs", unconstitutionally sending out the military to take charge of policing, initiating violent assaults on suspected narco gangs and (also unconstitutionally) inviting armed US agents into Mexico.

In the short run this hard-line approach did boost Calderón's popularity – a friend in Michoacán told me in 2007 "this man will solve the problem of gangs and violence" – but predictably, the crude shoot-first-and-ask-questions-afterwards approach simply led to a catastrophic rise in the homicide rate, with thousands of innocent victims killed or maimed. The annual number of homicides rose from less than 10,000 to over 27,000 a year from 2007 to 2011.[9]

Worse still, it subsequently emerged that Calderón's head of Public Security, Genaro García Luna, had made a deal with the Sinaloa cartel to work with them (indeed, for them) while waging war on the competition. It took time, but García Luna was finally arrested in the US in December 2019 on charges of conspiracy, money laundering and false testimony; in February 2023 he was found guilty on five counts by a Federal Court in New York.[10] The legal ramifications of the case are far from over: under AMLO, Mexico has been pursuing a claim for compensation from the proceeds of properties in Florida purchased by García Luna and his associates with funds derived from embezzlement of Mexican public resources.

An obvious question arises regarding Calderón's own responsibility: the ex-President, now ensconced in Spain and constantly spewing propaganda against AMLO and the 4T Transformation, must surely have known what his security chief was up to. AMLO declares that of all Mexico's reactionary politicians, Calderón "towers above all others": an unabashed admirer of Spanish dictator Francisco Franco, he is "the quintessential embodiment of right-wing hypocrisy".[11]

What saved AMLO and the democratic opposition in these years of brutal violence and corruption was not so much the fruitless attempt to impede the imposition of Calderón as de facto President, but AMLO's unceasing commitment to communicate in person with the people and to work with them to organise a country-wide movement. For nearly three years, from 4 January 2007 to 20 November 2009, he travelled the length and breadth of Mexico, visiting all 2,452 municipalities, holding meetings in communities big and small to tell people of his programme for real national transformation and to listen to their concerns.[12] It is said that at one point Calderón asked what his former opponent was up to,,and when told that he was addressing tiny meetings of 50 people, he laughed at what he regarded as a futile irrelevance.

It was also under Calderón that there occurred the first serious attempt to privatise the national oil company PEMEX (a neoliberal goal which would be attempted again in 2013). AMLO was among those leading the creation in January 2008 of the National Movement in Defence of Petroleum, which would have a significant impact on public opinion and on Congress over the next few years, including an occupation of Congress to prevent passage of a privatisation law.

By 2011 divisions within the PRD were intensifying and a new party, the Citizens' Movement (*Movimiento Ciudadano*, MC) appeared. Possible candidates for the presidency in the 2012 elections included AMLO, Cuauhtémoc Cárdenas and Marcelo Ebrard who was finishing a term as Head of Government of the Federal District. A compromise was arranged between Ebrard and AMLO and the latter was chosen as candidate for the PRD, MC and the Workers' Party, but Cuauhtémoc went his own way. It was also in November 2011 that AMLO announced the creation of Morena (*Movimiento de Regeneración Nacional*, National Regeneration Movement), but initially as an association rather than a party.

These divisions and manoeuvres did not favour the left, but at the same time Calderón had become extremely unpopular, and the PAN, even with the novelty of a woman as candidate (Josefina Vázquez Mota) had lost credibility. It was in these circumstances that the old governing party, the PRI, made an unlikely comeback with a victory for its candidate Enrique Peña Nieto: a victory based on superficial charisma and lavish, corrupt campaign spending far exceeding the legal limits.

AMLO, who came second more than six points behind, once again alleged fraud, but the democratic movement lacked the unity and strength to contest the results as in 2006. The extent of the left's crisis became clear when the day after his inauguration in December 2012 Peña Nieto proclaimed his "Pact for Mexico" with cross-party support from PRI, PAN and PRD. Much of the PRD simply abandoned their principles and joined a pact based on massive corruption.

The Pact included a whole series of legislative proposals, several of them being constitutional reforms. The most controversial were the Educational Reform which opened public education to private interests and abolished teachers' job security; and the Energy Reform which opened up the oil and gas sector and electricity generation and distribution to private interests, undermining the much-valued public institutions PEMEX and CFE (*Comisión Federal de Electricidad*, Federal Electricity Commission).

The Energy Reform was at least opposed in Congress by the left, and the PAN initially had partisan reservations although fundamentally in favour of privatisation. It was subsequently revealed that the notorious Brazilian Odebrecht corporation, involved in bribery scandals across Latin America, had lobbied in favour of the Reform and provided $10 million to PEMEX Director Emilio Lozoya Austín and $6 million to PAN Senators to pass the measure; photos were later published of wads of cash changing hands.

These events, which confirmed that both political corruption and neoliberalism had reached unprecedented extremes, and that the PRD had sold out, confirmed Morena's decision at a National Congress on 20 November 2012 to become a political party; it formalised its request to the Federal Electoral Institute in January 2014 and this was approved in July.

The task faced by Morena was Herculean: as expressed by the distinguished writer Lorenzo Meyer five years later, when AMLO had just taken office: "Today, in our country, corruption has reached levels for which concepts like *scandalous* or *uncontrolled* are inadequate. The tolerance and complicity of the network of institutions which theoretically ought to restrain and punish those responsible…is in reality a system created over time to prevent holding the great corrupt and corrupting individuals to account." Meyer also quotes another author, Javier Sicilia, who declared that "Politics in Mexico [is] no less than the continuation of crime by other means".[13]

To create an effective mass party of the left was a formidable task, and only determined and coherent leadership combined with nation-wide popular organisation could achieve it. It was only AMLO´s indefatigable work over 30 years which made this possible. Popular rejection of the political system was overwhelming, but as in many countries, this rejection was accompanied by profound scepticism towards all politicians. What AMLO finally achieved was to overcome this scepticism and inspire mass participation to initiate real transformation through the electoral process.

AMLO´s extraordinary success

By late 2017 it was clear that in the following year's elections the main contenders would be the PRI, the PAN and Morena. All formed alliances with smaller parties; in the case of Morena, the factionalism and opportunism of the PRD ruled it out and the MC (Citizens' Movement) was also too inconsistent. The only other parties with coherent positions were the PT (Workers' Party) and the PES (*Partido Encuentro Social*, Social Encounter Party); together they formed a coalition with the name *Juntos Haremos Historia* (Together We Will Make History).

From the beginning in late 2017 polls indicated that AMLO was in the lead, followed by PAN candidate Ricardo Anaya and José Antonio Meade for the PRI, who were neck-and-neck some ten percentage points behind AMLO. But from March 2018 onwards AMLO's lead increased, and panic set in for the establishment. The usual lies and insults were directed at AMLO: he would turn Mexico into "another Venezuela" or he was backed by the Russians.

As in the US – the source of some of these wild accusations – mention of Russia was accompanied by classic anti-communist tropes, despite the fact that Russia had not been Communist for over 20 years. AMLO's response demonstrated his quiet confidence as well as an acute sense of humour: he released a short video in which he declared that his name was now "Andrés

Manuelovich", and that he was at an undisclosed location on the Gulf coast of Mexico where he was waiting for the arrival of a submarine bearing Russian gold. It was a highly effective response to such absurd hostile propaganda.

As polling day approached and AMLO's lead only increased, the PAN put pressure on the PRI to withdraw its candidate so as to unite the establishment vote. But neither PRI as a party nor outgoing President Peña Nieto would agree to this. The result was a truly historic popular triumph with 53% for AMLO, 22% for Anaya of the PAN and 16% for Meade of the PRI.

In the Senate, Morena and its allies won a majority with 69 of 128 seats, and also in the Chamber of Deputies (Lower House) with 306 out of 500. Foreign recognition, by the US, the European Union, Latin American countries and others followed swiftly. In the long (five months) transition period the establishment finally accepted the inevitable, that it would for the first time since 1940 have to accept a government of the left or the popular movement.

AMLO's inauguration on 1st December 2018 observed much of the usual protocol with a formal address to Congress in the presence of national institutional dignitaries and foreign diplomats. But the new President, while respecting protocol, set forth explicitly his plans for radical change, which he would repeat in greater detail a few hours later before a mass audience in the central Zócalo: 100 specific pledges, with a highly symbolic ceremony in which he accepted a *bastón de mando* (staff of office) from indigenous leaders.

Lorenzo Meyer puts it succinctly: "Morena would not have been created as a party in 2014 if it had not been for López Obrador's determined opposition, his pilgrimage through Mexico's 2,458 municipalities, his refusal to be coopted or intimidated."[14] It was natural that his adversaries should call him a *caudillo*, a populist, a "Tropical Messiah": this was simply recognition of the essential role of effective leadership which for the first time in living memory permitted tenure of the highest office by a true representative of the popular movement.

NOTES

1. James J Kelly, "Article 27 and Mexican Land Reform: The Legacy of Zapata's Dream", Columbus Human Rights Law Review 541 (1993-1994), pp 543-4. https://scholarship.law.nd.edu/cgi/viewcontent.cgi?article=1693&context=law_faculty_scholarship, consulted 8 May 2024.
2. Aldo Musacchio, "Mexico's financial crisis of 1994-1995", Harvard Business School Working Paper, no. 12-101, May 2012; https://nrs.harvard.edu/urn-3:HUL.lastRepos:9056792. Consulted 13 April 2024.
3. Andrés Manuel López Obrador, *A New Hope for Mexico: Saying No to Corruption, Violence and Trump's Wall*. London, 2018: Pluto. Translated by Natascha Ullmann. pp 61-2.
4. AMLO, *A New Hope for Mexico*, pp 59-60.
5. AMLO, *A New Hope for Mexico*, p 63.
6. https://static.nuso.org/media/articles/downloads/2339_1.pdf Asa Cristina Laurell, "Pronasol o la pobreza de los programas contra la pobreza", *Nueva Sociedad* Nro 131, mayo-junio 1994, pp 156-170.
7. https://datanoticias.com/2023/07/20/que-hizo-amlo-jefe-de-gobierno/ Consulted 6 May 2024.
8. Andrés Manuel López Obrador, *¡Gracias!*, México, Planeta, 2024, pp 125-154.
9. Lorenzo Meyer, *El poder vacío: El agotamiento de un régimen sin legitimidad*, México 2019: Debate, pp 126-7.
10. edition.cnn.com/2023/02/21/us/genaro-garcia-luna-drug-trafficking/index/html. Consulted 6 May 2024.
11. AMLO, *A New Hope for Mexico*, pp 67-8.
12. www.gob.mx/presidencia/estructuras/andres-manuel-lopez-obrador. Consulted 6 May 2024.
13. Lorenzo Meyer, *El poder vacío*, p 112.
14. Lorenzo Meyer, *El poder vacío*, p 179.

Voters line up at a polling station for the 2024 election

Computer facility, Teotongo Utopia

3

'Civic austerity' and fighting corruption

The inauguration came with enormous expectation, and the new president's list of 100 specific pledges aroused great hopes. One of his first executive actions was to reduce his own presidential salary by more than 50% and to declare that he wanted to end many of the privileges of office. He would sell off the huge official airliner (indeed, would put it up for auction and sell tickets to the public with the proceeds going to fund hospitals) and would travel economy class on normal commercial flights; would stay in modest hotels and eat in ordinary popular restaurants. A law on remuneration of public servants would require all high-ranking officials, whether elected or appointed, to do likewise: no first-class travel, no luxury hotels or expense-account lunches.

This was one of AMLO's most misunderstood policies, *Austeridad Republicana*, perhaps best translated as "Civic Austerity": as he declared, "We cannot have a rich state alongside a poor people", the fight against waste and corruption must begin at home, in the government itself. This not only saved a vast amount of money but had great symbolic significance.

Another key measure, linked to Civic Austerity but of broader significance, was the dissolution of the Presidential Guard, the elite praetorian force of 8,000 special troops which, as we have seen, had been used to impose arbitrary rule and repression, often overriding the regular Armed Forces. AMLO would rely on a small civilian security team and where necessary, a modest escort of regular troops.

To combat corruption and impunity the new government reinforced the *Unidad de Inteligencia Financiera*, the Financial Intelligence Unit of the Finance Ministry (*Hacienda*) and the Solicitor General's office (*Fiscalía*): as

AMLO said, no-one would be persecuted, but if the authorities had evidence of corruption, or such evidence was brought forward by any citizen or organisation, investigation would take place and legal action would follow if appropriate.

Similarly, the President surprised many (especially on the left) by saying that he would not raise taxes (in a country where tax rates on the wealthy were quite low), but he declared categorically that everyone must pay their taxes, there would be no exemptions or exceptions. Ultra-rich individuals and corporations, national or foreign, must pay up. To this end the SAT (*Servicio de Administración Tributaria*, Tax Collection Office) was also greatly reinforced. As a result revenue collected increased very significantly; to give just one example, Walmart Mexico was persuaded to pay some $350 million USD in tax arrears.

The campaign against organised crime and corruption was prioritised with constitutional reforms imposing forfeiture of illicit gains and preventive detention for serious crimes, which would now include tax evasion, corruption and electoral fraud (none of which had been considered "serious" offences previously, having been excluded from this category by PRI President Salinas). Public security was also made a priority with reorganisation of the Department of Security and Civil Protection and creation of a National Guard with both military and human rights training to replace the notoriously corrupt Federal Police.

Civil rights and democratic guarantees were strengthened with constitutional amendments for gender parity in public office, recognition for the first time of the Afro-Mexican community, the right of presidential recall, and the right of public consultation on key issues.

Constitutional reforms require a two-thirds majority in both Houses of Congress, which Morena and its allies in the *Juntos Haremos Historia* (Together We Will Make History) coalition did not have, but in the first 18 months of AMLO's presidency sectors of the opposition were willing to negotiate on many issues and even to "cross the floor" (a situation which would subsequently change).

AMLO declared that to fight corruption it was necessary, "like sweeping the stairs", to begin from the top downwards. In this respect an immediate obstacle was that both current and former presidents enjoyed constitutional immunity from prosecution. There was a general belief that all of the presidents of the neoliberal era, from Salinas de Gortari (1988-94) to 2018, were profoundly corrupt, but to expose them to prosecution would arouse immediate opposition from their partisan associates.

AMLO's approach was to start by removing only the current president's (his own) immunity: an idea which was greeted with natural reluctance by his own supporters. But faced with his insistence, the governing bloc in Congress accepted the proposal.

To remove the immunity of former presidents, AMLO resorted to the new device of a popular referendum or consultation; in September 2020 he presented such a proposal to the Senate, for a referendum or consultation to take place either on 6 June 2021 (coinciding with the mid-term elections) or on 1 August 2021.[1] The proposal aroused fierce opposition from conservative interests in the media and in Congress; they claimed that it was unconstitutional, and then (contradictorily) that the charges of corruption, fraud and violence against the former presidents no longer applied due to a statute of limitations.

After being passed by Congress the proposal was subject to prolonged procedural examination by the National Electoral Institute (*Instituto Nacional Electoral*, INE), a very powerful body which constituted one of the principal obstacles to change. The consultation was finally allowed and took place on 1 August 2021, but with a question drastically revised by INE and the Supreme Court so as to be almost incomprehensible: where AMLO's original text asked voters if they agreed with appropriate legal investigations and sanctions of possible crimes committed by ex-presidents Salinas, Zedillo, Fox, Calderón and Peña Nieto (with their full names), before, during and after their terms of office, the actual text asked voters only if they agreed with appropriate legal actions "to clarify the political decisions taken in the past by political actors", in order to guarantee justice and the rights of possible victims. No mention of presidents, certainly not by name, nor of crimes, just "decisions" taken by "political actors".[2]

AMLO explained patiently in his press conference a couple of days before the vote that he would recommend a "Yes" vote, and indeed 97.72% voted Yes; but with such an obscure question, and with the INE doing all it could to discourage the exercise, participation was only 7.11%.[3] The result was not mandatory because participation did not meet the 40% threshold legally required, but it did have moral impact.

Despite this AMLO himself indicated that he was not in favour of prosecuting his predecessors, since "revenge is not my strong suit". He was all in favour of investigating and exposing the misdeeds of previous officials, from presidents on downwards, but regarded generalised prosecutions as a diversion from the urgent tasks of implementing new projects and reforms. What mattered was that previously officials not only got away with their crimes, but "they didn't even lose their respectability": their misdeeds should be exposed and above all there should be no repetition, corruption and abuse of human rights should be completely unacceptable in current and future administrations.

What this apparently futile exercise did was to reinforce the growing conviction of the President, of the Morena Party and of the majority of voters that sooner or later there would have to be thorough reform of both INE and the justice system. AMLO declared that democracy had not failed, what had failed was the administrative system, and what really mattered was that injustices should not be repeated.

The anti-corruption drive affected a wide variety of institutions which, according to AMLO, had been promoted and used by the neoliberals for private profit, thus facilitating corruption. One category that was singled out for thoroughgoing reform and in many cases, elimination, were *fideicomisos*, trust funds: in October 2020 no less than 109 of them were identified and eliminated by Congress through a government initiative[4]. Without giving a detailed list, some key examples will illustrate their significance; they included institutions in education, research, culture, sport and other fields (the total number of trusts was subsequently given as 191).

A typical example was CONACYT, the National Council for Science and Technology, and its local affiliates in individual states; 44% of CONACYT funds were transferred to the private sector, including such national and international companies as Intel, Whirlpool, Volkswagen, Kimberly Clark, FEMSA, Bayer, Monsanto, IBM, Honeywell, Bimbo and Mabe[5]. Also 91 trust funds related to CONACYT received from 2000 to 2018 65,335.70 million pesos or more than $3 billion USD, equivalent to almost three times its annual budget.

In 2014 a "Programme of Schools of Excellence" was created as a trust to install 31,000 drinking fountains; only 20,500 were installed, and by 2020 only 1,000 were functioning. Also in 2014 a trust was created to help fund the Central American & Caribbean Games in Veracruz, but 44% of the funds were lost, presumably to corruption.

In Querétaro State a trust called Centromex was created in 2017; it lasted only one year but spent 392 million pesos (about $17 million USD) on international travel.

These are just a few of the most scandalous examples; others might appear more plausible, funding genuine research, sporting and cultural activities, but were not subject to adequate budgetary control. Not surprisingly there were vigorous protests from beneficiaries of these programmes, but the Finance Minister (*Hacienda*) gave reassurance that all programmes of real value would continue to be funded, with the difference that the resources would come directly from the public purse and would be properly budgeted.

AMLO pointed out that the multiplication of trusts and similar autonomous institutions was part of the neoliberal obsession with privatisation; many of these functions could be carried out more economically and with stricter control by the public sector.

Other autonomous institutions, not legally registered as trusts, were also a target of the drive against corruption. One such is the INAI, *Instituto Nacional de la Transparencia, Acceso a la Información y Protección de Datos Personales* (National Institute of Transparency, Access to Information and Protection of Personal Data), supposedly the organ most concerned with preventing corruption and, as its name implies, guaranteeing transparency. It was founded in 2014, replacing a similar institution founded in 2003. But AMLO insists that INAI is a sham, a pretence, created to give an appearance of transparency while in fact being corrupt and doing precisely the opposite.

The idea of eliminating or restricting INAI came to a head in January 2021; it aroused fierce criticism in Mexico and abroad. AMLO responded that it was natural they should defend themselves, but pointed out that among those who received INAI contracts were the in-laws of former president Carlos Salinas de Gortari, notorious for their corruption[6]. He pointed out that it was a matter of urgency to provide more assistance to the poor and to small businesses as they emerged from Covid. There existed over 200 autonomous organisations with budgets totalling over 500,000 million pesos (some $25 billion USD), a serious burden on public resources.

The continued offensive against trust funds and autonomous agencies naturally led to accusations, even from leftist observers, that AMLO was engaging in *real* austerity with negative consequences for public services and the poor. The impact of COVID also had a serious negative impact in 2020.

All of these issues were leading to a change in the political landscape from mid-2020 to mid-2021, leading up to the mid-term elections of 6 June 2021. As the extent and ambition of AMLO's Fourth Transformation became clear, the willingness of sectors of the opposition to collaborate came to an end; PAN and PRI began to unite in practice against Morena and its allies in the governing bloc, and smaller parties like the PRD also began to work with a united opposition.

The mid-term elections included the entire Chamber of Deputies (Lower House), consisting of 300 members directly elected and 200 from proportional lists; 15 of 32 state governors; 16 mayoralties (*alcaldías*) of boroughs of Mexico City; 30 state assemblies and many local mayoralties. In late December 2020 the PAN, PRI and PRD formed the *Va Por México* (Go For Mexico) coalition, and as before, Morena, the PT and the PVEM formed *Juntos Hacemos Historia* (Together We Make History). The *Movimiento Ciudadano* (Citizens' Movement) was the most significant of four other registered parties. But the "Go For Mexico" coalition represented the first time that the main opposition parties had united, and as such implied a more serious threat to the governing bloc.[7]

This is where institutional roadblocks became important. The electoral institute INE, already mentioned, far from being impartial, was controlled by a cabal of longstanding members who scarcely tried to disguise their sympathy for the old establishment. It is also, as AMLO pointed out, the most expensive electoral commission in the world: its councillors pay themselves vastly inflated salaries (as much as three times that of the President, which is supposed to be unconstitutional since the Civic Austerity reform) and luxury expenses, plus an extensive bureaucracy.

INE imposed a gagging order on the president during the campaign period, forbidding him from discussing party politics or claiming credit for welfare programmes; it also used its powers of supervision over party campaigns in blatant discriminatory fashion, disqualifying 49 Morena candidates for minor infractions while ignoring similar errors by other parties. There also exists a Federal Electoral Tribunal which supposedly acts as a check on INE, but in fact shares the same bias.

As AMLO insists, "only the people can guarantee democracy", and mass mobilisation at polling stations and to observe the count was necessary in 2021 just as it had been in 2018. To an extent the president was able to obtain progressive decisions from the judiciary, having managed to appoint a reforming Chief Justice, Arturo Zaldívar, but his term of office was limited.

As might be expected, the opposition also received help from certain "civil society" organisations, the most notorious being "Mexicans Against Corruption and Impunity" (which as AMLO points out, does the opposite) and "Article 19", both of which receive substantial funding from USAID and the US National Endowment for Democracy. This is contrary to the Mexican Constitution, and on May 6 Mexico sent a formal diplomatic note in protest, but received no response.

Not surprisingly, *The Economist* published an appalling hatchet piece on Mexico[8] at this time, to which Foreign Secretary Marcelo Ebrard issued a vigorous reply.

In the circumstances the election results were a modest victory for Morena and its coalition, although with setbacks in the major cities. Its total in the Chamber of Deputies was 198, compared to 191 in 2018, so actually a modest gain (on occasions previously it had won the two-thirds majority necessary to pass constitutional amendments, but only when opposition members "crossed the floor", something they were no longer willing to do).

Of the 15 State Governor positions in contention, all but one were previously held by the opposition, but Morena won 11 and its PVEM allies won one, so this was a major gain. With its allies it also won majorities in 19 of 30 state assemblies.

Where Morena and its allies did not do so well was in Mexico City, where the opposition won half of the 16 boroughs; and in Jalisco state (home to the country's second city, Guadalajara) and Nuevo León state (with Monterrey, the third city). Both of these remained opposition strongholds due to effective manipulation of regional sentiments.

There is no doubt that these relative setbacks (or limited gains) were in part due to the emergence of a united opposition coalition. AMLO had to some extent encouraged this, saying that it was better to have a clear binary choice: "you are either with me or against me". This might have a temporary political cost, but in the long run it worked: over the next two to three years, in other local elections and then in the major 2024 elections for the succession, the united opposition declined steadily, and indeed by joining the right-wing PAN, the formerly leftist PRD virtually disappeared and the PRI also entered a steep decline. It became clear that these other parties had nothing to offer except conservative hostility to change.

As we shall see in the next chapter, AMLO's policies were given credibility by the reality of new social programmes reaching working people directly for the first time, without conditionality. AMLO was also moving to re-establish national control over oil and electric power, to end false sub-contracting of workers and to promote gender parity and indigenous rights. Moreover, the lifestyle and work ethic of AMLO and his team were visible and had no parallel in living memory. Not since Lázaro Cárdenas, who left office more than 80 years previously, had there been a president who really lived modestly, who worked six or seven days a week, who communicated constantly with the people and showed a firm commitment to favour workers, peasants, the poor and marginalised, women and indigenous people, Afro-Mexicans and students. Moreover, the government's policies were in general effectively implemented, not only in terms of welfare measures and democratic rights but also public works, something which the left in many countries failed to carry out efficiently.

Perhaps most important for many middle and upper class voters was the government's economic success, as in 2021 the country recovered from the impact of Covid and indeed in the following two years became one of the most successful economies in the Western Hemisphere, with a currency which not only avoided devaluation but appreciated more than any other against the dollar, from a low of nearly 23 pesos in 2020 to 16.5 pesos per dollar in late 2023. This was unprecedented in 50 years.

NOTES

1. *Expansión Política*, 15 septiembre 2020: https://politica.expansion.mx/presidencia/2020/09/15/amlo-propone-enjuiciar-ex-presidentes-por-corrupcion-fraude-y-violencia, accessed 13 July 2021.
2. *Expansión Política*, 28 julio 2021, https://politica.expansion.mx/mexico/2021/07/28/pregunta-de-la-consulta-popular-juicio-expresidentes, accessed 13 July 2024.
3. *Informador.Mx*, 20 octubre 2021, https://www.informador.mx/mexico/Consulta-popular-INE-valida-resultados-del-ejercicio-del-1-de-agosto-20211020-0132.html, Accessed 13 July 2024.
4. www.elfinanciero.com.mx/nacional/estos-son-los-109-fideicomisos-y-fondos-que-se-extinguiran, 01 octubre 2020, consulted 11 July 2024. The figures vary according to the source and the precise date.
5. www.gob.mx/presidencia, conferencia de prensa matutina, 21 octubre 2020, accessed live on 21/10/2020.
6. www.gob.mx/presidencia, conferencia de prensa matutina, 14 enero 2021, accessed live 14/01/2021.
7. For this account of the elections, see David Raby, *https://morningstaronline.co.uk/article/f/cruch-time-in-mexico*, 1 June 2021, and https://morningstaronline.co.uk/article/f/victory-in-mexico, 9 June 2021.
8. www.economist.com/leaders/2021/05/27/voters-should-curb-mexicos-power-hungry-president, *accessed 14 July 2024*

4

Creating a welfare state in the context of a pandemic

'For the Good of All, but First, the Poor' was not an empty slogan, and it implied immediate action to create effective programmes to provide universal benefits which were lacking: truly universal, but of greatest value to the poor and excluded. The aim was to improve and complete what was always a very limited and inadequate welfare system, but also the empowerment of the popular sectors, enabling workers and marginalised groups to become active participants in social transformation.

Before AMLO the situation of senior citizens from deprived sectors in Mexico was dire. Only in 2007 did the Federal Government begin a public pension system to cover those not included in the official public sector and unionised worker pension schemes, so that more than 20% of the old-age population received nothing at all, relying on family and charity support. The 2007 system was still completely inadequate, and although it was gradually improved down to 2015, an official evaluation in 2018 showed that it did not even reach minimum subsistence level.[1]

One of the president's first priorities was therefore the "Pension for the Welfare of Senior Citizens", officially launched in late February 2019. It covered all of those over 68 years of age (65 in indigenous communities) not covered by other private and public schemes, delivering more than twice the amount of the previous federal pension.[2]

By March 2021 more than 8 million seniors were benefiting from it, and as with other benefits introduced by the current government, it is paid directly by bank transfer from the Finance Ministry to each individual, without intermediaries (more on this later). Registration is guaranteed by home visits undertaken by Welfare Ministry officials. The amount has been increased every year by substantially more than the inflation rate, a total increase of 417%, reaching 6,000 pesos every two months in January 2024.[3] The age limit has also been lowered to 65 for all citizens.

Another essential measure introduced by the government was Incapacity Benefit for the disabled, limited at first to children and young people under 30, and indigenous or Afro-Mexicans or those in extreme poverty; it was gradually extended to other sectors.

Then came *Jóvenes Construyendo El Futuro*, "Young People Building the Future", which provides one-year apprenticeships for those aged 18 to 29 in neither education nor employment. AMLO was scathing about previous governments which had dismissed these "Ni-Nis", Neither-Nors, as worthless, and had given them no support.

The apprenticeship scheme was carefully designed to ensure real benefit to participants: both applicants and employing companies or institutions have to register with the Labour Ministry, and as with other benefits, it is paid directly to the beneficiary so it cannot be withheld or discounted by the employer. It is also the young person who chooses the employer and makes the first approach. As of 2024, after annual increases, apprentices receive 7,572 pesos a month, with medical insurance; so far it has assisted nearly 3 million young people, over half of them women, and 6 out of every 10 have found productive occupations as a result. All kinds of work and enterprise are included, from community health to arts and crafts and aerospace technology.[4]

Then there is an educational scholarship or grant system, the Benito Juárez Educational Welfare Grants, at three levels, Basic (pre-school, primary and secondary), Medium-High (Further Education/Pre-University), and Higher Education (University). They are directed at low-income families or those in marginalised areas.

Access to higher education was also improved with the creation of "Benito Juárez Welfare Universities" in communities characterised by extreme poverty and marginalisation. The scheme began in March 2019 and by early 2020 there were 101 such campuses operating in all states of the Republic, with over 45,000 students and 36,000 teaching staff registered, although not yet fully functioning[5]. They work closely with local communities in these areas, and offer access to higher education to those who would otherwise be excluded. By 2024 there were 203 such institutions offering courses in community health, sustainable development and careers relating to agriculture, fishing, forestry and other relevant areas.

In addition there is a very original programme, *La Escuela Es Nuestra*, "The School Is Ours", covering all levels from pre-school to upper secondary (some 170,000 schools in all), which aims to devolve financing and administration to each school. Each institution has a Participatory Administration Committee (*Comité Escolar de Administración Participativa*, CEAP), to administer the budget for maintenance and general management.

The CEAP has a parent as Chair, a parent or member of teaching staff as Secretary, a parent (mother or female guardian, but always a woman) as Treasurer, two more voting members (parents or teachers) and one non-voting student from the fourth form or above. The members of the CEAP are elected by a School Assembly consisting of parents/guardians, teachers and staff, students from the fourth form upwards and community members, and the CEAP must report back to the Assembly.[6]

The radical democracy of this initiative is remarkable, as is the fact that the treasurer of each CEAP has to be a woman (AMLO says they tend to be more honest). Of course all schools must still conform to the general guidelines of national educational policy, and the organisation of the assembly and election and functioning of the CEAP are assisted and guided by an Authorised Facilitator. This official must register the composition of the CEAP with the Education Ministry and supervise the school administration and accounting.

By the beginning of May 2020 a total of 48,163 schools had elected CEAPs and begun to implement the programme; this has now (2024) extended to almost all schools in the country, some 170,000. As well as being a radical democratic experiment it stimulates local enterprise, as the CEAP can hire local firms and workers to carry out construction and maintenance and provide supplies: another instance of community empowerment.

Popular education has also benefited from the Free Textbook programme which distributes millions of books to schools throughout the country and which received special recognition by UNESCO.

Originally introduced in 1960, the textbook programme had been neglected by the neoliberals, but AMLO revived it and appointed an independent commission to completely revise the textbooks for today's context, encouraging free and open discussion of social and cultural issues of all kinds, including indigenous and Afro-Mexican cultures and gender identities.

When the new textbooks were ready in July/August 2023 there was uproar from the opposition, especially the conservative PAN which said they were "communist": the PAN leader Marko Cortés, without apparently even having read them, called on parents to tear offensive pages out of the books, and opposition governors in some states (Chihuahua, Coahuila, Guanajuato, Jalisco) banned their distribution.[7]

The government pointed out that these actions (and some judicial decisions supporting the bans) were unconstitutional, and some progressive teachers' and parents' groups protested against the conservative state authorities. AMLO pointed out that much the same had happened back in 1960 when the first set of free textbooks was launched: conservative attitudes had not changed in over 60 years. After a few months the opposition subsided and the textbooks were distributed almost everywhere.

Health Care and the Covid Pandemic

In Mexico as elsewhere the Covid pandemic had an enormous impact from February 2020 onwards. Before AMLO's inauguration in December 2018 Mexico had a patchwork and incomplete health system which had never covered the entire population and which had been seriously run down by the neoliberal governments of the previous three decades. A Social Security Institute for State Workers covered public sector employees; another Social Security Institute covered most private sector workers in formal employment; the Armed Forces and the national oil company PEMEX had their own systems; others who could afford it had private insurance; and the rest of the population, above all the huge informal sector, had to fend for themselves.

Neoliberal governments had splashed public money around with abandon, appearing to address problems while encouraging patronage and corruption as never before. Scores of new hospitals were announced but never completed, or built but not properly staffed or equipped. López Obrador's team found 217 health centres and 110 hospitals abandoned. By May 2020 54 of the health centres had been completed, 56 were in process of reconstruction and 107 had been condemned as unfit for use; of the hospitals, 18 had been completed, 50 were in process of reconstruction and 42 condemned.[8]

The government's aim was to integrate these diverse institutions and create a universal free service, a Mexican NHS. In mid-2019 AMLO began systematically visiting hospitals in the most deprived areas so that his team could gather information on their shortcomings and the needs of local communities. His government prepared a legislative initiative to reform Article 4 of the Constitution (which deals with social security in general), among other things to establish the universal right to health care as a fundamental principle; this was passed by both Houses of Congress and officially became law on 4th April 2020 following approval by a majority of State assemblies.

With this decision, the health budget was increased by 40 billion pesos (about 1.8 billion dollars), and a new institution, the INSABI (*Instituto de Salud para el Bienestar*, Institute of Health for Welfare) was created to provide free services for those not covered by existing programmes. To make this functional would require massive effort and investment; it would eventually become *IMSS-Bienestar*, the Health for Welfare programme of the *Instituto Mexicano del Seguro Social*, the Mexican Institute of Social Security, which is still in process of completion in 2024.

While these plans were being announced, the country faced severe problems in dealing with the pandemic. In mid-April 2020 the government announced an agreement with private hospitals to provide free treatment to non-Covid patients so as to allow public institutions to concentrate on Covid.

The arrival of Covid in Mexico was eagerly seized upon by the opposition and the international media as a stick with which to beat AMLO and his progressive plans: scarcely had the first cases been reported than the media began to accuse the President of complacency and to compare him (with no justification) to Brazil's Bolsonaro.

From the beginning AMLO insisted that Mexico would avoid panic and repressive measures: he would be guided by medical and scientific advice at all times. In his morning press conferences he began to be accompanied by leading figures from the Ministry of Public Health, notably Dr Hugo López-Gatell, Deputy Secretary of Health, whose clarity, knowledge and attention to detail are outstanding. Communication with the population was exemplary: in addition to the morning press conferences, Dr López-Gatell also gave afternoon briefings with exhaustive information.

The President, with the agreement of the Deputy Secretary, refused to impose a compulsory lockdown, advising people to avoid contact wherever possible, but recognising that lockdown would cause massive disruption and hardship for many Mexicans who depend on small businesses and precarious employment for survival. AMLO was also much criticised for refusing to wear a face mask, relying instead on social distancing: this was a reflection of the importance of communication for his political style.

Unfortunately for those who accused López Obrador and his government of complacency, as early as 4 February 2020, when Mexico had yet to report any Covid cases, WHO international advisor Jean-Marc Gabastou declared that "Mexico was the first country [in the world] to react and to activate its emergency system along the lines established by international health regulations".

In March Dr López-Gatell outlined a clear three-stage plan for dealing with the pandemic. A National Safe Distancing Plan was decreed, with an iconic superwoman, "Susana Distancia" as mascot (*Su Sana Distancia* means "Your Safe Distance").

Unlike many countries that have used draconian decrees and police repression to enforce restrictions during the pandemic, Mexico relied on persuasion and cooperation to achieve distancing, staying at home and closure of non-essential enterprises. AMLO quoted Benito Juárez, "Nothing by Force, Everything by Reason and Law"; he praised the Mexican public for their public spirit and good sense, and this positive social psychology seemed to work.

AMLO made personal contact with President Trump and with Chinese President Xi Jinping to request assistance with the supply of medical equipment. A formal agreement with China created a special air link to supply ventilators, test kits and protective equipment (PPE), and Trump also agreed to facilitate a ventilator deal with a US company.

The first flight from Shanghai arrived with 200 ventilators on 8 April, and weekly flights brought more supplies. These were commercial purchases at favourable prices, but Mexico also received free donations from China, the US, South Korea, Denmark and Switzerland.

None of this diminished the right-wing propaganda campaign against Mexico and the 4T Transformation. On 8 May 2020 the New York Times published a sensationalist article by Azam Ahmed with the title "Hidden Toll: Mexico Ignores Wave of Coronavirus Deaths in Capital"[9], and similar articles then appeared in the Washington Post, Wall Street Journal and El País of Spain. The article alleged that real deaths were much higher than official figures and that patients were dying in corridors or on the street while seeking treatment. But it was based entirely on hearsay, without a single piece of hard evidence, and its arguments for questioning official statistics could be applied to virtually any country. It was unfortunately one of the first examples of how the NYT would abandon all ethical standards of journalism to attack AMLO and Mexico, and how most of the international media followed suit like sheep. This journalistic malpractice by the NYT has continued down to the present.

The opposition claimed that the emergency must mean an end to the 4T Transformation, and predictably advocated classic neoliberal measures such as tax breaks for corporations and further privatisations. The President on the contrary insisted that the crisis made the Transformation more urgent, not less.

Starting on 5 April 2020 AMLO announced a slew of measures to protect the poor and most vulnerable and to lay the basis for economic recovery, or at least economic resilience, with priority for those at the bottom of the scale and not at the top.

Existing programmes like "The School Is Ours" and "Young People Building the Future" were to be increased or accelerated, and new emergency schemes would be launched to address the situation. The aim, he declared, was to rebuild the economy "from the bottom up".

A total of 22 million Mexicans would benefit from one social programme or another, amounting with their families to 70% of the population, and the top 30% would also benefit indirectly from the increase in demand. "Hope", said AMLO, "is a very powerful force".

Payments of pensions for seniors, incapacity benefits and grants and scholarships for students were increased and/or brought forward, and the government introduced several ambitious new schemes. One of the most important consists of 25,000 peso loans (about $1,100 US) to small business owners, payable over three years with a grace period of three months, at 6% interest (the lowest available inter-bank rate); they are *Créditos a la Palabra*, on trust (i.e. without collateral). Over 1 million small entrepreneurs would receive them, and 98% of them ran micro-businesses with from one to five employees.

A further 600,000 would receive "Solidarity Credits", also of 25,000 pesos over three years and at 6% and "on trust", but in this case for slightly larger businesses; although larger and having more resources, they were deserving because they had not dismissed any workers despite the crisis, hence the term "Solidarity Credits". Their data must be registered with IMSS (the Social Security Institute) to confirm eligibility.

A third such microcredit scheme is *Tandas para el Bienestar*, "Wagers for Welfare", aimed at the most deprived living in the most marginalised areas. If they are 30 to 67 years old and have a small non-agricultural family business which has been operating for at least six months, they could receive a one-year credit of 6,000 pesos on trust *and at zero interest*. They received free training and advice, and if they completed repayment punctually they would be eligible for a second loan of between 10,000 and 25,000 pesos depending on circumstances. "Wagers for Welfare" began on a small scale in 2019 and was later greatly expanded to reach 500,000 people by the end of 2020.[10]

In the same way, mortgage credit was made available on easy terms through various schemes, with similar principles: rather than the state contracting with large developers and construction companies to build social housing, mortgages are made available direct to workers for them to use as they see fit (subject to regulations on building standards, the environment, etc). Existing institutions – INFONAVIT and FOVISSSTE[11] – were made to offer more flexible terms to their clients.

In other words, each individual, with their family, hires local builders, architects, designers and tradespeople. There are no intermediaries and minimum bureaucracy, and local enterprises and employment are stimulated.[12]

As with "The School Is Ours" and the credits for small businesses, these housing credits were designed to create hundreds of thousands of local *Frentes de Trabajo*, employment initiatives to stimulate activity by working people throughout the country.

There are also several programmes to assist agriculture, peasants and rural workers, the most notable being *Sembrando Vida*, "Sowing Life", an agroforestry scheme designed to help small peasant farmers improve cultivation of subsistence crops in combination with planting fruit and timber trees, and in some cases durable hardwoods; they receive financial support and technical advice. This programme is so important that it (and other agricultural schemes) will be examined in detail in another chapter.

As previously mentioned, a crucial aspect of all welfare and social programmes is that the benefits are transferred to individual beneficiaries direct from the Finance Ministry (*Hacienda*). At first this required using the services of a private bank, but over a five-year period the government created a public Welfare Bank, *Banco del Bienestar*, with 2,700 branches throughout the country; all beneficiaries receive personal debit cards for this bank which guarantees them a minimum level of financial independence. In July 2024 I visited a local branch of the Welfare Bank in the heart of the capital; I was able to interview an employee from the Welfare Ministry who assisted clients using the bank, Juana Angélica Vargas, she explained that her job was to help people with procedures, especially those using the bank for the first time, claiming pensions, disability benefits, apprenticeships, Benito Juárez educational grants and several other benefits.

Every two months when payments are due, given the huge numbers of recipients, several days are set aside and people are summoned by alphabetical order on specific days, hence the need for organised queuing and assistance. The benefits also include a Working Mothers' grant for single mothers. Also in rural areas the Welfare Bank distributes the monthly payments of *Sembrando Vida* and other agricultural support programmes, and in remote areas, for older people with mobility problems or the disabled, welfare workers ("Servants of the Nation" is the term used) make home deliveries of the payments.

I was also able to interview two senior citizens and a disabled person who were receiving their payments and who commented on the importance of the benefits for them.[13] In time it will become easier for most recipients to make withdrawals at their convenience with the Welfare Bank debit cards they will all have. Another facility offered by the bank is for clients to open savings accounts.

What should be clear from this summary of the most important welfare programmes introduced by AMLO's government is not only their scope but also in many cases their originality: they contribute enormously to the practical living standards of the most deprived sectors of the population, but by means which do not necessarily conform to conventional socialist or social-democratic policies. Their financing also derives from fighting corruption and applying "Civic Austerity", meaning cutbacks in public-sector waste and ineffective showboating programmes which looked good but really only benefited privileged groups. Also tax rates have not increased, but tax collection has risen through preventing evasion. All of these unorthodox tactics affect privileged groups, but in unexpected ways, which explains the hostility to AMLO from those who cannot accuse him of socialism or radicalism as normally understood. By not raising tax rates or public sector borrowing the government has maintained private sector confidence, avoiding the classic debt and inflationary traps which typically plague leftist governments. Currency or balance of payments crises would ruin the very real positive impact of AMLO's wide-ranging welfare measures, and he has wisely acted to maintain financial stability while directing benefits to those in greatest need. That he was able to do this despite the enormous challenge posed by the Covid pandemic demonstrated that the Transformation was real.

Returning to the question of the pandemic, emphasis should be placed on Mexico's international role. On 26 March 2020 AMLO participated in a virtual meeting of the G-20 countries, in which he pointed out the relationship of the pandemic to issues of inequality and the need to address this.

On 1 April at the United Nations Mexico presented a resolution in support of the WHO, calling on all countries to stop commercial speculation in medicines and medical equipment and to ensure universal access to any vaccine or treatment for the virus. This resolution was passed on 20 April with the support of 179 out of 193 countries.[14]

Then on 5 May AMLO published an article which was translated into English and French and widely distributed on social media, with the title "Some Lessons from the Covid-19 Pandemic"[15]. It did not pull any punches. "First, it is a fact that, during the neoliberal period, public health systems were not a priority for most governments in the world…" and it was clear that:

> – We must strengthen the public health systems, in the understanding that – just as with education and social security – health cannot simply be a commodity or a privilege but is rather an inherent right of all human beings.
>
> – We must urgently address the serious problems of chronic diseases which are, de facto, the pandemics that have caused the most deaths in the world…many more lose their lives because of heart attacks, obesity and diabetes than those who, tragically, will die from the coronavirus…
>
> – We need a more caring world in order to strengthen universal brotherhood, and we should start by putting an end to the stockpiling of food, medicine and hospital equipment… States must stop using a model that creates wealth without wellbeing…It is the responsibility of the state to reduce inequalities. We cannot continue to leave social justice off the governments' agenda…

AMLO's statement was a manifesto for fundamental global change.

NOTES

1. dof.gob.mx/nota_detalle.php?codigo=5551445&fecha=28/02/2019, accessed 30/05/2020
2. www.gob.mx/bienestar/acciones-y-programas/pension-para-adultos-mayores?state=published, accessed 30/05/2020
3. www.gob.mx/bienestar/prensa/2024-inicia-con-aumentos-a-pensiones-de-bienestar-anuncia-ariadna-montiel?idiom=es
4. jovenesconstruyendoelfuturo.stps.gob.mx, Secretaría de Gobernación, Diario Oficial, 10-20-2020, accessed 31/05/2020; and www.gob.mx/stps/articulos/preguntas-frecuentes-jovenes-construyendo-el-futuro, 08 de marzo de 2024, accessed 19/07/2024
5. ubbi.gob.mx/registro, accessed 06/06/2020, and www/gob/mx/cms/uploads/attachment/file/465578/Programa_de_Universidades_para_el_Bienestar_BJ.pdf, accessed 21/07/2024
6. www.sep.gob.mx/dgticDatos/LEEN/escuelas.html, accessed 02/06/2020
7. See www.gob.mx/presidencia for the morning press conferences (conferencias matutinas) of 03/08/2023, 08/08/2023 and 14/08/2023.
8. www.gob.mx/presidencia/, Morning Press Conference, 12/05/2020
9. www.gob.mx/presidencia/, Morning Press Conference, 11/05/2020, accessed live.
10. www.gob.mx/presidencia/es/articulos/version-estenografica-de-la-conferencia-de-prensa-matutina-jueves-7-de-mayo-de-2020, accessed 04/06/2020.
11. INFONAVIT: *Instituto del Fondo Nacional de la Vivienda para los Trabajadores*, Institute of the National Fund for Workers' Housing; FOVISSSTE, *Fondo de la Vivienda del Instituto de Seguridad y Servicios Sociales de los Trabajadores del Estado*, Housing Fund of the Institute of Security and Social Services of State Workers.
12. www.gob.mx/presidencia, Morning Press Conference, 06/05/2020, accessed 05/06/2020.
13. David Raby interviews, 5 July 2024, Banco del Bienestar Correos/Reforma branch, with Juana Angélica Vargas Álvarez, Adrián, Jorge and Wilma.
14. www.gob.mx/presidencia/, Morning Press Conferences, 17 & 22/04/2020 accessed live.
15. www.gob.mx/presidencia/, Morning Press Conference, 08/05/2020, accessed live.

5

Universal health care becomes a reality

As explained in the last chapter, universal free health care was the government's intention from the beginning, and it was incorporated into Article 4 of the Constitution early in 2020, just when the Covid pandemic made it more urgent and simultaneously more difficult. We also saw how neoliberalism had made a chronically inadequate health system more shambolic than ever, with many health centres and hospitals half-built, ill-equipped or abandoned.

Covid continued to be a major concern in Mexico as throughout the world, with the second and third waves and with vaccination becoming available. Mexico was among the most active countries in obtaining supplies of vaccines, whether from the US, Europe, China, Russia, Cuba or wherever; it also took the lead in cooperation with other Latin American countries to ensure equitable distribution of vaccines, especially to the countries in greatest need.

In late January 2021 there was great concern because AMLO himself came down with Covid; but with treatment from a specialist Institute of Nutrition he recovered remarkably well and was back in regular activity within a fortnight.

But the major concern was more and more to develop the country's overall health system, with investment in new clinics and hospitals and in training and hiring doctors, nurses and all kinds of personnel. This was not only a matter of money and commitment; political and organisational problems were constantly arising. Thus in December 2020 Zoé Robledo, the Director of the Social Security Institute IMSS, reported that its laboratory services and blood banks had been privatised under the previous regime, so to recover them would require not just investment but complex legal procedures.[1]

Another serious obstacle to the adequate development of the health system was the supply of medicines: in March 2021 AMLO denounced what he described as a "medicine mafia" of pharmaceutical companies which controlled supplies of medications, manipulating prices and limiting availability.[2] Indeed, as was later explained by AMLO and the Health Minister, ten companies monopolised supplies of medicines, but they were not even pharmaceutical companies, simply distribution agencies linked to corrupt civil servants; a law had now been passed to change the system.[3] Another such problem was the existence of "adjunct consultancies" attached to pharmacies, which were under pressure to promote commercial sale of medications.[4]

INSABI (*Instituto de Salud para el Bienestar*, Institute of Health for Welfare) was established in January 2020 to provide services for all those not covered by the State Workers' system ISSSTE or the Social Security Institute IMSS. But it would require enormous investment to become really effective, and in February 2022 AMLO recognised that he was having to spend one day every week on meetings dealing with the health sector, to get new hospitals completed and more health workers hired.[5]

One of the logistical problems affecting the sector was that Mexico had a chronic deficit of medical specialists in certain fields, and it would take years to train sufficient new staff. In May 2022 an agreement was announced with Cuba for Mexican doctors to train there in certain specialisms, and for Cuban specialists to work in Mexico.[6] By July 2024 there were nearly 1,000 Cuban doctors working in Mexico, and more were on the way.

Another organisational problem complicating the reorganisation of health care was that state governments exercised a significant degree of control over the sector. It was clear that in order to achieve the kind of universal coverage that was the goal, federalisation would be necessary. The government therefore began to negotiate federalisation on a state-by-state basis, something which was of course resisted by opposition-controlled states. In this respect Morena's victories in several state elections in June 2021 was very helpful, and indeed in June 2022 another six state governorships were up for election, all of them held by the opposition, and Morena won four of the six, confirming the growing popularity of AMLO and the 4T Transformation.[7]

Federalisation of health care began in a few small states (Nayarit, Colima, Tlaxcala) and by the end of 2022 had spread to Baja California Sur, Sonora, Sinaloa and Campeche.[8] By July 2024 it had reached 23 of the 32 states, all of those governed by Morena and its allies, although even in those 23 there was still more to do in terms of completing hospitals and hiring more staff. Organisational progress was reflected in the transformation of INSABI into *IMSS-Bienestar* which is now the official designation of the system which covers all those not registered in previously existing public programmes.

What became clear was that in order to achieve a really effective universal system it was necessary to focus improvements at local level and to involve patients in the process: in the words of Zoé Robledo, the very capable and dedicated Director of IMSS-Bienestar, "the President told us to design 'The Clinic Is Ours', a programme to improve conditions of infrastructure and equipment of units at the first level of treatment, where most of the population seek assistance and where 80% of illnesses can be resolved"[9]. Starting in April 2024 a process began to create 11,816 Committees of Health for Welfare, each one elected by a community assembly and provided with a budget to improve their local clinic in consultation with medical staff. This was similar to the model adopted previously in education, "The School Is Ours". As Zoé Robledo went on to say, "We are sure that when decisions are collective, when they are taken with the people and in a democratic manner, they transform reality". On 30 July 2024 he gave a state-by-state statistical breakdown of IMSS-Bienestar hospitals and local Health Committees.[10]

It was therefore particularly relevant that in June 2024 I was able to visit two local clinics to see for myself the progress that was being made. In Lerma, an industrial town in Campeche state dependent on oil (PEMEX) and fishing, the Health Centre has been transformed with new investment in equipment and staff. It functions seven days a week, with three consulting rooms, equipment including electrocardiogram and ultrasound machines, its own pharmacy with the most essential medications, and dental service five days a week, all free of charge. The staff includes five GPs and seven nurses as well as a dentist.

Lorena Méndez, the state coordinator of IMSS-Bienestar, emphasised the importance of "The Clinic Is Ours" in involving local people in administering and supervising implementation of health care and ensuring transparency. It is also relevant that the treasurer of the committee is always a woman.

The members of the committee were meeting when I visited and were full of enthusiasm for the new programme which gives them real influence in decision-making. They commented on how the clinic, which had existed but was severely neglected under the previous regime, was now being positively transformed.

Another clinic I was able to visit is in Tlahuac, a working-class community in the outer suburbs of Mexico City. This clinic (the Ampliación Selene Health Centre) had existed since 1980, run by the Mexico City (Federal District) Health Service, but only offered free treatment to those enrolled in official programmes under the neoliberal regime. This has now changed, any local resident can register and receive treatment free of charge, and in emergencies anyone will be treated even if they are not registered.

The Health Centre, which serves a population of over 18,000, functions seven days a week from 8 am to 8 pm, with dentistry from Mondays to Fridays. It has seven doctors, three dentists and eleven nurses working in rotation, and also offers social service with a woman visitor working in the community, another worker in residence and an epidemiologist who monitors infections.

A monitoring service at the clinic entrance, known as *Salud en tu Vida* (Health in your Life) offers rapid checks of blood pressure, temperature, pulse and other basic vital indices, with medical referrals when necessary. A poster publicised a community campaign against measles, German measles and mumps.

A Health Committee elected as part of "The Clinic Is Ours" had been functioning for a month and a half when I visited; it meets once a week and evidently has lively discussions. Community engagement is clearly very active and this new scheme is transforming health care in Mexico.

The drive to improve community services is continuing: at the end of July 2024 AMLO and President-Elect Claudia Sheinbaum announced a new plan for regular home doctors' visits for the elderly.

As of 29 July 2024 *IMSS-Bienestar* was operating in 23 of 32 states, and it is to be expected that more states will affiliate depending on political conditions; thus Yucatán, previously governed by the PAN, was won by Morena in the June 2024 elections and is now in process of affiliation to the new medical service. A total of 576 hospitals have been transferred to *IMSS-Bienestar*, and 10,501 health establishments altogether, with 53,625 health professionals formally employed by the service.[11] Registered patients are entitled to free quality medical care including hospital care of all kinds; free medical examinations and laboratory tests; and free medicines and medical supplies.

The system includes (as seen in the clinics I visited) community action with an intercultural perspective. This includes a local Health Committee with a president and five more members dealing with general health, basic health education, nutrition and sport, hygiene, and social monitoring. Health volunteers are recruited, each to make regular visits to between 10 and 15 homes. Where possible traditional medical practitioners using indigenous or other remedies, and traditional midwives, are incorporated on a voluntary basis.

Registration in the system is available to all individuals not already covered by the health services of the Social Security Institute IMSS, the public sector workers' service ISSSTE or other institutions. In September 2024 Zoé Robledo, the Director of the new service, announced that as of 1 October *IMSS-Bienestar* cards would be distributed to 53 million people;[12] this would be done by home delivery, although it was also possible to register at clinics and hospitals. Each individual would have to provide official ID and proof of residence (utility bills).

There is also a system of coordination for all the public institutions providing health care, including *IMSS-Bienestar*, IMSS, ISSSTE and others; it is called *MAS-Bienestar* and is operated by the federal Department of

Health. It is responsible for prevention, supply of resources, quality of service, coordination, community involvement and rehabilitation.

NOTES

1. www.gob.mx/presidencia/ Morning Press Conference, 15/12/2020, accessed live.
2. www.gob.mx/presidencia/, Morning Press Conference 09/03/2021, accessed live.
3. www.gob.mx/presidencia/, Morning Press Conference 27/05/2021, accessed live.
4. www.gob.mx/presidencia/, Morning Press Conference 16/08/2022, accessed live.
5. www.gob.mx/presidencia/, Morning Press Conference 02/02/2022, accessed live.
6. www.gob.mx/presidencia/, Morning Press Conference 09/05/2022, accessed live.
7. https://www.jornada.com.mx, 6 de junio de 2022, "Morena triunfa en 4 gubernaturas: PAN-PRI, en dos". Accessed 06/06/2022.
8. www.gob.mx/presidencia/, Morning Press Conference 15/11/2022, accessed live.
9. www.gob.mx/imss/articulos/la-clinica-es-nuestra, 11 de junio de 2024, accessed 01/08/2024
10. www.gob.mx/presidencia/, Morning Press Conference, 30/07/2024, Accessed live.
11. www.imssbienestar.gob.mx Accessed 24/11/2024.
12. vanguardia.com.mx/informacion/para-que-sirve-la-credencial-imss-bienestar-2024-fecha-de-entrega-y-como-recibirla-BG13400634, 29/09/2024. Accessed 24/11/2024.

6

'Sowing life': rural communities as a priority

If support for the poor was AMLO's priority, the rural poor had to be front and centre. Although Mexico is a highly urbanised country, rural communities – largely indigenous or mestizo – are still of great importance, especially in the central and southern states. Subsistence and small-scale commercial agriculture remain very significant and are part of the heritage of last century's revolution with the agrarian reform based on *ejidos*, communal farms.

The agrarian reform suffered a fatal blow with Carlos Salinas' constitutional reform of Article 27 in 1993, which gave individual members of *ejidos* the right to sell or rent out their parcels of land, and allowed commercial enterprises to buy the land. Although in many cases *ejido* members have refused to sell (which is interesting), the aim and the effect was to destroy any remnant of agrarian collectivism in law and policy.

AMLO's response to this situation was typical of the man in both clarity and originality. *Sembrando Vida*, "Sowing Life", combines social, environmental and economic goals. It addresses simultaneously the problems of rural poverty, environmental degradation and agricultural decline. An agroforestry programme, it provides financial support, technical advice and environmental guidance to small peasant farmers.

Sembrando Vida revives local economies, generates employment, restores the environment and promotes community cohesion. It does this by selecting applicants who own or have access to 2.5 hectares of agricultural land in municipalities with a serious level of social deprivation. Preference is given to those of indigenous or Afro-Mexican background, and at least 20% must be women.[1]

They must sign a four-year contract agreeing to work the land in an agroforestry system of timber and fruit trees (*Sistemas Agroforestales de árboles maderables y frutales, SAF*) and/or of subsistence crops interspersed with fruit trees (*Milpa Intercalada con Árboles Frutales, MIAF*), or preferably both.

In return they receive a monthly stipend and scientific and cultural advice. While in some cases this may be done on an individual basis, the preference is to integrate them into Farming Apprenticeship Communities (*Comunidades de Aprendizaje Campesino, CACs*), consisting on average of 25 individuals working together (with their families). They will have access to Community Nurseries (*Viveros Comunitarios*) and Bioindustrial installations (*Biofábricas*) producing compost, natural fertilisers and other organic inputs.

The programme was designed taking into account that rural areas with great agricultural potential had in recent decades suffered seriously from deforestation and over-exploitation of resources, causing degradation of soils and negative effects on local microclimates. This was leading to further impoverishment of the population and out-migration to cities or abroad.

Agroforestry systems have the advantage of increasing agricultural productivity and reducing inputs such as fertiliser, improving soil quality and biodiversity, and providing improved incomes and employment opportunities.

As of 30 December 2023 *Sembrando Vida* had benefited 455,749 individuals and their families, of whom 31% were women; it was operating in 24 states out of 32; and it had improved 1,139, 372 hectares of land.[2]

A total of 18,500 Farming Apprenticeship Communities had been created, with active participation in democratic decision-making and cooperation; they benefit from collective marketing of their products, notably fruit and timber. 36% of the committee members are women and they constitute 40% of the savings, education and sustainability sub-committees.

Ill-informed or prejudiced critics of the programme have suggested that it might actually increase deforestation because the poor would be tempted to clear land by burning or felling trees in order to have their 2.5 hectares to qualify: this is specifically forbidden in the regulations, and recently-cleared land is not accepted for inclusion. Already forested land cannot be included either, it may qualify for other support schemes.

Since *ejidos* do continue to function in many places despite Salinas' privatisation reform, members of *ejidos* can apply to participate in *Sembrando Vida* using their ejidal plots, but only with the express permission of the *ejido* Assembly.

In a recent visit to southeastern Mexico I was able to see this remarkable programme in operation. In Palenque (Chiapas) Victoria Cruz Damas, who was selling fruit and juices she had prepared, explained that she had been able to affiliate with *Sembrando Vida* on an individual basis, and for nearly six years had been able with her husband and daughter to produce timber trees and fruit trees (limes, oranges, mango, guava, and chico zapote), and also beans and cacao from which they made a pozole drink. This had given them subsistence and a modest business, as well as the monthly grant which started at 4,000 pesos and increased to 6,250 at present (government policy provides for annual increases). This was a total contrast from former governments which provided nothing.[3]

A more typical (and more relevant) example of *Sembrando Vida* in action is the Farming Apprenticeship Community (*Comunidad de Aprendizaje Campesino*) "Rebuilding the Countryside" (*Reconstruyendo el Campo*) on the outskirts of the town of Champotón in Campeche, which I visited on 12 June 2024. It has a nursery (*vivero*) of some 20 hectares where 23 peasant farmers and their families have seen a real transformation of their lives in the past three years.

The Secretary of the group, Mario Alberto Poscaya Delgado, explained that where previously communities like theirs felt abandoned and small peasant farmers would neglect their plots of land and consider selling them, now they are able to cultivate and improve the land and work with others to grow new crops. Marginalised areas are now green and productive, and thousands of peasants have received support with grants and assistance from scientists and technicians. AMLO gave them the opportunity to develop their own land in ways which they could not imagine.

Each farmer is now able to grow subsistence crops like maize and beans more reliably, with more varied vegetable production and also diversification by planting fruit trees for consumption with a small commercial surplus: limes, mangos, avocados, guava, and more, and also timber trees. The monthly subsidy provides cash in hand and also helps to pay for inputs.

Mario Alberto explained that while each farmer tends his or her own plot, they work as a team with each member responsible for certain tasks: to allocate plants from the nursery according to the specific needs and possibilities of each plot; to prepare compost; to prepare biodegradable fertilisers; to develop natural insecticides; to repair tools, etc. They do not use chemicals, everything is organic, and by teamwork and with technical advice they have succeeded in three years in growing 50,000 trees and bushes in the nursery for reforestation of their land.

The group accommodates the methods of older members who use traditional composting and planting seasons; the flexible combination with modern techniques has been beneficial. They have been able to produce enough of a surplus to donate trees to schools and neighbouring communities (and plant them) in what they describe as a form of "social work".

In recent years they have given preference to drought-resistant plants because of the lack of rainfall, in the words of one older member, "we must not allow plants to die". They have a natural well which they use for irrigation and also a reserve cistern to ensure water supply. After the vegetable harvest, when they have their supply of cucumbers, radishes, lettuce, chillies and other greens, they allow the land to rest in the dry season and when the rains come again they plant trees including fruit and timber trees like rosewood (*maculí*) and *cedro* (for timber), also mahogany.

Another member of the team showed me where they had been growing avocados in some quantity, also coconuts, tamarinds, *chico zapote* (soap apple), aloe vera, mamey and ciruelo fruit, and timber trees such as the drought-resistant *siricote* (borage), rosewood and *cedro*. For this they had improvised another small irrigation system. They had suffered from drought and even fire on one occasion, but were still producing a wide variety of fruit and timber.

Mario Alberto insisted on the great benefits of the "Sowing Life" programme and their gratitude to President López Obrador, to Campeche Governor Layda Sansores and to the Welfare Secretary. It is essential that the programme continue, it has rescued their community from poverty.

An official report in July 2024[4] indicated that in nearly six years *Sembrando Vida* had received an annual investment averaging $2 billion USD. The 1.2 million trees planted included 637,000 (so slightly over half) timber trees like mahogany, pine, *cedro* and rosewood, to be commercialised in a sustainable manner. It is also producing 277,000 agroindustrial trees such as coffee, cacao, nopal cactus, annato dye (used for textiles but also as food colouring and flavouring), and 252,000 fruit trees including lime, peach, guava, guanábana and mango, and spices such as cinnamon, pepper and chillies.

The programme has also led to the creation of 15,115 *biofábricas* (ecological installations producing non-chemical composts, fertilisers and insecticides), producing 62 million litres of liquid inputs and 472,000 tons of solid inputs.

It has helped to promote agricultural self-sufficiency, producing 819,000 tons of maize per year (90% for subsistence and 10% for sale). Among 115 different fruit varieties grown, *Sembrando Vida* has increased national lime production by 6.2%, apple production by 39.25%, oranges 8.1% and mango 15.8%; and in other crops, coffee by 20%, cacao by 40% and agave by 46.7%.

The social, economic, environmental and cultural value of the programme is immense, and it is one of the most important components of AMLO's 4T Transformation of Mexico. It has even been extended to neighbouring Central American countries in a very generous act of disinterested foreign aid.

Sembrando Vida began in the neglected and impoverished southeastern region, and it is where its benefits are most apparent. It has been recognised by the UN Development Programme for its contribution to carbon capture, aquifer restoration, soil improvement and biodiversity conservation, as well as reducing poverty and migration, improving food security and restoring the social fabric. Étienne von Bertrab, a Mexican lecturer in Political Ecology at University College London, studied the impact of *Sembrando*

Vida along with other policies such as the Tren Maya in the southeastern region; he points out that despite being based formally on individual grants and contracts, it reinforces social bonds including traditional methods of collective work (*mano vuelta* and *tequio*). Through the CAC Farming Apprenticeship Communities it develops practices of dialogue, cooperation and self-government, and leadership capacity especially among women, although sometimes causing an excess work burden.[5]

As explained by Von Bertrab, in reforestation *Sembrando Vida* is not only one of the biggest projects in the world but one of the most effective: unlike many such projects which are based on monoculture, it promotes diversity of species, especially native varieties, with multiple benefits, not just carbon capture. Each tree is cared for by a specific individual and each participant in the programme has to maintain 2,500 trees (so 1,000 trees per hectare) on his or her 2.5 hectare plot. With some 450,000 participants in Mexico as a whole, this means more than 1,000 million trees planted in six years on previously degraded lands. In social and economic terms this has benefited above all communities previously suffering from moderate to extreme poverty and marginalisation, above all indigenous and Afro-Mexican. They still face problems such as the marketing of their produce, but without doubt it has led to a great improvement in their prospects and opportunities; Von Bertrab noted in the south of Quintana Roo that a significant number of participants had been able through *Sembrando Vida* to escape from exploitative work in the tourist enclaves and return to their communities. The result has been a restoration of dignity and autonomy as well as economic betterment.

NOTES

1. https://www.gob.mx/bienestar/acciones-y-programas/programa-sembrando-vida Accessed 08/08/2024
2. www.gob.mx/cms/uploads/attachment/file/878464/PSV2024.pdf Accessed 08/08/2024
3. Video interview in Palenque, 7 June 2024.
4. www.jornada.com.mx/noticia/2024/07/26/sociedad/se-han-invertido-38-mil-928-mdp-cada-ano-en-sembrando-vida-8021 Accessed 26/07/2024
5. http://gatopardo.com/noticias-actuales/legado-amlo-en-mexico/ *Fin de sexenio: una mirada desde el sur,* 17.9.24 Étienne von Bertrab.

7

Public Works: the *Tren Maya*

Another fundamental aspect of AMLO's programme and a key component of his success is the implementation of major public works projects to benefit the nation and above all neglected regions and sectors of the population. These include roads, irrigation works, ports, airports, a new oil refinery, railways, public parks, environmental reserves and a major solar energy installation.

All of them have been criticised as wasteful, inefficient, unnecessary, economically unviable or environmentally destructive, criticisms which are generally incorrect and frequently reflect vested interests. The most vocal and sustained attacks have been directed at the new Mexico City Santa Lucía airport, the Dos Bocas oil refinery in Tabasco, and the Tren Maya, a 1,550-km railway looping round the Yucatán peninsula and adjacent areas of the southeast.

The new Santa Lucía airport (officially *Aeropuerto Internacional Felipe Ángeles*, AIFA, named after a revolutionary General) was urgently needed to supplement the existing heavily overloaded Mexico City Benito Juárez International Airport. The previous government was planning to replace the existing airport with a much bigger one nearby, on the wetlands of the former Lake Texcoco, causing enormous environmental damage and costing nearly three times as much. The project favoured real-estate speculation and corruption, and the AIFA, a public enterprise built by military engineers in record time, is already a success, contrary to opposition propaganda.

As for the oil refinery, it has to be pointed out that where the PEMEX public enterprise had been a mainstay of the Mexican economy for decades, neoliberal governments had been trying to privatise it while pumping out more and more crude oil for export and importing refined products: as AMLO said, "like exporting oranges and importing orange juice".

AMLO's policy has been to restore national refining capacity to achieve self-sufficiency in refined petrol and diesel while exporting less; it does not negate the need for transition to renewables. The Dos Bocas refinery, now complete, is another triumph of Mexican public-sector engineering.

The *Tren Maya* railway has to be seen in this context, not only for its benefits to the economy and society of the neglected southeast but as part of the restoration of Mexican industrial capacity and the public sector. It is indeed a major project, connecting extensive areas of five states, Tabasco, Chiapas, Campeche, Yucatán and Quintana Roo. It will service the tourist coast of Cancún and the "Mayan riviera" as well as urban centres like Mérida and Campeche and the great Mayan archaeological sites of Palenque, Edzná, Uxmal, Chichén Itzá, Calakmul and others. It will encourage tourism and get tourists to venture beyond the beach resorts, and also serve the general economy of the region, agriculture, industry and business of all kinds. Local people are already benefiting from skilled and well-paid employment in construction and in running the railway, and in selling their own produce.

You would not know this, however, from most of the mainstream media, whether Mexican or international, which conducted a sustained campaign against the *Tren Maya* from the beginning. in this they were backed by opposition politicians and misguided environmentalists, anthropologists and NGOs claiming to defend indigenous peoples, peasants and the natural heritage.

None of AMLO's projects has been the object of more ferocious and sustained criticism than the *Tren Maya*. Critics allege that it will destroy the region's sensitive environment, that it rides roughshod over indigenous culture, that it deprives peasant communities of land and promotes uncontrolled neoliberal development, and that it is a high-speed train for big business.

The Zapatistas (EZLN) declared (in the words of Subcomandante Moisés) that "The capitalist hydra" had arrived, "the beast will swallow in one mouthful entire villages, mountains and valleys, rivers and lakes, men, women, boys and girls"[1]. In July 2020 researchers from 65 Mexican and 26 international institutions signed "Observations on the Environmental Impact Assessments of the Mayan Train" claiming it would cause "serious and irreversible harm"[2]. Prominent intellectuals said it was a manifestation of "savage capitalism" which robs the native people of land, destroys the environment, exploits migrant and native labour, "favours the introduction of pig 'factories', allows the production of genetically-modified soya and hothouse crops using large amounts of toxic chemicals, and turns a blind eye to the clearing of the forest". Drug trafficking, criminality and prostitution were central to this model and they alleged would only grow with the Mayan Train, whatever the government's good intentions[3].

There was almost no evil which critics did not attribute to the railway. The chorus of criticism generated with haste when the project was just beginning was repeated in 2023 when it was fast advancing: on 23 May 2023 the *Guardian* carried an article with the provocative title "'A megaproject of death': fury as Maya train nears completion in Mexico"[4].

So comprehensive are these denunciations that it seems inconceivable that anyone progressive could support the Tren Maya; but careful examination shows that the allegations are almost entirely false, and reflect a coordinated political campaign.

Most of the Yucatán peninsula is a low-lying limestone platform which naturally erodes to create sinkholes known as *cenotes*, with underground rivers and lakes where groundwater accumulates. It is indeed ecologically sensitive, but this did not prevent the ancient Maya from building great pyramids or the Spanish from developing colonial cities like Mérida and Campeche.

Where this vulnerable environment has been wantonly destroyed is in the massive uncontrolled development of Cancún and the "Mayan riviera" stretching for some 150 km along the Caribbean coast. Fifty years of speculative investment has created the biggest tourist complex in Latin America, bringing abundant wealth to a handful of national and (mainly) transnational interests with no concern for Mayan or indeed Mexican culture. *Tren Maya*, with all of its associated public initiatives, is just the beginning of an attempt to reappropriate some of this wealth for the Mayan and Mexican people.

It is not possible here to make a detailed refutation of all the criticisms, but it should be emphasised that virtually all the problems attributed by opponents to the *Tren Maya* began long before. The best answer came from a Yucatecan woman anthropologist, Paloma Escalante Gonzalbo, writing four years ago about the pre-existing situation:

> ...the ancestral territories were lost centuries ago, [the farming communities] produce less and less due to the droughts of recent years, they find themselves obliged to migrate to the tourist areas or elsewhere to find work...We find forests devastated by clandestine logging and poachers who even start fires to drive out the game... highways where heavy lorries drive at great speed and run down animals... The local inhabitants are clear about one thing: paradise hasn't existed for many years, and we cannot go on doing nothing about the situation. If transformation is what the government is offering, then that's what has to be our hope...[5]

Cancún and the "riviera" consists of typical nondescript resort architecture, with privatised beaches, anonymous hotels and highways, poor to non-existent public transport, hidden or damaged *cenotes* and mangroves replaced by manicured lawns swallowing up scarce water supplies. Also, chronically deprived *barrios* for insecure and marginalised local workers.

I was able to observe the reality of the situation on a recent visit to the area facilitated by a Mexican colleague, Étienne von Bertrab of University College London, with his colleagues and students who were studying the project. In an intensive ten-day field trip in May 2023 we were able to visit construction sites, tour the region and interact with local communities, government officials, NGOs, academics and ordinary people.

What we found was a much more balanced picture of a project which represents the first serious attempt in 50 years by federal authorities to counterbalance uncontrolled and destructive neoliberal development and generate an alternative based on collective interests, with publicly owned infrastructure integrated with social, cultural and environmental initiatives to benefit local communities. It deserves serious consideration and not hysterical denunciation. Local people we spoke to had many questions about the railway, but most were optimistic about its benefits; surveys indicate that a substantial majority of the region's population favour the Train.

To set the record straight we should list some of the positive features of the Train, as follows:

> 1] Most obviously, it's a *railway*, and as such will take both passenger and goods traffic off the roads, reducing pollution. Almost 50% of the route is electrified and the hybrid locomotives will use ultra-low-emission diesel on the rest of the track.
>
> 2] It will have many stations, 20 plus 14 *paraderos* (which we would call local stations) for a total of 34, thus serving tourists and local people as well as business travellers.
>
> 3) Indeed it is misleading to call it a "high-speed train": it is very modern and efficient, but there will be only a few limited-stop express services, with a maximum speed of 170 km/hour, similar to fast inter-city trains in the UK and Europe but only about half the speed of the French TGV or similar high-speed lines elsewhere in Europe, Japan and China.
>
> 4) Fares for local people (of the five states where the railway operates) are lower than for other Mexicans, and much lower than those for foreign visitors; there are also discounts for senior citizens, students, teachers and the disabled. Local people are already using the train to get to work or for other needs.

5) Restaurant cars and cafeterias on the trains, and food offerings at the stations, give priority to local cuisine.

6) Local independent businesses will be given preference in commercial concessions at and around the stations.

7) Both in construction and in operation of the completed railway, local people are being employed as far as possible, with skilled and well-paid jobs far superior to the precarious employment which predominates in the private tourist industry. Investment in Tren Maya (without counting related development projects, discussed below) amounts to 515 billion pesos, about $26 billion US.

8) Courses in railway engineering have already begun at universities and technical colleges in Palenque, Campeche and Quintana Roo.

9) Locomotives and rolling stock – 42 train sets with 219 coaches – are being manufactured at the Alstom plant in Hidalgo state in central Mexico, a major industrial complex dating from the mid-twentieth century. Although majority owned by a French multinational, it is comparable to the largest such plants in the world and for the *Tren Maya*, has increased Mexican national input to 70% (whereas previous neoliberal governments had been running it down).

10) The railway is built with hundreds of green underpasses for the local fauna to cross safely, unlike the existing motorways where animals are constantly being run down.

11) In one coastal section in Quintana Roo with particularly vulnerable foundations, a long section of the track is elevated, supported by columns with very advanced technology.

We were very impressed by the dedication and enthusiasm of those involved in construction, from both public agencies and private contracting companies. We were able to visit three of the stations being built, at Teya, Maxcanú and Calkiní, where work was going ahead despite the intense heat (and with appropriate protection and frequent breaks for the workers).

Given the scale of the project the track was built in seven sections by different consortia combining Mexican and foreign companies and military engineers. The finished railway is Mexican public property, run by the military. Almost half the route uses the abandoned line of a former railway, the *Ferrocarril del Sureste* (Southeastern Railway) begun by the great President Lázaro Cárdenas in 1937 and completed in 1950; it provided good service for some 40 years but was run down by neoliberal governments. When Ernesto Zedillo privatised the railways in 1997 (and the private companies abandoned passenger services), the Southeastern Railway was not even included in the privatisation but was simply closed down, reflecting the elite's contempt for the southeastern region. This at least was an advantage when AMLO initiated the *Tren Maya*: the existing route remained public property.

While the railway is a massive and ambitious undertaking in and of itself, it is in fact only part of (and the beginning of) a comprehensive development project for the Mexican Southeast as a whole. It represents by far the biggest public investment ever in social and cultural development for the region: it is a huge attempt to change direction from the chaotic and destructive neoliberal model which had prevailed for 50 years. With all the related projects it has generated about 600,000 jobs in the region, many of them much better paid than previously existing work in tourism, agriculture or logging; indeed, it has caused a shortage of labour in various sectors.

Tren Maya is closely linked to implementation throughout the region of all the government's social programmes and of *Sembrando Vida*, and there is further reforestation implemented as part of the railway project itself. It is also linked to other infrastructure and urban improvement projects, notably those carried out by SEDATU (*Secretaría de Desarrollo Agrícola, Territorial y Urbano*), the Ministry of Urban, Agricultural and Regional Planning. SEDATU already existed but had a limited budget and little impact; AMLO gave it a much broader mandate, and under a very creative and dynamic young architect, Román Meyer Falcón, it has carried out hundreds of urban and rural improvement projects in deprived communities throughout the country, winning more than 200 architectural design awards for its high-quality work on a total of more than 1,000 public works. Its projects include parks, recreation and sports grounds, community centres, markets, schools, libraries and theatres, and it has been very active along the route of *Tren Maya*. In collaboration with state and municipal governments it has helped to bring comprehensive improvements to many neglected communities in the region. Access to all of these facilities is free (except for a small charge for toilet access in some cases). For local people the benefits are tangible and unprecedented.

We visited some of these projects in the deprived southern suburbs of Mérida, including two small parks with play equipment for children, and a community centre which offers many activities for local women including embroidery and crochet but also computer courses for both women and men.

SEDATU's Urban Development Programme operates nationally, but has devoted special attention to the south and southeastern region. Étienne von Bertrab points out that some of its projects are more ambitious, such as the Jaguar Park in Tulum and the Chetumal market, involving local firms, providing thousands of jobs and developing new skills in the workforce; he was impressed by the sense of pride and dignity of the engineers, architects and other workers, and the participation of women.[6] One concern arising from Tren Maya was the expansion of the tourist industry, no longer confined to Cancún and other beach resorts but extending inland and to many of the ancient Mayan sites, with speculative commercial urbanisation. But here another aspect of SEDATU's work is particularly important, its regional planning mandate. By an agreement signed in December 2020 between the federal government, the five states and 17 municipalities directly impacted by the railway, it was decided to create the *Programa de Ordenamiento Territorial de la Región Sur-Sureste* (Organisational Plan for the South-Southeastern Region), developing a pattern for state and municipal plans (something which almost none of them had previously). Over the following years there was intense work on developing plans from regional to very local level.

This coordinated effort helped to eliminate corruption at local level, for example in Tulum where the environment ministry Semarnat condemned a previous plan which would have allowed urbanisation of 19,000 hectares of jungle. Some deforestation was inevitable with the railway and the new Felipe Carrillo Puerto airport, but very much less, and the Jaguar Park included recognition of new natural reserves.

In both Mérida and Campeche, as they are historic cities with a valuable historic heritage, it was not possible to build a modern railway in the centre, so the *Tren Maya* stations are some distance away. In both cases light rail lines are being built to connect the urban centres with the *Tren Maya* stations.

The *Tren Maya* is linked to other new and or modernised railways currently nearing completion in southern Mexico. The most notable of these, now complete, is the Trans-Isthmian corridor which traverses the Isthmus of Tehuantepec, the narrowest point where the Atlantic (Gulf of Mexico) can be linked to the Pacific. With modernised ports at Coatzacoalcos in southern Veracruz and Salina Cruz in Oaxaca (both redeveloped under AMLO) this railway, primarily for freight, offers an alternative to the Panama Canal. Another route runs from Ciudad Hidalgo near the Oaxaca coast, along the Pacific coast of Chiapas to the Guatemalan border. These routes will all be connected, giving the southeastern region a relatively complete publicly-owned passenger and freight network.

Much of the opposition comes from private interests wanting to maintain their own transport monopoly and exploitation of cheap labour and resources. As AMLO has pointed out, nine of the NGOs most active in opposition to *Tren Maya* have received funds from US foundations; already in 2020 they had received a total of $14 million.[7] While this is no more than circumstantial evidence, it is relevant when considering that the railway will remain Mexican public property and that construction contracts have gone to several Mexican, European and Chinese firms. As for local farmers affected by expropriation in some parts of the route, they are small and medium cultivators of mixed race, often settlers from other parts of the country, and have received adequate compensation.

Much publicity has been given to the opposition of the Zapatistas (EZLN), but as we have seen their support base is concentrated in the Chiapas highlands, some distance away from the railway. The population of the Yucatán peninsula most directly affected by the railway are also indigenous Maya, heirs to the great revolt of the mid-19th century and of the Socialist Party of the Southeast, active protagonists of the Mexican Revolution who from 1916 to 1924 carried out a remarkably advanced land reform along with secular education and feminist reforms throughout the peninsula. Their leader was a bilingual Mayan worker named Felipe Carrillo Puerto, and the new Tulum airport in Quintana Roo (on the route of *Tren Maya*) is named after him.

The peninsular Maya have a different history to those of the Chiapas highlands. In President López Obrador's press conference of 12 June 2023 a representative of the Maya Cruzob – cultural and political heirs of the 19th-century revolt and of Felipe Carrillo Puerto and the Socialist Party of the Southeast – spoke at length, in both Mayan and Spanish, in favour of the *Tren Maya*, while requesting the removal of neoliberal bureaucrats who were still perverting AMLO's social and environmental reforms at local level. He also demanded implementation of a programme of indigenous justice which had been promised by the President.

AMLO listened attentively and promised to implement the plan of indigenous justice not only in Quintana Roo but throughout the region. In other words, what we have here is an advanced social and political project with active local indigenous engagement and support; indigenous identity does not correlate necessarily with either opposition to or support for *Tren Maya*. It is a question of political orientation.

Under previous administrations, environmental protection was promoted in some areas, but it was implemented by decree with no consultation, leaving a number of communities isolated and subject to arbitrary restrictions. Now under AMLO local consultation was the order of the day, and it was recognised that conservation was a priority of the rural and indigenous population; by including them in environmental projects the results were much more effective. As Von Bertrab points out, the local people realise that the Tren Maya is of real benefit to them, and the opposition claim that it is "not Mayan" rings hollow when none of the previous capitalist projects inflicted on the region were Mayan: neither the hotels, nor the highways, nor the golf courses or luxury restaurants. The "white city" of Mérida (the regional capital, so called for its architecture, but also a bastion of the creole elite) was not Mayan, nor were the henequen plantations which dominated the regional economy before the revolution and the extraordinary government of Felipe Carrillo Puerto and the Socialist Party of the Southeast from 1921 to 1924. The Tren Maya with its benefits for the local people is a fitting contemporary memorial to this Mayan revolutionary legacy. Much remains to be done to ensure that future development in the region is beneficial to the working people, whether through a new type of tourism or other activities, but the balance sheet so far is overwhelmingly positive.

Finally, the new (2023) Governor of Quintana Roo state, a young bilingual woman called Mara Lezama, has launched an ambitious state programme of support for local communities and cooperatives to give them priority of access to commercial opportunities linked to the railway, and Campeche Governor Layda Sansores is doing the same.

When in late 2023 the first trial runs of the train occurred with AMLO and members of his cabinet on board, hundreds of cheering spectators lined the route. In June 2024 I was able, with my partner, to take the train from Palenque to Campeche, a very comfortable four and a half hour trip. The train is a great success, and AMLO announced that he wants to see passenger train services restored throughout Mexico. His successor Claudia Sheinbaum also favours this, and has announced that she wants to install 3,000 km of passenger lines during her presidency, a complete transformation of public transport with emphasis now on the centre and north of the country. Passenger railways are in general of obvious environmental and social benefit, and Tren Maya is an outstanding example of this.

NOTES

1. Claro y Directo MX, "EZLN avisa que va vs el Tren Maya", www.cydnoticias.mx/2020/01/02/ezln-vs-tren-maya/, accessed 11/10/2020
2. www.jornada.com.mx/ultimas/politica/2020/07/30/mia-del-tren-maya-sin-valoracion-suficiente-sobre-impacto-expertos-9545.html, accessed 11/09/2020
3. Luis Hernández Navarro, "Tren Maya, desarrollo y presencia estatal", www.jornada.com.mx/2020/03/03/opinion/017a1pol, accessed 11/09/2020
4. x.com/guardian/status/1660899232121868288, 23 May 2023, Accessed 16/08/2024
5. *La Jornada Maya*, 18/06/2020, "¿Nos robará el tren el paraíso?", Paloma Escalante Gonzalbo, www.lajornadamaya.mx/opinion/843/--nos-robara-el-tren-el-paraiso-, Accessed 10/09/2020
6. http://gatopardo.com/noticias-actuales/legado-amlo-en-mexico, 17.9.24, "Fin de sexenio: una mirada desde el sur", Étienne von Bertrab. Courtesy of the author.
7. *Financiamiento de OSC opositoras al Tren Maya*, twitter.com/JesusRCuevas/status/1299368891525804032/photo/1, accessed 28/08/2020.

8

Justice for the native people

International publicity for the EZLN gave many people the false impression that AMLO and his government were hostile to the indigenous population or at least indifferent to their predicament: nothing could be further from the truth. "For the good of all, but first, the poor": the indigenous people are for the most part the poorest and most marginalised in Mexico, and are of course at the centre of the Fourth Transformation.

As we have seen, the EZLN have support from many of the Maya of the Chiapas highlands and neighbouring areas of that state, but have little presence elsewhere. There are more than 60 different native groups in Mexico with a wide variety of languages and cultural characteristics and specific historic and political experiences.

From the beginning AMLO identified the Yaqui people of Sonora as the most oppressed and abused nationality in the country. Conquered in colonial times like the rest of the indigenous population, they had been forcibly deprived of their remaining lands in the 19th century and then brutally suppressed when they revolted, and under Porfirio Díaz thousands of those who remained were deported to the Yucatán (3,000 km away), in effect as plantation slaves. In the late 1930s as part of the agrarian reform Lázaro Cárdenas had restored much of their land and rights, but in subsequent decades they once again lost most of these gains.

Early in his presidency AMLO announced his intention to discuss the situation directly with Yaqui representatives, and promised a "Justice Plan for the Yaqui People". On 27 October 2020 he decreed the creation of a Presidential Justice Commission for the Yaqui People, with representatives from the National Institute of Indigenous Peoples and several key government departments as well as the Traditional Governors and Secretaries of the eight Yaqui towns, Vícam, Pótam, Lomas de Guamuchil-

Cócorit, Loma de Bácum, Tórim, Ráhum, Huírivis and Belem. It was to meet regularly and investigate the situation of the lands, territories and waters of the Yaqui people and other indigenous peoples.[1]

A first key session on site took place in the Indigenous Children's House of Tórim, Sonora from 23 to 25 January 2021 with the participation of 20 federal agencies and the traditional Yaqui authorities. The agenda was to promote the integral development of the Yaqui People, beginning with artisan roads to remote municipalities as in Oaxaca, investment in traditional medicine, in a radio station and in new refectories for indigenous girls and boys so as to reduce school absenteeism.[2] The Ministry of Agriculture presented a strategic project for indigenous economic development with investment of more than $11 million in the first year, with active participation of all communities.

The Secretary of Ráhum, Crisóforo Valenzuela Ahumada, served as interpreter and also insisted that development must start from below and not with "salomonic" ideas imposed from central offices. This was a point he would emphasise repeatedly in later meetings.

The work of the Presidential Justice Commission produced a first formal agreement on 28 September 2021 with a bilingual event in Vícam Pueblo[3]. There were formal welcomes by the indigenous Governor of the town and the State Governor Alfonso Durazo, who declared it was an historic occasion. The Chair of the Justice Commission recalled the crucial 1937 and 1940 decisions of President Lázaro Cárdenas to return lands to the Yaqui People, and AMLO's first visit of October 2019. A decree now signed by the President included a first transfer of 2,943 hectares of land and the guarantee of drinking water, and that Irrigation District no. 18, with over 126,000 hectares, would be directly administered by the Yaquis. As originally promised by Lázaro Cárdenas, 50% of the waters of the River Yaqui basin would be for the native people. A Yaqui University would be established in Vícam Pueblo, and a Regional Hospital in Vícam Estación, with six rural medical units; also a radio station, the Voice of the Yaqui People. The initial investment amounted to some $500 million.

The Justice Plan for the Yaqui People was formally signed by all parties at the conclusion of the event. AMLO spoke eloquently of the history of repression, quoting the Governor of Sonora at the time of Porfirio Díaz who admitted that 15,000 Yaquis had been slaughtered in crushing the revolt (as against 200 soldiers), and thousands more died in the deportations to Yucatán that followed. The survivors and their descendants would now at last receive their lands, waters and rights.

The Secretary of Tórim community, Jesús Patricio Varela, quoted the Spanish conquistador Nuño de Guzmán as saying that he had never encountered a nation so determined to defend its territory as the Yaquis. Together with the Secretary of Ráhum, Crisóforo Valenzuela Ahumada, he presented the proposed constitutional reform on indigenous rights: "We want to thank [everyone] and celebrate this new era of reconciliation and peace with all our indigenous and Afro-Mexican sisters and brothers; that's why representatives of all the original peoples are here before you [Mr President], and together we are presenting you the constitutional reform proposal". There were 68 indigenous peoples represented at the event.

A prominent veteran of the INI (*Instituto Nacional Indigenista*, National Indigenist Institute) who had worked closely with AMLO many years ago, Salvador Nahmad y Sittón, spoke forcefully of the need for all indigenous peoples to have their autonomous territory and self-government.

Also present was Cuauhtémoc Cárdenas, son of Lázaro Cárdenas and former leader of the PRD, who insisted that the water issue was still not adequately resolved because of an aqueduct which was operating illegally and taking part of the Yaqui basin water for other purposes.

But AMLO repeated that the Irrigation District would be directly administered by the traditional Yaqui authorities, and nothing was being done without consulting them.

A fortnight later, on 15 October 2021, Sonora Governor Alfonso Durazo visited Vícam Pueblo to meet with indigenous leaders. In response to the Secretary of Tórim he declared:

> I respect, I will respect and I will work with the community to strengthen the autonomy of this ethnicity and of other native peoples. I always refer to the traditional authorities, governors of the Yaqui people, I refer to them as colleagues, because I recognise in their condition as governors a representation similar to my own, which the people of Sonora have entrusted me with just like their communities...I think we face a historic opportunity for the State of Sonora...I am completely willing to establish working groups to analyse the aims of resources for the people...[4]

An indigenous woman pointed out that a representative of Ráhum was also present, together with Church representatives; but never before had a State Governor visited them, this was historic. She noted also the presence of the mayors of Guaymas and Cajeme municipalities (six of the Yaqui towns are in Guaymas municipality and two in Cajeme). The municipal rates (taxes) were collected from them but were not reflected in public works to benefit the Yaquis, they hoped this would change. Both the mayors promised this would be the case.

The Yaqui Secretary of Tórim declared that they must celebrate this agreement, and that what they were receiving was not "welfarism" but was theirs by right.

Governor Durazo added that they could save 500 million pesos (about $25 million) by reducing the cost of running the State Congress (no doubt in line with AMLO's Civic Austerity policy), and use it for a scholarship fund for Sonora university students. He would also ensure that the issue of local rates was resolved. There was also a dispute about highway tolls, gas pipeline and railway charges of which the Yaqui wanted a share, all of this was open to discussion.

Then on 21 May 2022 AMLO visited Cajeme again with the State Governor and other officials to check on progress.[5] The Governor stressed the need to work among the Yaquis to ensure unity, and different officials reported on what had been achieved.

Ramón Meyer Falcón, head of the Regional Development Ministry SEDATU, said that 79% of infrastructure work was complete; more than 1,700 houses had been built; 2,900 hectares of national lands had been handed over, and several sports facilities were ready. The head of the National Water Commission CONAGUA reported that the Yaqui Aqueduct was advancing through eight municipalities and 50 communities, it would have a total length of 241.7 km with a water purification plant and should be complete in September 2023.

The Director of the National Indigenous Institute gave details of progress on other projects, including the University of the Yaqui People and infrastructure for a Yaqui Fishing Cooperative. He insisted on the need for unity, showing that differences existed among local people.

Finally AMLO declared that the agreements must be fulfilled, there were sufficient funds and he as President authorised payment for transfer of the entire 30,000 hectares of land promised to the Yaquis as soon as possible. Similarly with the work for expansion of the Irrigation District, pumping and other equipment must be installed. The same with housing, roads and health. He was going to visit again on 30 August 2022 and wanted matters resolved by then.

The Justice Plan for the Yaqui was indeed fulfilled and celebrated in 2023, and it was only the first (but in a sense the most important, a real landmark) of similar plans for other native peoples. On 22 May 2022, the day after the progress inspection in Cajeme, AMLO and his team were in Pitiquito, Sonora to inaugurate the Integral Development Plan of the Seri-Comcá-ac People. The traditional coordinator of the Seri, Joel Barnett Morales, spoke in his own language and in Spanish, saying that the "Men of Sand" as they called themselves were pleased to receive the President.[6]

A local woman explained how they were driven out by the Spanish and lived only on Tiburón/Kunkaak island, and the present ceremony was taking place in Desembarque (Landing) community where they had first reclaimed a presence on the mainland years ago. They lived from fishing, hunting wild sheep, and also now tourism.

The Justice Plan for the Seri began with a desalination plant for drinking water, then also 80 new fishing boats and commercial facilities for marketing fish, a photovoltaic solar plant, electrification and road building, housing and health centres. The health plan included support for traditional medicine. Education would be improved, including two refectories for local school students. AMLO pointed out that since there was also mining in the area, the law would be changed to include profit-sharing for local people.

Justice Plans and Development Plans have since been created for many indigenous peoples in different regions of Mexico.[7] These include four peoples in the state of Sonora, four in Chihuahua, four in Jalisco, Durango and Nayarit, and at least one in each of Veracruz, Chiapas, Querétaro, Guanajuato, Oaxaca, Guerrero and Baja California.

The importance of these specific plans is self-evident, but they are only the most visible and practical manifestation of AMLO's commitment to the indigenous cause. He repeatedly refers to Mexico's indigenous roots as a fundamental part of his vision for the country. If we have survived as a nation, he says, and if we have avoided the worst aspects of social disintegration which afflict the United States and Europe, it is because of our traditional values with roots going back before the Conquest, before the Spanish invasion. The maintenance of community and family cohesion is what distinguishes Mexico from many other countries in the modern world.

AMLO defines the guiding principle of his project, its theoretical basis, as Mexican Humanism. It is manifested in the communal cultivation and usufruct of land; in the principle of mutual help; and in a libertarian spirit. These values are inherited from the ancient cultures of Teotihuacán, the Olmecs, Maya, Toltecs, Zapotecs and others, and all negative and prejudiced judgements about them must be dismissed:

> …It is a great lie to assert that the European invaders brought civilisation to a region of the world where civilisation had existed for many centuries…That's why we are promoting the recovery of memory and of the historic heritage, and at the same time we are applying justice plans to indigenous peoples and communities…to all the original peoples of Mexico and to the Afro-Mexican peoples and communities.[8]

Although individualism has been imposed, traditional communal ideals continue, along with the practice of collective labour and solidarity. Moreover – and here AMLO's conception is a radical rejection of the widely-held stereotype derived from Hollywood – he maintains that honesty is a fundamental Mexican characteristic:

> …another one of the good precepts or elements we inherited from the first inhabitants of pre-Hispanic Mexico is an innate inclination to honesty, which is still the greatest value of our country. Corruption is a relatively new phenomenon, begun with the foreign invasion and fomented by greed and

profit which almost always accompany the desire for gain, superiority, command and domination.

The heroes of Mexican Independence, of the Liberal Reform and the Revolution all repudiated corruption and exalted values of honesty, cooperation and equality.

In this respect there was great symbolic and political importance in the ceremonial commemorative events organised for the year 2021, supposedly the 700th anniversary of the foundation of México-Tenochtitlan by the Aztecs/Mexica, the 500th anniversary of the most important events of the Spanish Conquest, the 200th anniversary of the formal consummation of independence and the 100th anniversary of the fall of Porfirio Díaz. No less than 15 special events were to be held during the year.

The first such event was held on 14 February 2021 in the small town of Cuilapam, Oaxaca; it marked the 190th anniversary of the death of Vicente Guerrero, one of the insurgent leaders of the struggle for independence from Spain. Born in Tixtla, Guerrero (the state which is named after him), he was of African and indigenous descent, and worked as a mule-driver before becoming leader of the armed insurgency after 1816.[9] He became President in 1829 and governed for eight months; his rule was distinguished by the official abolition of slavery and promotion of education and agrarian reform, but he was overthrown in a coup by the conservative Anastasio Bustamante and after more than a year's armed resistance was captured and executed in Cuilapam.

The commemorative event was attended by AMLO along with the governors of Oaxaca and Guerrero and also Martin Luther King III who declared that Guerrero was a hero of the abolitionist movement. King declared that like Guerrero, they were working for justice, equality and dignity, and he thanked the Mexican President for "the opportunity to participate in this incredible event". The Governor of Guerrero pointed out that the figure of Vicente Guerrero had been neglected in the country's historiography.[10]

The next event, just ten days later on 24 February 2021, was the anniversary of the Plan of Iguala,[11] a compromise which made possible formal recognition of Mexican independence by agreement between insurgent leader Vicente Guerrero and royalist commander Agustín de Iturbide; it provided for independence but with Iturbide as Emperor, an arrangement which not surprisingly did not last, giving way to a Republic in 1824.

Much more in keeping with the spirit of self-determination and indigenous identity was the third event on 25 March 2021, the anniversary of the battle of Chakán Putum (modern Champotón, Campeche), a naval encounter in 1517 where Mayan war canoes defeated a Spanish naval force.[12] This symbolic victory is a cause of celebration and AMLO often repeats the defiant cry "Take your Champotón!" against overweening foreigners.

3 May 2021 saw the next such event, commemorating the end of the "Caste War of Yucatán", a major uprising of the Mayan people of the peninsula which lasted off and on from 1847 to 1901.[13] The native people were inspired by the "Speaking Cross" as interpreted by their leaders, and the place in modern Quintana Roo state where this Cross was located was known as Chan Santa Cruz, later renamed Felipe Carrillo Puerto after the revolutionary leader of the Socialist Party of the Southeast who played a key role from 1916 to 1924. The commemoration was led by AMLO together with the President of Guatemala, the governors of the five southeastern states and key government ministers. AMLO made a formal apology to the Mayan people, and spoke of the paradox by which the territory of greatest repression, Quintana Roo, has now become a tourist paradise.

Only ten days later came a very different commemoration, also of great significance for the country's indigenous identity, the 700th anniversary of the foundation of México-Tenochtitlan by the Aztecs or Mexica.[14] The event took place in the ruins of the Great Temple just north of the Zócalo. AMLO spoke of the achievement of "this fragile Chichimeca tribe" which in 200 years succeeded in building a great dominion over much of what is now central and southern Mexico; this is reflected in the fact that 48% of Mexican place names are in Nahuatl, the Aztec language. Whatever their methods, there was no justification for the brutalities of the Spanish Conquest.

Several other commemorative events followed, most notably 13 August (the date of the final fall of Tenochtitlán to the Spanish, and the beginning of 500 years of indigenous resistance); 16 September (celebrations always begin on the night of 15 September), Independence Day, the day of Father Miguel Hidalgo's *Grito* (Shout) of rebellion in 1810; 28 September, the date of Justice for the Yaqui People; and 30 September, the birthday of Father José María Morelos, the second great insurgent leader after Hidalgo. Several of these commemorations took place in the presence of important international guests.

The year 2021 was also marked by efforts (which continue) to obtain the return of national treasures held in museums or private collections in Europe and the US, such as the Aztec and Maya codices (pictographic records of their history and culture), and Moctezuma's ceremonial head-dress, held in the Vienna Ethnology Museum. Mexico also requested a formal apology from Spain for its actions in the Conquest, which is controversial in Spain and has not been forthcoming. There was also controversy over the excommunication by the Catholic Church of Fathers Hidalgo and Morelos, although the Church maintains that these excommunications had already been withdrawn.

Such symbolic commemorations had occurred previously in Mexico, but never on such a scale and with such intensity. Even more important, however, was the implementation of programmes to benefit today's indigenous peoples, the Justice Plans and other plans to recognise their rights in practice and give them the place they deserve in national life. The use and teaching of indigenous languages, first implemented in a limited way under Lázaro Cárdenas in the 1930s, is now being encouraged as never before.

As previously mentioned, but deserving further attention, AMLO is the first president ever to give explicit recognition to Afro-Mexicans. The presence of African slaves, their exploitation and their cultural contribution is well-known in many countries in the Americas, most notably the USA, Brazil, Colombia, Cuba, Haiti and the Caribbean islands in general, but they were also present in colonial Mexico. Their presence was proportionately less because of the size of the indigenous population, but they were certainly significant on the Gulf coast (particularly in the state of Veracruz) and parts of the Pacific coast (Guerrero and Oaxaca).

From the beginning AMLO referred to the Afro-Mexican community and the need for its long-overdue recognition, and insisted on a constitutional amendment to that effect which took effect on 11 August 2019[15]. He has also shown practical recognition of communities with a strong and visible African presence.

On 26 August 2023 the President visited the town of Cuajinicuilapa, known as the Black Pearl of the Pacific, to supervise the advance of welfare programmes in the area. He was given an enthusiastic welcome by local inhabitants.[16] Nearly a year later, on 29 July 2024 the same town was visited by AMLO together with President-Elect Claudia Sheinbaum and the Governor of Guerrero, Evelyn Salgado Pineda. They inaugurated the modernised Federal Route 200 from Las Cruces to Pinotepa Nacional in Oaxaca, and 682 km of artisan roads in the coast and the mountains, benefiting 500,000 inhabitants in 23 municipalities.[17] "These are signs of such a significant advance for our indigenous and Afro-Mexican peoples", said the Governor who praised AMLO and his philosophy of Mexican Humanism. AMLO affirmed that "to change a reality of injustices, of oppression, to achieve a real change, a transformation, you must have the people. The people is the motor of change…" Claudia Sheinbaum promised to continue the transformation with new programmes of pensions for women aged 60 to 64, the extension of the Benito Juárez grants for pre-school, primary and secondary students to be universal and no longer means-tested, and home health visits for seniors. There were words of thanks from the mayors of Cuajuinicuilapa, Metlatónoc and Tlapa, and the event closed with the traditional "Devils' Dance".[18]

In February 2024 it was announced that as a result of the process of consultation and dialogue which took place from 2019 to 2021 and subsequently, another constitutional reform would be included in AMLO's 2024 list of 20 reforms which he wished to push forward if Morena and its allies achieved the necessary two-thirds supermajority in the 2 June elections.[19]

This was the reform giving constitutional status to the Indigenous and Afro-Mexican Communities, with significant territorial rights, a large degree of self-government, linguistic and cultural rights, traditional agricultural practices and rights to consultation on economic development. Since this supermajority (which many thought impossible) was indeed achieved, the new amendment which reinforces the constitutional rights of indigenous and Afro-Mexican inhabitants was indeed passed and formally adopted on 31 October 2024. Mexico's multi-ethnic identity was finally recognised as never before.

NOTES

1 www.gob.mx/cms/uploads/attachments/file/588300/decreto-comision-presidencia-de-justicia-para-el-pueblo-yaqui-2020-10-27-MAT-inpi-pdf. Accessed 18 August 2024.
2 https://www.gob.mx/presidencia/prensa/gobierno-federal-y-pueblo-yaqui-acuerdan-inversion-para-desarrollo-integral-de-comunidades, 26/01/2021. Accessed 19/08/2024
3 www.gob.mx/presidencia/prensa/gobierno-de-mexico-acuerda-plan-de-justicia-del-pueblo-yaqui-y-recibe-propuesta-de-reforma-indigena 28 de septiembre de 2021/Comunicado Accessed 21/08/2024.
4 twitter.com/AlfonsoDurazo/status/1449131216540733440, 15/10/2021. Accessed 22 August 2024.
5 https://lopezobrador.org.mx/2022/05/21/version-estenografica-plan-de-justicia-para-el-pueblo-yaqui-desde-cajeme-sonora/ Accessed 23/08/2024
6 www.gob.mx/presidencia/es/articulos/version-estenografica-plan-de-desarrollo-integral-del-pueblo-seri?idiom=es, Accessed 29/05/2022
7 www.inpi.gob.mx/planes-de-justicia/, Accessed 24/08/2024.
8 Andrés Manuel López Obrador, *¡Gracias!* , México, 2024, Planeta, p. 447.
9 https://es.wikipedia.org/wiki/Vicente_Guerrero, Accessed 26/08/2024.
10 twitter.com/lopezobrador_/status/13611013988654391300, 2021/02/14. Accessed 16/02/2021
11 https://cultura.gob.mx/recursos/sala_prensa/pdf/202102/cpm_conmemoraciones_emblemaamp769ticas_2021_05feb21_compressed.pdf, Accessed 27/08/2024
12 www.mexicodesconocido.com.mx/batalla-de-champoton-o-cuando-los-mayas-vencieron-a-los-espanoles.html, Accessed 27/08/2024
13 www.gob.mx/conmemoraciones/es/articulos/fin-de-la-guerra-de-castas-peticion-de-perdon-por-agravios-al-pueblo-maya?idiom=es, Accessed 27/08/2024
14 www.publimetro.com.mx/mx/nacional/2021/05/13/tenochtitlan-amlo-celebracion.html, Accessed 27/08/2024.
15 www.animalpolitico.com/analisis/invitades/anotaciones-cinco-anos-reconocimiento-pueblos-comunidades-afromexicanas, Accessed 28/08/2024.
16 https://es-us.noticias.yahoo.com/amlo-supervisa-avance-programas-costa-… Accessed 28/08/2024.
17 www.elfarodelacostachica.com.mx/2024/07/evelyny-amlo-

inauguran-ampliacion-de-carretera-a-pinotepa/, Accessed 28/08/2024.

18 Also useful is www.worldbeatcenter.org/exploring-the-hidden-treasures-of-afro-mexican-culture-in-costa-chica-oaxaca, Aug 26, 2023, by Volunteer, Accessed 28/08/2024.

19 www.gob.mx/inpi/articulos/iniciativa-de-reforma-indigena-y-afromexicana-es-un-acto-de-justicia-social-inpi-358411?idiom=es, 21 de febrero de 2024, Accessed 28/08/2024.

The author, second from right, pictured at "Sembrando Vida", complex in Champotón

9

Dealing with the Colossus of The North

In previous chapters we have examined in detail some of AMLO's key policies in order to make clear what the Fourth Transformation is really about and what a remarkable positive impact it has had for all Mexicans, but first, the poor. In later chapters there will be more on the 4T and its benefits, but first it is necessary to examine how Mexico has succeeded in achieving so much despite its close, indeed some would say overwhelming, relationship with its great northern neighbour, the USA.

A common border of more than 3,100 km, a trade treaty which has reinforced economic integration so that the US accounts for more than 80% of Mexico's trade, and something like 40 million first- and second-generation Mexican migrants living and working in the US: this might seem to make independent policy impossible. Moreover, when AMLO took office in December 2018 – indeed, during his election campaign early in that year – he was facing in Donald Trump the most right-wing and apparently anti-Mexican US President in generations.

With Trump expressing open disdain for Mexicans and talking of building a wall to keep them out, the prospects seemed grim. In August 2017 AMLO had published a book with the title *Oye, Trump* (Listen, Trump)[1] denouncing the Republican President's policies, and he toured Mexican and Latin American communities in the US expressing solidarity with migrants:

> …Trump's persecution of migrants is mere electoral demagogy; he has deceived many US citizens with the narrative that Mexicans are stealing their jobs…But he knows perfectly well that the US economy cannot sustain itself

without migrant labor…The pretence of building a wall follows this hypocritical logic. If it is ultimately built, this wall will not staunch the flow of workers from one country to another; it will simply make things much more dangerous. This is a criminal idea.[2]

AMLO condemned Trump as a neofascist, and filed a formal complaint with the UN Office of Human Rights in New York.[3]

Despite this AMLO recognised the need for and the possibility of negotiations. Trump was threatening to tear up NAFTA, the North American Free Trade Agreement of 1994, and while AMLO like much of the Mexican Left had condemned this neoliberal treaty, it seemed likely to be replaced with something even worse if Trump got his way.

Once in office, AMLO surprised most observers (and probably the US administration) by seeking good relations from the word go. Despite the imbalance of forces, the Mexican leader and his team correctly calculated that Washington would not really want to exclude migrant workers completely or to disrupt the closely integrated economy of the border regions and of major production chains like the automobile industry.

While totally opposed to neoliberalism, AMLO realised that with 80% of Mexico's foreign trade being with its northern neighbour the idea of tearing up NAFTA was a non-starter. The only viable solution (though far from easy) was to seek revision of the treaty, but in ways beneficial to Mexico.

Rather than indulge in futile anti-imperialist gestures, AMLO sought to engage with the vain and irascible occupant of the White House by a combination of flattery and hard bargaining. Trump's preference for personal dialogue and deal-making could be used to Mexico's advantage.

On his election in 2018 AMLO contacted the US President proposing a new stage in bilateral relations "based on mutual respect", and Trump responded in kind, with warm congratulations on AMLO's victory. Shortly afterwards a high-level US delegation arrived to push trade negotiations forward.[4] While domestically AMLO advanced with his 4T agenda, he also sought rapprochement with Mexico's hegemonic neighbour.

Eighteen months later, in July 2020, the inconceivable happened: a new trade treaty, (USMCA, the US-Mexico-Canada Agreement) was approved, with significant benefits for Mexico; and AMLO visited Washington as a favoured guest of President Trump. Moreover, despite scepticism from many on both sides of the political spectrum, this gesture may well go down in history as a triumph of Mexican diplomacy.

In the 18 months following his inauguration, AMLO and his remarkably capable Foreign Secretary Marcelo Ebrard discreetly but firmly undertook a radical reorientation of Mexican foreign policy. Rather than a supine submission to Washington and a steady rightward drift, as had been the case with the neoliberal presidents of the previous 30 years, they have reasserted

Mexico's historic tradition of non-intervention and respect for sovereignty, and combined it with an active and protagonistic role promoting peace and multilateral cooperation on the international stage.

While quietly negotiating with Washington, Mexico showed an apparently contradictory desire for closer relations with progressive governments in Latin America. Formerly a leading member of the conservative "Lima Group" of Western Hemisphere governments (formed in August 2017 to increase hostile pressure on Venezuela in line with US policy), Mexico now withdrew from the group. This new trend in Mexican policy faced a potential crisis in late May 2019, when after months of growing Central American migration through Mexico towards the US, Trump suddenly threatened to slap 25% tariffs on all Mexican products if the flow of migrants was not halted.[5]

Rather than respond with hostile rhetoric, AMLO called for dialogue and sent Marcelo Ebrard to Washington for talks. A week later Ebrard emerged triumphant, with a bilateral agreement to work together to manage migration from Central America (and elsewhere), and an understanding that tariffs and migration were separate issues.[6] Trump abandoned the tariff threats and trade negotiations resumed.

Mexico also made it clear that while it wanted close collaboration on economic and migration issues, military involvement of any kind was not acceptable. Legal action against corruption under former President Felipe Calderón raised the issue of the "Fast and Furious" intervention of 2009, a raid by armed US agents which violated Mexican sovereignty and was authorised by Calderón's government. Marcelo Ebrard sent a diplomatic note on 8 May 2020 requesting clarification of recent revelations on the subject.[7]

Also on 18 June 2020 AMLO reminded his audience that under former President Enrique Peña Nieto (2012-18) the US had provided helicopter gunships to Mexico to help in the fight against crime, but "with all due respect, we do not want this".[8]

To Washington with Prestige and Dignity

Mexico's initiatives for international cooperation in the fight against Covid, and for cooperation on migration, were reflected in the country's election to the UN Security Council's rotating membership by a near-unanimous vote, and its appointment to ECOSOC, the UN Economic and Social Council.

Global diplomatic success combined with the assertion of legal and military sovereignty meant that the Mexican President could arrive at the White House with his head held high, not as a supplicant but as leader of an independent country with growing prestige.

The visit was not generally expected until almost the last minute. AMLO had maintained from the start that he did not want to travel internationally and that "the best foreign policy is made at home". In late March 2020 he received invitations from both Trump and Xi Jin-ping of China, but expressed reluctance to travel for health reasons. He was still saying this early in June.[9]

But AMLO likes to keep his cards close to his chest, and it should not have come as a surprise when ten days later he was talking of the visit to Washington as a strong possibility. When the visit finally materialised, his capacity for surprise and audacity was revealed yet again in the unprecedented decision to take an ordinary commercial flight. While it was well known that he was selling the luxurious presidential plane as part of his "Civic Austerity" drive, and was travelling by very modest means in Mexico, it had been assumed that if he did go to Washington he would go in a Mexican Air Force plane for security reasons.

The event itself, from the evening of 7 July to the afternoon of 9 July, followed the choreographed ritual of such events. AMLO made formal tributes at the monuments to Abraham Lincoln and Benito Juárez, underlining the good relations that had prevailed at a crucial moment in the history of both countries (the US Civil War and abolition of slavery, and the French invasion of Mexico). This could be seen as a subtle but significant gesture given Trump's association with white supremacists, made more palatable by the fact that Lincoln was a Republican. It also marked a very rare instance in which the US actually defended Mexican sovereignty.

Following the official meeting of the two presidents on 8 July, the formal speeches in the White House Rose Garden were remarkably cordial. Trump spoke of "my good friend" and said the two countries now enjoyed "an outstanding relationship...which had never been so close", praising the contribution of Mexican-Americans in many fields of US life.

AMLO's speech also focused on the positive, but was longer and more substantial. "We want to privilege understanding...setting aside differences, or solving those differences through dialogue and mutual respect" – "Some thought that our ideological differences would inevitably lead to confrontation. Fortunately, that bad omen was not fulfilled." He outlined the benefits of the new trade treaty, and stressed the gains for workers and for small and medium enterprises. He also thanked the US President for help in obtaining ventilators for dealing with the Covid pandemic.

AMLO also politely but pointedly stressed several historical episodes: a remark by George Washington to the effect that no nation should take advantage of another's weakness; the close relationship between Juárez and Lincoln and the rejection of the French invasion; and the good relations between Lázaro Cárdenas and Franklin Delano Roosevelt in avoiding conflict over the 1938 oil expropriation.

AMLO repeatedly referred to friendship and good relations between the two countries "despite some grievances which cannot be forgotten"; and "what I appreciate the most is that you have never sought to impose on us anything that violates our sovereignty...You have not tried to treat us as a colony; rather, you have honoured our status as an independent nation".[10] Not surprisingly, Trump described his visitor as "tough but fair".

The visit concluded with a gala dinner and more speeches; among those attending were leading business representatives, a sign of the new treaty's real commercial and economic significance.

Critics, allies and saboteurs: what was really at stake

As was to be expected, the visit was subject to intense criticism from all sides, but particularly from the left. Those who had denounced NAFTA as a neoliberal agreement destroying workers' rights, depressing wages, turning Mexico into a branch-plant economy and harming the environment, saw no benefit in the new treaty. A typical Mexican leftist journal, *La Izquierda Diario*, accused AMLO of "grovelling" with a "display of flattery" in the face of Trump's "unlimited cynicism". In the US the Democrats inevitably accused the Mexican President of unwarranted interference in the election campaign, and the liberal media in both countries rehashed all of Trump's unsavoury qualities and the alleged benefits for Mexico of a Democratic victory in the elections. [11]

What the critics fail to consider is that a failure to engage with the US on trade when Trump was denouncing NAFTA for his own nationalist reasons, and even more when global economic crisis threatened to see Mexico crushed by US protectionism, would have been disastrous. As for migration, open confrontation with Trump could only lead to brutal retaliation which would leave the migrant community in a much worse situation.

The new USMCA Treaty also has real benefits which the critics fail to consider. Unlike NAFTA, it includes a chapter on labour which explicitly recognises union rights, calls for internal union democracy and for higher wages in Mexico. It also includes small and medium enterprises, explicitly providing for their participation in exchanges between the three countries; and it respects Mexico's energy sovereignty, previously threatened by US proposals for a free energy market. To have won these concessions from Washington is no small achievement.

But where the critics are most wide of the mark is in terms of the political context, both domestic and international. Anyone familiar with US Latin American policy in recent decades will realise that the Democrats, despite their liberal rhetoric and their much more presentable manners, are in practice no less interventionist than the Republicans. As for migration, under Obama a record number of Mexicans – nearly two million – were deported.

In Mexican domestic politics the right-wing and old-guard opposition to AMLO was completely outmanoeuvred by the Washington visit. They were trying desperately to tar him with the leftist brush as an irresponsible populist, an enemy of business, a castro-chavista bent on turning Mexico into another Venezuela. Now he had most of the country's leading entrepreneurs on side, transnational companies like Walmart agreeing to pay overdue taxes to finance the 4T Transformation, a new trade treaty and a good relationship with the most notoriously unpredictable US President in living memory.

What the Mexican right wing (and much of the US establishment) wanted was to provoke AMLO into a confrontation which would have enabled them to generate a middle and upper class revolt with significant support, leading to regime change as in Brazil or Bolivia, or at least serious unrest as in Venezuela or Nicaragua. Instead they were faced with a moderate consensus for real progressive change in a democratic and peaceful manner, a positive example which could only be beneficial for the entire Latin American and Caribbean region (and even – dare one hope – for the US itself).

Viewed in this context, AMLO's Washington visit could be seen, in the words of John Ackerman, as "a strategic triumph of reason over politics" and "a diplomatic master-stroke" comparable in US politics to Nixon's visit to Beijing in 1972.[12] The more thoughtful and analytical intellectuals in Mexico realised this: Victor Flores Olea wrote of "AMLO's tour-de-force in dangerous territory" and quoted veteran Senator Porfirio Muñoz Ledo: "this is the most complete and illuminating speech I have ever heard from a Mexican president in the United States…" Muñoz Ledo also pointed out that "Trump didn't say what he thinks, but what he had to say, while López Obrador said exactly what he thinks and what I believe all Mexicans think".[13]

Moving on to deal with the Democrats

When Trump's term came to an end AMLO had to tread very carefully to avoid accusations of political interference in the explosive US presidential succession. When Donald Trump refused to accept Joe Biden's victory, AMLO – unlike many other heads of state and government – abstained from taking a position until 15 December 2020, when the US Electoral College had formally confirmed Biden's victory, and only then did he send a letter congratulating the Democrat on his victory.[14] Then on 20 December AMLO had a phone conversation with Biden, which he said was friendly; they discussed migration and the need to provide support to the people of Central America and southern Mexico in order to limit migration.[15]

When the Washington Capitol riot of 6 January 2021 occurred, AMLO's only comment was to lament the violence and say that it was an internal US affair.[16] But following Biden's inauguration he did indicate agreement with key points of the new US President's agenda, such as the economic stimulus, the intention of making US citizenship available to millions of migrants and of dedicating $4 billion to development in Central America.[17] Then in February he was able to celebrate Biden's declaration that he would not continue with building a border wall, something which not only Trump but other US presidents of both parties had done.

It was also in February 2021 that AMLO first presented his Electricity

Reform plan, to reinforce the powers of the Mexican Federal Electricity Commission (CFE by its Spanish initials), beginning to reverse the effects of privatisation. The negative reaction of the Governor of Texas, threatening to cut off energy supplies to Mexico in the crisis caused by a winter storm, was not shared by Biden, indicating a more cooperative approach at federal level.[18]

Then on 1 March 2021 the two presidents had their first full personal meeting (by virtual means) which confirmed positive cooperation on economic and trade matters, migration and human rights. In the following months the debate on electricity, and on energy reform in general, became heated, with fierce criticism of AMLO's proposals from private interests in Mexico and the US and from the media, and legal injunctions against the CFE and the government. But AMLO stood his ground, and it was notable that the Biden administration did not intervene for the time being.

These were issues that would continue to create tensions over the next three years. The opposition's use of the courts and the problem of judicial corruption would become the biggest obstacle to progress and would dominate the 2024 elections; in 2021 it was already a problem but looked as if it might be resolved because for the time being the Supreme Court had a progressive Chief Justice, Arturo Zaldívar, who was pushing through a judicial reform package.

As for relations with the US, it was already apparent that friendly dialogue with Biden and his cabinet did not prevent interventionist habits and tendencies from various US agencies from continuing. As explained in chapter 3, in May 2021 it was revealed that two of the most active NGOs promoting hostile propaganda against AMLO, Mexicans Against Corruption and Impunity (which as AMLO declared, does the opposite) and "Article 19", were being financed by the US Embassy. A diplomatic note of protest was sent but there was no reply, and the same issue would be raised again in 2024. Funding such organisations through USAID and the National Endowment for Democracy, whether in Mexico or elsewhere, is institutionally established in Washington and it would take a really radical US administration to change this.

In the June 2021 mid-term Mexican elections the OAS (Organisation of American States), notorious for its submission to Washington and to the most interventionist interests, insisted on sending observers. Although AMLO was open in his criticism of the OAS, even playing the satirical song by Cuban Carlos Puebla *Como no me voy a reír de la OEA, Que es una cosa tan fea* ("How can I stop laughing at the OAS, When it's such an ugly thing?), he nevertheless allowed their observers in, saying that freedom of speech and the press were for Mexico absolute values.

With Mexico insisting that respect for sovereignty and non-intervention are the foundation of its foreign policy, being very open in its criticism of the blockade of Cuba, but equally very willing to negotiate with Washington on trade, migration and judicial matters, it is very difficult for the US to take really hostile action. As Trump realised, the extremely close commercial and economic relationship works both ways.

Furthermore AMLO's financial orthodoxy – the fact that he has financed his ambitious welfare and infrastructure projects by eliminating corruption and waste, avoiding tax increases or borrowing – means that the IMF and other international financial agencies have no leverage over Mexico.

Another crucial factor – of which more later – is AMLO's very close and positive relationship with the Mexican military, for which he has been much criticised by some sectors of the left but which means that a coup (no doubt always on the wish list of the radical right in Washington) is not on the cards.

It is instructive to examine further AMLO's handling of relations with the Biden administration in the last three years. On 18 November 2021 he attended the 9th North American Leaders' Summit in Washington with Biden and Canadian PM Justin Trudeau.[19] AMLO went to Washington with a clear agenda, insisting (as he had previously with Trump) that it was time for another "Good Neighbor Policy" like that of Franklin D Roosevelt. Biden responded – and this had a powerful impact on the audience – that "It's no longer a Good Neighbor Policy, we're absolutely equal, we're equal countries"; how this would translate into practice remained to be seen, but it was a very important declaration.[20]

While Covid was still on the agenda, AMLO pointedly mentioned a US health problem, the 100,000 annual deaths from opioids. Also when gang violence was mentioned, he recognised that it was a problem in Mexico but pointed out that arms smuggling from the US was a major factor; indeed, Mexico had presented a lawsuit in Massachusetts against US arms manufacturers for criminal negligence causing bloodshed south of the border, turning the tables in terms of responsibility for cartel violence.

The official final declaration of course included platitudes about economic growth and "building back better together", but it also mentioned explicitly no less than four times the need to promote small and medium enterprises and their participation in the benefits of cross-border trade, a point stressed by the Mexican President. AMLO also repeated explicitly in public his request to Biden to keep his promise to legalise the situation of 11 million undocumented Mexican migrants in the US, a difficult issue in the US Congress.

The next big event where AMLO and Joe Biden – and many other hemispheric leaders – were supposed to get together was the Summit of the Americas in Los Angeles from 6 to 10 June 2022, basically an OAS event. But in the preceding months there was diplomatic tension because the US made it clear it would not invite Cuba, Venezuela or Nicaragua which it regarded as undemocratic. Mexico, and many other regional governments, were not in agreement with this.

In May Mexico took its own initiative as AMLO visited Guatemala, El Salvador, Honduras, Belize and Cuba, promoting its own development aid for these Central American countries and expressing solidarity with Cuba against the blockade (see next chapter). In his declarations on this trip AMLO made it clear he would not attend the Los Angeles Summit if any countries were excluded. When Washington insisted on the exclusion of the governments it disliked, many regional leaders refused to attend: as well as AMLO, the presidents or prime ministers of Honduras, Guatemala, El Salvador, St Vincent and the Grenadines, Bolivia, Uruguay and Grenada.[21] Most sent lower-level delegations, but the event was clearly a failure for the US. Of those who did attend, Alberto Fernández of Argentina was vocal in his criticism of US policy.

But AMLO still wanted dialogue and productive relations with the US, and so he arranged for another official visit to Washington, the second in eight months, from 11 to 13 July 2022.[22] Along with Foreign Secretary Marcelo Ebrard and other leading members of his cabinet, he had a full schedule of meetings, and it was clearly AMLO who set the agenda.

Never had it been clearer that the main obstacle to further advance in bilateral cooperation was congressional opposition to Biden's agenda, fuelled by the media and powerful financial interests. AMLO's final advice to Biden was very clear: "Faced with the crisis, the solution isn't in conservatism but in transformation. To act boldly, to transform the situation, not to maintain the status quo". AMLO clearly understood that the real obstacles to change lay in the Republican Party, but also some of the Democrats like Bob Menéndez.

On the economic front AMLO had begun to implement an anti-inflation plan which was more effective than anything yet undertaken by Washington. By promoting energy self-sufficiency he had been able to control petrol and diesel prices which were lower than in neighbouring US states, and also regulate domestic gas and electricity prices; Mexico had the lowest energy price inflation of all 30 OECD countries. Mexico offered to facilitate purchases of fuel south of the border by US drivers, and use of its border-area gas pipelines to ship natural gas from Texas to California. It called for a joint plan for public and private investment in all energy sectors (and mentioned AMLO's decision to nationalise lithium, for which he did not apologise).

Judicial collaboration was another key area of cooperation with the US: more and more corruption cases revealed cross-border criminal links, and Mexico was actively pursuing its legal action against US gun manufacturers for criminal liability. Here Mexico's priorities tied in with the Biden administration's agenda on gun control. On women's rights there was also a common agenda: the Mexican Supreme Court had recently decriminalised abortion, although access varies from state to state as in the US.

The joint communiqué which followed emphasised robust actions to control inflation; Mexico to buy large amounts of fertilisers (for small farmers) and powdered milk at favourable prices; joint investments in strategic areas such as semiconductors and IT; joint actions against trafficking in arms, drugs and human beings; and recognition of the need for development aid for Central America and southern Mexico to address the root causes of migration.

A weak figurehead of a declining superpower, Biden cannot openly accept the multipolar world which is fast emerging, hence his pernicious confrontation with Russia and China. But he knows he has to make concessions to Latin American and Caribbean autonomy, and fluctuates between negotiation and interventionism.

The high point of Mexico-US engagement was the 10th North American Summit, from 8 to 10 January 2023 in Mexico City. President Joe Biden arrived on the evening of 8 January at the AIFA,[23] the new Mexico City airport which was one of AMLO's key infrastructure projects, built by military engineers and inaugurated only some six months before. It had been a special request of AMLO that the US President should land there and not at the old airport which still handled most traffic: this was a symbolic gesture, and when questioned on the subject, Biden declared "Whatever the President of Mexico says". It was a clear indication that whatever their differences, the two leaders (and Canadian PM Justin Trudeau) were seeking constructive dialogue.

The summit produced a final declaration with high-sounding clauses on indigenous and gender rights, environmental protection, promotion of key industries like semi-conductors and electric vehicle batteries, migration, health and security. AMLO obtained Biden's agreement to extend the temporary visa programme for Venezuelans to Cubans, Nicaraguans, Colombians and Haitians. There was also agreement in principle on Mexico's argument for more development support for Central America, although whether the US would deliver on this remained doubtful.[24]

In the early months of 2023 in the US Congress, and among some state Governors, verbal attacks on Mexico over issues of migration and drug trafficking intensified, mainly but not exclusively by Republicans, with talk of mass deportations and even military intervention. AMLO declared that if they continued with such hostility Mexico would have to undertake an information campaign by all its consulates, advising Mexican-Americans not to vote Republican; and they would also have to denounce the matter at the United Nations.[25]

This growing hostility led the Mexican President to take a bold and decisive political move, making the annual commemoration of the Petroleum Expropriation by Lázaro Cárdenas on 18 March 1938 a mass rally in defence of Sovereignty.[26] On that date in 2023 hundreds of thousands of patriotic Mexicans filled the Zócalo and neighbouring streets for several blocks around in an impressive demonstration of unity and commitment to national independence, resource sovereignty, democracy and social justice.

The message to the US was crystal-clear: Mexico is an independent, free and sovereign country, not a colony or protectorate of anyone.[27] Cooperation, yes; intervention or imposition, never. This was a direct response to Republican members of Congress who falsely accused Mexico of being the main source of the opioid fentanyl and of allowing cartels to operate with impunity, and to Senator Lindsey Graham who said that if Mexico did not "clean up its act" he would introduce legislation to declare the cartels "terrorist organisations" and authorise the use of military force against them. Republicans also expressed outrage over the kidnapping of four US citizens and murder of two of them by a criminal gang in Tamaulipas.

While the Biden administration remained open to positive cooperation, the media, including supposedly liberal papers like the New York Times and Washington Post, had become very critical of Mexico. The liberal establishment was also critical of AMLO's proposals for electoral reform of the corrupt INE (*Instituto Nacional Electoral*, National Electoral Institute), an interventionist attitude which they would display time and again. Another key cause of tension (to be examined in a later chapter) was Mexico's assertion of energy sovereignty, of which the Petroleum Expropriation was a direct reminder.

In response AMLO asked why there was no investigation of cartels and corruption in the US, as if only Mexico were to blame. The drug trade was fuelled by demand: why was there so much addiction in US society? They could learn from Mexico's social programmes which helped prevent loneliness, poverty and despair. As for US victims of crime, he expressed sympathy but asked why there was no such scandal when Mexicans were killed in the US, as happened frequently.

AMLO also now acted on his earlier declaration and sent Foreign Secretary Marcelo Ebrard to Washington for a special meeting with all 52 Mexican consuls in the US, providing them with maps, data, audio-visual and other materials to distribute to Mexican-Americans in their districts explaining Mexico's efforts to combat drugs and its demand that the US halt arms trafficking which foments violence south of the border.

The complexity of the Mexico-US relationship was underlined by the fact that just two days later AMLO and members of his team held a meeting in Veracruz with 12 US members of Congress from both parties. The meeting was very respectful with discussion of migration, cooperation for development and security; it was agreed that US agents could not enter Mexico without permission, and that hostile legislation about drug cartels would not after all be introduced in the US Congress. But simultaneously the State Department made another critical statement, showing that the US establishment was divided on these matters.

These controversies continued unabated, but intense diplomatic engagement led to further agreements on migration (with increased legal migration), action by Biden against arbitrary measures by the Republican Governor of Texas, and discussion of arms control, in a diplomatic meeting on 24 July. Then on 5 October in the Mexican capital AMLO and his security team met with US Secretary of State Blinken and other prominent US officials and signed further agreements. When AMLO declares that the two governments have good relations, he is correct; the problem is that the fundamental issues are never really resolved, and powerful interests in the US maintain interventionist pressures regardless of diplomatic discussions. This would become clearer than ever as crucial general elections approached in Mexico (in June 2024) and the US (in November).

But before discussing the electoral and succession processes, it is necessary to examine Mexico's intimate ties with its Latin American neighbours, which AMLO rescued from oblivion and greatly reinforced in ways which were often not to Washington's liking; and the essential matter of resource sovereignty, a fundamental component of AMLO's transformational project which was even less welcome to US interests. These questions will be examined in the next two chapters.

NOTES

1. www.planetadelibros.com.mx/libro-oye-trump/253646, Accessed 29/08/2024
2. Andrés Manuel López Obrador, *A New Hope for Mexico: Saying No to Corruption, Violence and Trump's Wall*, translated by Natascha Uhlmann. London, 2018, Pluto, pp 76-77.
3. The next seven pages are reproduced with slight modifications from my article "AMLO in the Lion's Den", https://prruk.org/amlo-in-the-lions-den/, Public Reading Rooms UK, 15/7/2020.
4. www.washingtonpost.com/es/post-opinion/2020/07/07/la-reunion-trump-amlo-es-un-triunfo-estrategico-de-la-razon-sobre-la-politica/, Accessed 08/07/2020.
5. "Trump castiga con aranceles a México por no Frenar Migración", www.jornada.com.mx/2019/05/31politica/0031pol, Accessed 08/07/2020.
6. "Mexico's Ebrard says Talks with U.S. focused on Migration Flows, not Tariffs", www.reuters.com/article/us-usa-trade-mexico-ebrard-idUSKCN1T62WS, June 6, 2019, Accessed 08/07/2020, and www.migrationpolicy.org/research/one-year-us-mexico-agreement, Accessed 08/07/2020.
7. www.gob.mx/presidencia/ Morning Press Conference 08/05/2020, Accessed live.
8. www.gob.mx/presidencia/ Morning Press Conference 18/06/2020, Accessed 10/07/2020.
9. www.gob.mx/presidencia/ Morning Press Conference, 10/06/2020, Accessed 10/07/2020.
10. Presidencia de la República, Comunicado, 09 de julio de 2020: www.gob.mx/presidencia/we-choose-to-march-together-towards-the-future-declares-president-lopez-obrador-during-an-official-work-visit-to-the-united-states Accessed 14/07/2020
11. www.laizquierdadiario.mx/historica-arrastrada-de-AMLO-ante-Trump-en-la-Casa-Blanca, 8 July 2020, Accessed 14/07/2020. "Alarde de zalamerías" de AMLO, "cinismo sin límite" de Trump. translation mine.
12. www.washingtonpost.com/es/post-opinion/2020/07/07/la-reunion-trump-amlo-es-un-triunfo-estrategico-de-la-razon-sobre-la-politica. Accessed 08/07/2020, translation mine.
13. www.jornada.com.mx/ultimas/politica/2020/07/13/la-proeza-de-amlo-en-tierras-peligrosas-victor-flores-olea-1884.html Accessed 14/07/2020, translation mine.
14. www.gob.mx/presidencia/ Morning Press Conference, 15/12/2020, Accessed live.
15. www.gob.mx/presidencia, Morning Press Conference, 21/12/2020,

	Accessed live.
16	www.gob.mx/presidencia/ Morning Press Conference, 07/01/2021, Accessed live.
17	www.gob.mx/presidencia/ Morning Press Conference, 23/01/2021, Accessed live.
18	www.gob.mx/presidencia/ Morning Press Conference, 18/02/2021, accessed live.
19	See my article of 20/11/2021, https://morningstaronline.co.uk/article/mexicos-diplomatic-activism-continues
20	www.gob.mx/cms/uploads/attachment/file/790555/NALS_Fact_Sheet_Achievements_2021-2023.pdf, Accessed 13/09/2024.
21	en.wikipedia.org/wiki/9th_Summit_of_the_Americas, Accessed 15/09/2024.
22	See my article "AMLO's Firm Diplomacy Advances Mexico-US Dialogue", https://labouroutlook.org/2022/07/18/amlos-firm-diplomacy-advances-mexico-us-dialogue/
23	www.sopitas.com/noticias/joe-biden-llega-aifa-primera-visita-mexico-amlo-fotos-videos 08/01/2023, accessed 08/09/2024
24	www.whitehouse.gov/briefing-room/statements-releases/2023/01/10/declaration-of-north-america-dna/ Accessed 08/09/2024
25	www.gob.mx/presidencia/ Morning Press Conference, 09/03/2023, Accessed live.
26	See my article: https://morningstaronline.co.uk/article/f/mexican-sovereignty-non-negotiable-amlo-rallies-thousands, 22/03/2023
27	https://es-us.noticias.yahoo.com/discurso-completo-amlo-85-aniversario-151426876.html, Accessed 19/09/2024.

10

Reviving Mexico's Latin American Identity

Despite rhetoric to the contrary, in the neoliberal era Mexico had shown no interest in Latin American integration or in the emergence of new anti-imperialist governments and the assertion of regional sovereignty. AMLO was determined from the start to re-engage with Mexico's Latin neighbours in a positive way.

This was shown very quickly with regard to the Lima Group, a conservative alliance formed in 2017 to exert hostile pressure on Venezuela in line with US policy. Under President Peña Nieto Mexico was prominent in this group, but on 4 January 2019 AMLO´s deputy Foreign Secretary declared at a meeting of the group that Venezuela's problems could only be resolved by dialogue, and Mexico did not attend any more meetings of the group (even if its formal withdrawal did not occur immediately).[1]

Bolivia and Evo Morales

Much more dramatic was Mexico's response to the coup against Evo Morales in Bolivia. It was on 10 November 2019, following more than a fortnight's violent right-wing protests against Evo's re-election, that the Bolivian President resigned to avoid further violence. But the violence continued and within hours it was clear that Evo's life was in danger.

AMLO immediately instructed Foreign Secretary Ebrard to contact Evo and offer him asylum. He also asked his Defence Secretary General Sandoval to prepare an aerial mission to rescue Evo.[2] Within hours a Mexican Air Force plane with the necessary long-distance capacity was being prepared, and given the urgency of the situation it was decided to fly over the Pacific Ocean to avoid the complication of seeking permission from other governments, except Peru whose air space would have to be crossed in the final approach to Bolivia. The aircraft, with a capacity for 18 personnel and medical equipment, would carry military and diplomatic staff but with minimal armament to demonstrate peaceful intent.

After refuelling in Lima the aircraft headed for Chimoré, Cochabamba, Bolivia; at first it was denied permission to enter Bolivian airspace, but further negotiations allowed this. Evo, his Vice-President Álvaro García Linera and Minister of Health Gabriela Montaño boarded the plane, but then the Bolivian military demanded that they return. The Mexican Air Force General who was piloting the plane went on to the runway, unarmed, to negotiate; he was hit by two of the Bolivian troops and one of them pointed his pistol at the pilot's chest. The Mexican looked straight at him and said: "Young soldier, the brave do not commit murder", and the Bolivian, taken aback, let him go.

After further negotiations and tense moments the Bolivians allowed the plane to leave. But shortly after take-off a rocket-propelled grenade was fired at the aircraft, and only a swift manoeuvre by the pilot prevented disaster. The plane was then, somewhat surprisingly, allowed to land in Paraguay and refuel, and was granted permission to cross Brazilian airspace. The Ecuadoreans did not grant permission, but by flying close to the Peruvian border and at very high altitude the pilot was able to reach international airspace over the Pacific and return to Mexico.

The Mexican Air Force pilot, Miguel Eduardo Hernández Velázquez, was later awarded a medal for his heroism, and Evo Morales has repeatedly expressed his gratitude to AMLO and to Mexico for saving his life. This extraordinary episode was the clearest possible demonstration of the Mexican President's stance in favour of human rights and non-violence, but also of his political sympathies.

CELAC & regional integration

In January 2020 Mexico assumed the rotating presidency of CELAC, the Community of Latin American & Caribbean States established originally by Venezuela and Brazil as an alternative to the US-dominated OAS (CELAC includes all the Latin American and Caribbean countries but not the US or Canada). Bolivia held the presidency when Evo Morales was overthrown, and it was agreed that Mexico should take over, and in fact Mexico held the position for two years, until January 2022.

The inauguration of a progressive government in Argentina in December 2019, headed by Alberto Fernández, reinforced Mexico's position in the region; Fernández inherited from the previous right-wing government a massive external debt, and AMLO helped arrange a more favourable deal with the IMF for Argentina. Just over a year later, on 22-24 February 2022 Fernández made a high-profile official visit to Mexico, addressing one of AMLO's morning press conferences, attending the symbolic commemoration of Afro-Mexican independence leader Vicente Guerrero, and signing an important joint declaration affirming a Strategic Association between the two countries.[3] There were a series of specific commitments including defence of sovereignty and self-determination, support for democracy in Bolivia and Ecuador, and Mexican support for Argentina's claim to the Malvinas (Falkland) Islands.

Both countries had given vigorous support to the restoration of democracy in Bolivia, where popular mobilisation had led to the downfall of the coup regime which had seized power from Evo Morales in November 2019; elections there led to the victory of a candidate from Evo's MAS party, Luis Arce Catacora, in October 2020. Mexico and Argentina also worked together on availability of Covid vaccines, and agreed to push in the G20 for a socio-economic recovery plan based on "solidarity, social inclusion and sustainable development".

A month later, from 23 to 25 March 2021, it was the Bolivian President who was AMLO's guest. Arce Catacora thanked the Mexican people for their solidarity and stressed the importance of AMLO's action in saving Evo's life.

Bolivia, like Argentina, signed an agreement on "strategic association" with Mexico, and agreed to work together in agriculture and energy (where both countries were promoting sovereign control).[4] In particular they would seek to collaborate on lithium, a strategic mineral of which both countries have important deposits. They sent a pointed message to the OAS on its obligation not to interfere in the internal affairs of sovereign states.

Cultural exchange between the two countries also featured prominently: a major Mexican cultural institute and publishing house would establish a centre in La Paz, and both governments would support the creation of an Ibero-American Institute of Indigenous Languages.

As with Fernández' visit, Arce also attended one of AMLO's morning press conferences and ceremonial events: a ceremony in honour of Mexican independence hero Vicente Guerrero, and the commemoration of the 1517 naval battle of Chakan Putum where the Mayans had defeated the Spanish. The latter aroused great enthusiasm in the Bolivian visitor who saw it as an inspiration to strengthen CELAC.

The procession of Latin American visitors continued with Brazilian ex-president Dilma Rousseff as guest of honour at the May 12-13 commemoration of 700 years since the foundation of Tenochtitlan, the Aztec capital which is now Mexico City.

Apart from cultural symbolism, these events could not be separated from ongoing tensions with Washington: criticism of the OAS, promotion of CELAC which excludes the US and Canada, and promotion of resource sovereignty. But a much more confrontational issue was about to take centre stage: Cuba.

Cuba and the blockade

From the beginning AMLO had made clear his opposition to the US blockade of Cuba; this in itself was not controversial because it is a position shared by the great majority of countries. But this changed in July 2021 when Washington intensified its pressure, and protests broke out on the streets of Havana, protests which were generally suspected to be orchestrated from the US. Very quickly, in response to a question at his 12 July press conference,[5] AMLO reaffirmed Mexico's principles of non-intervention and self-determination: "If they want to help Cuba, the first thing to do is suspend the blockade!" – "We express our solidarity with the Cuban people without hesitation!" He also declared that the island deserved a prize for dignity for its 61 years of resistance and should be declared a World Heritage site.

Actions followed words as on 25 July Mexico sent two naval vessels with 138 lorry-loads of medical supplies, food and diesel fuel from Veracruz to Havana (and more shipments followed later).[6] Then on the symbolic date of 26 July AMLO declared that all the nations that voted against the blockade at the UN should likewise take action to end it. As a local Mexican official declared, "We in Veracruz are almost Cubans" (as well as geographical proximity the port shares Cuba's African heritage).

Also on 24 July, at a CELAC meeting in Mexico City in the presence of representatives of 31 Latin American and Caribbean countries, AMLO celebrated the birthday of Venezuelan liberator Simón Bolívar and his call for regional unity. The model of domination imposed by the Monroe Doctrine had no future, and the US should accept a new relationship based on respect and equality.

More was to follow at the Mexican Independence celebrations on 16 September 2021: Cuban President Miguel Díaz-Canel was the guest of honour. AMLO and key members of his cabinet were accompanied to the podium on the Zócalo by Díaz-Canel and other Cuban officials.

The Cuban President stressed the close historic ties between the two countries, with details of Cubans who had joined in Mexican popular and revolutionary struggles and vice-versa. In 1868 Mexico under the great indigenous reformer Benito Juárez had been the first country to recognise Cuban insurgent leader Carlos Manuel de Céspedes in the revolt against Spain. Nearly a century later Mexico had been the only Latin American nation to refuse to break relations with Cuba in 1961 when the OAS, at Washington's behest, expelled the island. Mexico's great ex-president Lázaro Cárdenas had been among the first to show solidarity with the revolution by visiting Cuba early in 1959. "Mexico is a country which all Cubans should love like their own,"[7] said Díaz-Canel.

AMLO responded by emphasising Mexico's historic belief in social justice and its abolition of slavery. He repeated his belief that Cuba should be given a prize for dignity and his call on the US to end the blockade; if the perverse blockade strategy were to succeed in overthrowing the Cuban government – which was extremely unlikely – it would be a Pyrrhic victory and an indelible stain on Washington's reputation.

Then on 18 September Mexico hosted another CELAC summit, with Cuba taking pride of place. At the summit Mexico also persuaded other countries to increase the regional organisation's funding and to establish more ambitious plans for cooperation in trade, industry, agriculture, education and health, and to create a Latin American and Caribbean Space Programme.

Global diplomacy

September is the month when the UN General Assembly convenes, and many heads of state and government take the opportunity to address the world body and present their respective agendas. AMLO did not do this, but instead seized another opportunity: at this time Mexico was one of the ten non-permanent members of the Security Council, and for the month of November 2021 it was Mexico's turn to exercise the rotating presidency of this august organisation.

Most countries would just allow their diplomats to fulfil conventional protocol, but AMLO saw this as a unique opportunity, and arranged to chair a session of the Security Council himself on 9 November.[8] His theme was peace, security, exclusion, inequality and conflict. He quoted former US President Franklin Delano Roosevelt (one of the founders of the UN) on the universal right to a life free from fear and poverty.

The greatest obstacle to justice, he declared, is corruption: and it is corruption when international tribunals protect corporations that plunder resources, when wealthy individuals and corporations use tax havens, when hedge funds speculate at the expense of people's needs, all of this justified by neoliberal ideology. It would be hypocritical to ignore that the greatest of the world's problems is corruption, in all its forms: political, moral, economic, legal, fiscal and financial.

Never before had so much wealth been concentrated in so few hands, with the privatisation of goods and services which should belong to all. This was demonstrated with the maldistribution of Covid vaccines and the failure of the UN Covax scheme which had only managed to distribute 6% of vaccines.

AMLO then briefly explained Mexico's social programmes *Sembrando Vida* and Young People Building the Future, and how Mexico was sharing them with Central American countries and calling on the US to provide aid.

Mexico would now present to the General Assembly a World Fraternity and Welfare Plan to provide assistance to the 750 million poorest people on the planet. A census should be conducted to identify those most at need, and aid should be distributed directly to the recipients by international agencies so as to avoid bureaucratic obstacles or corruption. The plan should be financed by contributions of 4% from the fortunes of the 1,000 wealthiest individuals, 4% from the profits of the 1,000 biggest corporations and 0.2% of the GDP of each G20 country.

The immediate response from the other 14 members of the Security Council was predictable: favourable reactions from St Vincent & the Grenadines, Ireland, Niger, China and Russia, and indifference or deliberate avoidance from the US, Britain, France, India and others. But there was no overt hostility. On 10 November Foreign Secretary Marcelo Ebrard said over 40 countries in the General Assembly had expressed interest in developing the plan, as had a number of UN agencies and international bodies. But the key issue would be for those with real clout to press the global elite to accept a form of international taxation and redistribution, which would require a worldwide movement in support of the plan; and this of course did not happen.

Such international indifference would not prevent Mexico from continuing with its own actions to promote cooperation and welfare in Latin America and the Caribbean. The very next month saw victory for a young progressive candidate in Chile, Gabriel Boric, who evoked memories of the great Socialist Salvador Allende; the first high-level foreign visitor to meet Boric was Mexican Foreign Secretary Marcelo Ebrard on 5 January 2022. Subsequent developments would show that Chile's commitment to progressive causes under Boric was far from reliable, but for the time being it seemed like a promising ally for Mexico. From 5 to 8 May 2022 AMLO visited Guatemala, El Salvador, Honduras, Belize and Cuba. In Central America the key themes were migration and regional development, and in Cuba, solidarity against the blockade; and AMLO's statements and actions sent direct and explicit messages to Washington.[9]

At its own expense and with remarkable generosity, Mexico had begun applying two of its key social programmes in neighbouring countries, by agreement with their governments and regardless of ideology: *Sembrando Vida* and Young People Building the Future. As he had repeatedly said to President Joe Biden and other US officials, illegal migration and people-trafficking could not be halted by repressive actions alone, but only by improving conditions in the countries of origin so that people did not want to leave.

With the Guatemalan president AMLO emphasised "joint actions to reduce the structural causes of irregular migration", and also agreed to simplify procedures so that 30,000 Guatemalan migrants working on plantations in Chiapas could register for Mexican social security benefits. In El Salvador he pointed out that it is the Central American country which has advanced most in applying Mexico's programmes in the past two years, with 10,000 Salvadoreans already participating in *Sembrando Vida*, and another 10,000 in the apprenticeship scheme Young People Building the Future; surveys showed that many of them said that before enrolment they were considering emigration, but not any more.

In Honduras the Mexican programmes had not been accepted by the previous right-wing dictatorship, so they were only just being introduced under the new progressive president Xiomara Castro. The sympathy, indeed close bonding between AMLO and Xiomara was immediately apparent; AMLO said that both countries had now left behind "the long night of neoliberalism", and Xiomara declared that she was introducing an alternative economic model and celebrated Mexico's "object lesson of solidarity". She was introducing an electricity reform to bring this crucial resource into the public sector, just as AMLO was doing in Mexico, and the Mexican president did break diplomatic protocol to declare that he fully supported her initiative.

From Honduras, on to Belize, the small former British colony which has had a difficult relationship with both Mexico and Guatemala. Belizean PM John Briceño gave a warm greeting in fluent Spanish, and AMLO announced the removal of all Mexican tariffs, giving free access to Belizean agricultural produce. There was agreement for *Sembrando Vida* to be introduced, initially for 2,000 beneficiaries, a "game-changer" in Briceño's words.

In each country AMLO pointed out that Biden had promised to join in this effort to help Central America by contributing $4 billion to expand application of the Mexican programmes, but as yet, not a single dollar had arrived. This, said AMLO, was "inexplicable" when Washington had already approved $30 billion for the war in Ukraine.

The messages to Washington became stronger and bolder with the final leg of AMLO's tour, in Cuba on 8 May. In a joint press conference with President Díaz-Canel he repeated Mexico's firm opposition to the US blockade.[10] The model of domination and intervention "imposed on all of America two centuries ago is exhausted. It is time to explore another option, of dialogue with the United States to open up another type of relationship". In this respect Mexico would insist with President Biden not to exclude any country from the Americas Summit in Los Angeles in June.

AMLO proclaimed his identification with the Cuban Revolution's ideals of fraternity and equality and his belief that the revolution was engaged in a process of renewal which would be an example to the world. Cuba and Mexico signed a new healthcare agreement, providing for a number of Mexican doctors to undertake specialist training in Cuba and for several hundred Cuban doctors to work in remote areas of Mexico; Mexico would also purchase Cuban Covid vaccines for children.

In appealing for the US to accept the sovereignty and equality of Latin America and the Caribbean, he referred to the "unstoppable rise of China" and the need to avoid confrontation and war. This scenario implied in his view the need for integration not only of Latin America and the Caribbean but the US and Canada too, "something like a European Union for America" but with respect for the sovereignty of all. He must surely have realised that the US was most unlikely to accept such a radical change, abandoning completely its hegemonic pretensions; but this was in effect an heroic attempt to break the deadlock of North-South confrontation in the Western Hemisphere.

AMLO's balancing act with Washington continued, as we have seen, with another visit to Washington in July 2022 and hard-hitting talks with President Biden. His tough bargaining with the US President on this occasion won him praise from Latin American anti-imperialist leaders, notably Nicolás Maduro of Venezuela who declared that it was "historic, that's how I see it…the solid, clear, diplomatic, firm position" of the Mexican leader. "And we have to recognise that if President [AMLO] speaks of relations between the United States and Mexico, he is speaking of the relations between the United States and all of Latin America: a position of dignity, which we recognise publicly and applaud, of the President of Mexico, the President of Dignity, the President of Truth…"[11] Similar praise came from French left leader Jean-Luc Mélenchon who was visiting Mexico, and from Evo Morales of Bolivia and Pepe Mujica of Uruguay.

Colombia, Brazil, Peru and Chile

In the meantime AMLO, like many others, was able to celebrate a very positive regional development: the election of left candidate Gustavo Petro as President of Colombia, winning the second round of the elections on 19 June 2022. The very next day in his *mañanera* AMLO reported that he had already phoned Petro to congratulate him: "This with Petro is historic…the conservatives in Colombia have always been tenacious and tough", and he quoted Colombian José María Vargas Vila who said that the dictators there "dipped their daggers in holy water before committing murder". He gave a brief summary of Colombian history and said that in their conversation Petro had agreed with him on the need for regional integration with respect for autonomy and sovereignty, without discrimination.[12] What was needed was a horizontal relationship of integration as envisioned by Bolívar, and also with the US and Canada, but with respect for sovereignty and without hegemony, seeking justice and democracy with a social dimension.

A few months later, on 30 October 2022, came another progressive election victory of massive importance: that of Lula (Luis Inácio Lula da Silva) in Brazil. In the early 2000s Lula had been one of the pioneers of the so-called "Pink Tide" of progressive governments in Latin America, and his popular reforms were continued by his successor Dilma Rousseff, also of the Brazilian PT (Workers' Party). But Dilma's impeachment on dubious charges in 2016, followed by the imprisonment of Lula on equally specious charges in April 2018, were part of a right-wing offensive which paved the way for the election of retired military officer Jair Bolsonaro (president January 2019 – December 2022). Lula's release in November 2019 was a result of sustained popular pressure which would slowly reverse right-wing dominance in Brazil, leading to Lula's third election victory.

Lula's narrow victory on 30 October occurred despite anti-democratic manoeuvres by Bolsonaro supporters, particularly among the military police and some state governments. AMLO immediately phoned to congratulate him on 31 October, declaring that it was due to the support of "the common people, the poor people: it shows once again that the people are grateful, they never forgot you".[13] Lula responded that he was very pleased now to look forward to meeting AMLO as Mexican President and to strengthening the relationship of the two countries which was very important for Latin America. With new efforts for Latin American unity, said Lula, with the combined efforts of their two countries they could "take care of the people who suffer hunger and create good-quality jobs for the people"; AMLO replied that he was in complete agreement.

But the matter did not end there: after Lula's inauguration on 1 January 2023, on 8 January hundreds of Bolsonaro supporters assaulted the Congress building, the Presidential Palace and the Supreme Court in Brasilia.[14] Lula issued an emergency decree and regained control, but the attempted coup, similar to the Trump-inspired assault on the Capitol on 6 January 2021, was a sign of the strength of extreme right and anti-democratic forces in Brazil. AMLO expressed concern and congratulated Lula on his successful restoration of order, and the close alignment of Mexico and Brazil was reinforced.

On more than one occasion AMLO invited Lula to visit Mexico, and Lula reciprocated the invitation, but no such visit ever occurred, which must surely be seen as a serious failure of diplomacy between these two countries, the two progressive giants of Latin America.

Mexico's standing with progressive sectors in Latin America increased further with AMLO's bold reaction to the congressional coup against President Pedro Castillo of Peru in December 2022.[15] Castillo had been elected in July 2021 with a wafer-thin majority with a programme for progressive change, but Peru's Congress, dominated by profoundly conservative interests, had systematically sabotaged his government. Early in December 2022 he attempted, in desperation, to assume emergency powers to overcome the deadlock, but was impeached on 7 December. AMLO immediately denounced this as victimisation based on racism and class prejudice, and offered him asylum as reports indicated he was trying to reach the Mexican Embassy; but he was prevented from doing so and arrested.

Other progressive Latin American governments including those of Argentina and Brazil also condemned Castillo's arrest as a coup. AMLO demanded guarantees of Castillo's safety, and did grant asylum to his wife and children. Peru declared the Mexican Ambassador to be *persona non grata*, but Mexico did not break diplomatic relations because it wanted to be able to assist Mexican citizens there. But AMLO maintained his vocal condemnation of Castillo's overthrow and of repression in Peru by the new government of Dina Boluarte. He also recognised, and condemned, the crucial role of the US in the Peruvian process, and repeated his view that the Monroe Doctrine must be abandoned.[16]

AMLO in general avoided international travel, maintaining from the beginning that "the best foreign policy is made at home", and apart from a couple of necessary trips to the US and his brief tour of Central America and Cuba, this was still the case. But under pressure from progressive opinion at home and abroad, he did hint that before leaving office he would make a tour of some of the key South American countries: Brazil, Argentina, Colombia and Chile were mentioned. Finally in August 2023 he confirmed his intention of visiting Colombia and Chile in September.

The occasion was an invitation to attend a Latin American & Caribbean conference on the drug trade, its structural causes and how to combat it by peaceful means. The event was held in Cali, Colombia where AMLO arrived on 8 September, flying in a Mexican Air Force plane with Foreign Secretary Alicia Bárcena, Defence Secretary General Luis Cresencio Sandoval and Navy Secretary Admiral Rafael Ojeda Durán.[17] They discussed the Colombian peace process and social programmes to promote development; Alicia Bárcena signed an agreement to implement Mexico's *Sembrando Vida* and Young People Building the Future in Colombia. Also, with Colombian Vice-President Francia Márquez, Bárcena signed a memorandum of understanding to promote the rights of indigenous and afro-descendant communities in both countries.

On the evening of 9 September the Mexican delegation flew on to Chile, avoiding Peruvian airspace because of the diplomatic tension with Peru. The following day, after a private meeting with Chilean President Gabriel Boric in La Moneda Palace in Santiago, AMLO declared that the betrayal of President Salvador Allende by Augusto Pinochet on 11 September 1973 was "abominable, a stain which cannot be erased even by all the water of the oceans". He recalled the memory of Allende as a humanist, a pacifist and a democrat. Boric recalled how dozens of Chileans had sought refuge in the Mexican Embassy and the ambassador, with great courage, had personally gone to find Allende's family to give them refuge.[18]

On 11 September at the official commemoration, AMLO was accompanied by his wife Beatriz Gutiérrez Mueller, and they were greeted with enthusiastic chants from the crowd, *Es un honor estar con Obrador*, "It's an honour to be with Obrador!" just as supporters often chanted in Mexico. A Peruvian woman gave him a small present in recognition of his support for democracy in that country. Along with other international dignitaries AMLO paid tribute to Allende as an apostle of democracy, and declared that Mexico and Chile were united by the ideals of freedom, justice, democracy and sovereignty.[19] In another ceremony attended by Alicia Bárcena (who had previously spent several years in Chile working for the UN Economic Commission for Latin America and the Caribbean) she received tributes from Chileans grateful to Mexico for its solidarity in receiving large numbers of Chilean refugees.

After this AMLO would not make any more trips to Latin America and the Caribbean, but his remaining year in office was characterised by many tensions and conflictive events in the region, with threats of intervention by the US or its European allies, in which Mexico was obliged to take a stand. One of the most dramatic was the electoral victory in Argentina of extreme-right candidate Javier Milei who took office on 10 December 2023; well described as a fascist, Milei took pleasure in insulting progressive leaders like AMLO and Lula, regardless of the damage to trade relations which might be of great value to his own country. AMLO was quite explicit about his dislike for Milei, but recognised that he was the duly elected leader of his country.

The Mexican President was very clear in his condemnation of authoritarian, privatising, racist and classist policies, and pointed out the role in Milei's victory of the media which were even worse in Argentina than in Mexico. This was also what happened when progressive governments failed to meet the needs of the people, but it had to be recognised that Argentina's ineffectual centrist president Alberto Fernández (my description, not AMLO's) had been hamstrung by the legacy of the previous conservative ruler Mauricio Macri who had negotiated a huge (and probably illegal) loan from the International Monetary Fund, leaving a completely unmanageable debt.

Another right-wing victory which would lead to serious complications was the election in Ecuador of Gabriel Noboa, the young (36 years old) son of the country's richest man, who took office on 23 November 2023 and continued the extreme right-wing policies of former president Guillermo Lasso. One of the factors leading to Noboa's victory was the assassination during the election campaign of another conservative candidate, Fernando Villavicencio. This in itself had no direct impact in Mexico, but on 4 April 2024 during his morning press conference (and in the middle of the Mexican election campaign), AMLO in a discussion of media influence mentioned the Villavicencio assassination and how it had been exploited by the media to favour Noboa. This provoked a hostile reaction from Ecuador which declared *persona non grata* the Mexican ambassador Raquel Serur.[20] The Ecuadorean government was also persecuting the left, in particular former vice-president Jorge Glas who had served under progressive president Rafael Correa (now in exile in Belgium) years earlier. Glas sought refuge in the Mexican embassy and was granted asylum, but Ecuador did not accept this, and on the evening of 5 April, in an unprecedented action, Ecuadorean special forces broke into the embassy and seized Glas, assaulting embassy personnel including the new ambassador who had been appointed in the meantime. Mexico immediately broke diplomatic relations, not only AMLO and Morena but the Mexican opposition condemned this blatant violation of diplomatic immunity which amounted to aggression against Mexican sovereign territory.[21]

Other regional issues that complicated matters for AMLO were the impending elections in Venezuela (July 2024) where anti-imperialist President Nicolás Maduro was running for re-election in the face of US sanctions and attempts at destabilisation, and the continuing instability in neighbouring Colombia where AMLO´s friend Gustavo Petro was pushing forward his agenda for progressive change despite constant hostility from the country's conservative establishment.

All of these issues impinged on Mexico's own electoral process (even if the official campaign did not begin until March 2024) and of course the coming US elections. While avoiding interference in other countries' internal affairs, AMLO did point out (for example in relation to Milei and to the Colombian right wing) that Mexican conservative opposition politicians, journalists and intellectuals were enthusiastic in their praise for these fascist leaders. Spokespeople for the PAN, PRI and PRD parties in Mexico, who claimed to be democrats and even to accept some of AMLO's welfare reforms, suddenly expressed strong support for Milei's destruction of public services and privatisation of almost the entire Argentine economy and his brutal repression of popular protest. They would do the same with regard to some extreme reactionaries in Colombia and the violent protestors in Venezuela after the elections there.

AMLO's unwavering stand in favour of democracy, popular welfare, public enterprise and sovereignty did not go unnoticed. While he made no attempt to claim a leadership or vanguard position in Latin America, his prestige was constantly growing. As his term approached its end in August-September 2024, expressions of admiration came from progressive governments, movements, leaders and intellectuals across the region. Admiration and support for President-Elect Claudia Sheinbaum also grew, and she has continued AMLO's policy of solidarity with progressive governments and movements in Latin America. But before we examine the electoral process, there are several more aspects of the Fourth Transformation which demand attention, notably the crucial issue of resource sovereignty.

NOTES

1. www.nodal.am/2021/03/mexico-y-el-grupo-de-lima-cuestion-de-principios-y-de resultados-por-maximiliano-reyez-zuniga-especial-para-nodal/ Accessed 09/09/2024.
2. This account is based largely on that provided in Andrés Manuel López Obrador, *A la Mitad del Camino*, México 2021: Planeta, "La misión Bolivia", pp 138-174.
3. See my article of 05/03/2021, https://morningstaronline.co.uk/article/f/mexico-and-argentina-sign-landmark-agreement
4. See my article of 03/04/2021, https://morningstaronline.co.uk/article/f/mexico-and-bolivia-have-reinforced-their-push-regional-sovereignty.
5. www.gob.mx/presidencia/ Morning Press Conference, 12/07/2021, Accessed live.
6. https://laopinion.com/2021/07/27/mexico-envia-a-cuba-el-barco-libertador-cargado-con-ayuda-humanitaria/ Accessed 11/09/2024.
7. See my article of 18/09/2021, https://morningstaronline.co.uk/article/f/amlo-diaz-canel-raise-stakes-against-blockade
8. See my article of 13/11/2021, https://morningstaronline.co.uk/article/mexicos-welfare-plan-stuns-un
9. https://lopezobrador.org.mx/2022/05/09/presidente-destaca-resultados-de-gira-en-paises-centroamericanos-y-del-caribe/ Accessed 15/09/2024.
10. www.jornada.com.mx/notas/2022/05/08/politica/visita-de-amlo-a-cuba-el-punto-culminante-de-la-nueva-relacion/ Accessed 15/09/2024.
11. www.telesurtv.net/news/presidente-maduro-expresa-admiracion-amlo-biden-20220714-0002.html, Accessed 17/09/2024.
12. www.gob.mx/presidencia/ Morning Press Conference 20/06/2022, Accessed live.
13. *La Jornada*, 1 de noviembre de 2022. Accessed 01/11/2022.
14. www.politize.com.br/invasao-ao-congresso/, Accessed 22/09/2024.
15. https://es.wikipedia.org/wiki/Arresto_de_Pedro_Castillo, Accessed 18/09/2024
16. www.gob.mx/presidencia/ Morning Press Conference, 21/12/2022, Accessed live.
17. www.sinembargo.mx/08-09-2023/4407382, Accessed 21/09/2024
18. www.jornada.com.mx/notas/2023/09/10/politica/la-traicion-de-pinochet-fue-abominable-dice-amlo-en-chile/ Accessed 21/09/2024

19 www.infobae.com/mexico/2023/09/11/es-un-honor-estar-con-obrador-vitorean-a-amlo-en-santiago-de-chile/ Accessed 21/09/2024.
20 www.infobae.com/mexico/2024/04/06/que-dijo-amlo-que-desencadeno-la-ruptura-de-relaciones-diplomaticas-entre-ecuador-y-mexico/ Accessed 24/11/2024
21 www.jornada.com.mx/noticia/2024/04/05/politica/condenan-irrupcion-policial-a-embajada-mexicana-en-ecuador-9274 Accessed 24/11/2024.

11

Resource sovereignty: oil, gas, electricity and lithium

From the beginning a key component of AMLO's platform had been defence of national sovereignty and the public sector in hydrocarbons and electric power generation and distribution. The 1938 oil expropriation and 1960 electricity nationalisation were seen as great achievements, and both the PRD before 2012 and Morena from then onwards campaigned vigorously against the privatising efforts of neoliberal governments in these sectors.

Where from 1938 to the 1970s Mexico had developed its oil under the public enterprise PEMEX to supply its domestic needs and promote industrialisation with petrochemicals, the neoliberals had increased crude oil production for export while neglecting national refining capacity. The result, as AMLO said, was that the country was exporting crude while importing refined products, "which is like exporting oranges and importing orange juice". Hence his plan to renovate refineries, where possible, and to build a new one with the latest technology at Dos Bocas, Tabasco (all under public ownership).

This led to criticism from environmentalists who failed to see that transition to renewables was a process which could be much better managed by public control of PEMEX to satisfy domestic needs while limiting and then gradually reducing total output. It also led to a diplomatic crisis in April 2020 when OPEC (the Organisation of Petroleum Exporting Countries) agreed to a significant reduction in output in order to stabilise international oil prices.[1] Mexico, although not an OPEC member, was one of several collaborating non-members, and was asked to reduce its daily output by 400,000 barrels, but wanted a reduction of only 100,000 barrels. The higher figure would have obliged Mexico to greatly increase imports to meet its needs, and Rocío Nahle, AMLO's very capable Energy Minister, refused and actually walked out of the meeting. After several hours' stalemate Mexico's demand was accepted.

When AMLO began his term no new oil refinery had been built for 40 years; there were six in service, but all were old and inefficient. If Mexico were to achieve its aim of producing sufficient refined products to meet domestic needs, new industrial capacity was essential. AMLO's solution was to build the new plant at Dos Bocas (a major public investment) and to purchase outright an existing refinery at Deer Park, Houston, Texas, which PEMEX already shared with Shell but in which the Anglo-Dutch corporation was willing to sell its remaining shares. Deer Park became a fully Mexican enterprise early in 2022.[2]

As for Dos Bocas, construction began in June 2019 and it was inaugurated in June 2022, although production did not begin until several months later because the complexity of refineries requires a long trial period. It is designed to produce 340,000 barrels per day of petrol, ultra-low-sulphur diesel and other products, making it Mexico's largest refinery and one of the most advanced in the world.[3]

Political opposition to the project was constant, but the economic and employment benefits were obvious. The assertion of national control led to criticism from the US and Spain: on 22 October 2020 six US senators and 37 representatives wrote to President Trump complaining that Mexican policy impeded market access and contravened the USMCA trade agreement.[4] But this was not the case as Mexico had taken care to exclude the energy sector from the treaty, and AMLO gave a categorical response on 26 October: "I am paid to protect the public interest, not to help Repsol or Shell" (Repsol is a Spanish oil company favoured by the previous government).[5] Foreign companies were welcome if they accepted the conditions laid down by the government, which gave priority to the public sector. Not so long ago, 40% of the government's income came from petroleum (not from exports but from taxes on PEMEX and its affiliates).[6]

Very soon after this the other major component of the energy sector, electric power, became the focus of conflict. AMLO had already made clear his intention of restoring the capacity of the other great public enterprise of the sector, the CFE (*Comisión Federal de Electricidad*, Federal Electricity Commission). Like PEMEX it had been deliberately neglected, indeed sabotaged, by the neoliberal governments, restricting its ability to generate and distribute power. Thus Mexico had a very substantial hydroelectric system, but its capacity was in serious decline as old turbines were not replaced and private thermoelectric plants were given priority in exporting energy to the national grid. AMLO appointed a very capable engineer and administrator, Manuel Bartlett, as head of the CFE, with the aim of replacing old turbines to increase hydro generation.

Then on 1 February 2021, while still in quarantine for Covid, AMLO sent a formal proposal to Congress for reform of electric power legislation. The CFE would have priority in power generation, all contracts with private companies would be examined for corrupt or illegal clauses, subsidies to private operators would be eliminated and the aim would be to restore national self-sufficiency in the sector.

Mexico's leading progressive newspaper *La Jornada* described the electricity proposal as "probably the most important set of legal changes undertaken by the Fourth Transformation…we should celebrate the fact that today the authorities are seeking to return to the people the property and the energy sovereignty given away by the corrupt and unscrupulous political class that took over the country during the long neoliberal night".[7] Back in the 1980s the CFE generated all the country's electricity, but by 2018 this had fallen to 54% and the CFE had financial losses of about $90 million US in the first half of that year.

Giveaway contracts to foreign companies, in which the state built the infrastructure and transferred it to private operators for free, and also paid inflated rates for power generated (ripping off Mexican consumers in the process) are the explanation for these massive losses. The most notorious case was that of Spanish company Iberdrola which was later found guilty of bribery.

There was of course fierce criticism of the electricity reform from conservatives and private interests at home and abroad. When questioned, AMLO said that so far there had been no comment on the subject from Washington, and he showed the clauses of the USMCA trade agreement which recognised Mexican energy sovereignty. To make the matter crystal clear he showed the public letter to the Mexican people by President Adolfo López Mateos of 27 September 1960 when electric power was first nationalised, which concluded with this dramatic statement: "People of Mexico, I release you from any obligation to obey future rulers who may try to give away our resources…"[8]

As if sent from on high to confirm AMLO's views on energy sovereignty, in mid-February a massive snowstorm hit Texas, leading to serious power blackouts and leaving large numbers of people freezing, without electricity or gas and in some cases without water. The effects spilled over into northeastern Mexico (Coahuila, Nuevo León and Tamaulipas): although the snow did not reach far across the border, import dependency resulting from neoliberal reforms did have an effect. One journalist compared Texas to a "failed state" and pointed out that the disaster was not just due to the weather but to the extreme privatisation of the state's power grid which prevented a coordinated response. In the Mexican states affected, however, the unified grid of the CFE, even if not yet fully functional, prevented the worst. Where Mexico was affected was in supplies of gas: sellout contracts had privatised Mexican gas, the country had to import significant amounts from Texas and the gas plants there were out of action. As AMLO pointed out, this emphasised the importance of having an integrated energy sector.

It was precisely in relation to the electricity reform that the opposition, in league with foreign interests, began to use the justice system for political ends. In mid-March 2021 a judge granted an *amparo* (injunction) against the Electricity Reform Law.[9] AMLO declared, as always, that he would respect judicial autonomy, but he also pointed out that there was reason to suspect the intervention of corrupt interests which might invalidate the injunction: the judge in question had also acted in favour of ex-president Calderón in several cases. The government had to defend the general interest and could not allow justice to be manipulated to favour rapacious minorities: what was needed was the Rule of Law, not simulation. The hostile comments in the *New York Times* and *El País* of Spain amounted to political interference: they were entitled to their opinions, but defending corrupt corporations was unjustified.

AMLO had promised from the beginning that there would be no increase in the price of petrol or of electricity for consumers: this meant that speculation in the energy sector could not be permitted. How was it that a middle or lower class family paid a higher rate for electricity than Oxxo (a big chain of convenience stores)? it turned out that big companies like Walmart, Oxxo and Bimbo were linked to electric enterprises like Iberdrola and got subsidies supposedly intended for small investors in renewables.[10]

Peña Nieto's 2013 Energy Reform (passed in Congress by all the main parties through massive bribery) provided among other things that the CFE had to buy electricity from private generators at high prices and then pay the cost of distribution via the grid; the private companies were guaranteed these conditions for 25 years. Consumer electricity prices for Bimbo were 1.0 pesos per kilowatt/hour, for Walmart 1.1 pesos, and for a family home 5 pesos.[11]

AMLO's Electricity Reform was of course popular, but further injunctions and stays of execution followed and it soon became clear that the law could only succeed as a constitutional amendment. So on 30 September 2021 the president sent a revised set of proposals to Congress as a constitutional package. It explicitly restored the CFE as a policy-making federal agency (not as previously, a public company subject to market rules), generating 54% of energy (previously only 38%) and controlling tariffs and the national grid. Private companies could generate up to 46% but must sell to the CFE at regulated prices and receive no subsidies. The CFE would now be explicitly allowed to install new turbines in hydroelectric plants and generate hydropower at full capacity. Finally – and this was completely new – lithium, of which Mexico has substantial deposits, particularly in the northwest state of Sonora, was declared of strategic importance and subject to exclusive public control and exploitation.

Constitutional amendments require a two-thirds majority in both houses of Congress, so this was a high-stakes move by AMLO: the Morena party had a clear majority, but even with its two allies the PT and PVEM it did not have two thirds. But AMLO – always an astute tactician – did not negotiate with the opposition. Rather, he threw down the gauntlet to the PRI, the former dominant party, which before its surrender to neoliberalism had always based its appeal on nationalism and popular reforms. Did the PRI want to defend the heritage of Lázaro Cárdenas who nationalised the oil in 1938, and of López Mateos who nationalised electricity in 1960, or that of Enrique Peña Nieto who passed the privatising reform of 2013?

This was a real dilemma for the PRI since its alliance with the right-wing PAN was undermining its credibility and pointed to the danger that it might become simply a client of the PAN, a process which has been advancing since 2021.

Corruption was a major factor in the problems of the energy sector: after AMLO imposed military control of customs at border posts, and naval control of customs at ports, sales of petrol and diesel by PEMEX increased significantly; previously contraband had been big business.[12] PEMEX had also been responsible for fertiliser manufacture, but this had been privatised and purchases from private fertiliser plants were found to be seriously overpriced; in one case investigation led to 220,000 pesos being refunded to the public sector.

Knowing that the Constitutional Reform package on electricity would meet fierce resistance, AMLO did not ask for an immediate congressional debate and vote when he presented it on 30 September 2021, but began holding public debates and forums on the issue throughout the country, with mass rallies and discussions on social media. The idea was to create such pressure on the opposition, particularly the PRI, that they might be won over or at least abstain. But this did not work; the "Institutional Revolutionary Party" confirmed that it was no longer in the least revolutionary but thoroughly institutional, and when the package finally went to a vote on 17-18 April 2022 the entire opposition voted against it, so it won a simple majority but not two-thirds. Much of the population now saw them as traitors to the nation, and they would eventually pay a heavy electoral price for this, but they were shameless in their rejection of national sovereignty. AMLO deplored their lamentable failure to defend the national interest, and pointed out that privatisation had just led to serious increases in electric power tariffs in Spain and Algeria. As for those who criticised him for calling the opposition "traitors", he pointed out that Presidents Lázaro Cárdenas and López Mateos had done the same.[13]

As before, the electricity reform was now law and would be applied by the government, but as it was not given constitutional status it was still open to legal challenge through injunctions, and this political tug-of-war would continue for more than two years, until after the June 2024 general elections.

The very next day AMLO introduced a separate bill to reform the Mining Law so as to take control of lithium: it proclaimed categorically "Lithium is declared to be of public utility, so there will be no concessions, licenses, permits or authorisations on the subject...Those zones where there are lithium deposits will be considered mining reserves. It is recognised that lithium is the patrimony of the nation and its exploration, exploitation, processing and use is reserved for the Mexican people". Within 90 days the government must create a public body for lithium prospecting, mining and processing.[14]

This specific and detailed terminology was necessary because although in principle the Mexican Constitution has established since 1917 that subsoil rights are the property of the nation, it allowed in practice for the granting of concessions to private interests and was used – especially by neoliberal governments from the 1980s to 2018 – to give away 60% of the national territory in mining concessions. AMLO did not grant any more mining concessions and began seeking for means to limit or revoke some of the existing ones. The lithium proposal swiftly passed both houses of Congress and was celebrated by all except the unpatriotic minority.

There were two or three companies which claimed to already have lithium mining concessions which they would defend in court, such as Bacanora, a British/Chinese company operating in Sonora. But the government declared they would have to complete various procedures to make their claims effective.

The concessions typically indicated rights in a certain area to specific minerals, such as gold, silver, copper, etc; if they did not specifically mention lithium then it was excluded.

The debate on the electricity and lithium reforms also raised the question of renewables, especially since they involved annulment of many small wind-power concessions owned by OXXO and similar corporations. As we have seen, these were abusive tax-evasion arrangements by which the corporations used tax exemptions supposedly designed for miniature enterprises to boost their profits; what the government intended was to install large publicly-owned solar and wind farms instead. The biggest solar plant in Latin America was already being built in the Sonora desert.

In June 2022 there was a global forum of leading countries on Energy and Climate Action, and AMLO reported on Mexico's contribution. It included the modernisation of 16 hydroelectric plants; that PEMEX would invest $2 billion to reduce its methane emissions by 98%; to make 50% of vehicle production electric by 2030, hence the national control of lithium; construction of a 1,000 megawatt photovoltaic plant in Puerto Peñasco, Sonora, providing power to more than 200,000 households; an agreement with 17 US companies for investment in solar and wind farms with 1,854 megawatts capacity, for cross-border energy supplies; and the *Sembrando Vida* agroforestry programme, the biggest reforestation project in the world according to AMLO, permitting the absorption of 4 million tons of carbon dioxide.[15]

In July 2022 both the US and Canada requested consultations within the scope of the USMCA trade treaty regarding Mexico's oil and electricity legislation, but AMLO pointed out that these were normal procedures and the fact was that Article 8 of the Treaty recognised Mexico's energy sovereignty. This had been negotiated with President Trump in 2020, negotiations had been suspended for 15 days but in the end Trump accepted Mexico's position.[16]

In the meantime Mexico was advancing on the issue of lithium; on 4 August 2022 Foreign Secretary Marcelo Ebrard had a meeting with Evo Morales about cooperation with the Bolivians who were very advanced in the matter. The Mexican aim was to create a national enterprise under the Ministry of Energy and then work jointly with Bolivia to produce electric batteries.[17] However, there have been difficulties because the Sonora deposits are of lithium clay, and it is much easier to extract the mineral from lithium salt flats as in Bolivia, Argentina and Chile. LitioMX was created as a public company by decree on 23 August 2022, but had hardly any budget until it was decided in 2023 to seek public-private partnerships because of the very high cost of the technology for lithium clay processing.[18] [19] It may be that other lithium deposits will be discovered that are easier to exploit; the important point is that the Mexican public sector has primacy in exploitation.

On 17 February 2023 the first stage of the photovoltaic plant at Puerto Peñasco was inaugurated by AMLO with Sonora Governor Alfonso Durazo and CFE Director Manuel Bartlett; it would benefit 1.6 million inhabitants, and the second phase would be ready by June 2024; the next day, still in Sonora, the lithium nationalisation decree was signed (previous decrees had established public national control but not nationalisation as such). Durazo pointed out that Sonora also had large deposits of copper and graphite which were strategic minerals for electrical engineering.[20]

It should be emphasised that despite the real problems caused by the judicial sabotage attempted by the opposition, the government did succeed in implementing many of its energy reform policies. Hydroelectric plants were modernised, the CFE recovered its capacity to regulate electric generation and distribution, and consumer tariffs did not rise, in contrast to many other countries. PEMEX began to recover its refining capacity and was able to control petrol prices at the pumps. A very important achievement was the dramatic reduction of what was known as *huachicol*, the illegal tapping of PEMEX pipelines to sell fuel on the black market, which in previous decades had become big business: criminal gangs were doing this with direct collusion by corrupt officials who controlled this racket from the third floor of PEMEX headquarters in Mexico City. The amount stolen in November 2018, on the eve of AMLO's inauguration, was 81,000 barrels a day; within a year this was down to 6,800 barrels a day, a reduction of more than 90%, representing a saving of approximately $18 billion US by July 2024.[21]

The political conflict over energy policy, particularly electricity, did however continue. By mid-2023 it was clear that the opposition was going to make this a key issue in the 2024 general elections. This is why AMLO decided to organise the mass rally of 18 March 2023 in the Zócalo to defend Energy Sovereignty on the anniversary of the 1938 oil expropriation (already discussed in chapter 9): it sent a clear message both to the US and to the domestic opposition. Hostility to the electricity reform was coupled with hostility to AMLO's other proposed constitutional reforms, including that of the electoral system and above all reform of the corrupt judiciary.

As the election campaign got under way, the presidential candidate for the main opposition coalition (of the PAN, PRI and PRD parties), former PAN Senator Xóchitl Gálvez, gave a speech at the Wilson Center in Washington on 5 February 2024 in which she accused Mexico's "populist" government of "flirting with Russia and China" and urged US interference in the elections, hinting that if elected she would facilitate foreign access to energy, health, education, infrastructure and security in Mexico.[22]

Already in late 2023 the President was talking about the need in the forthcoming elections to win not just the presidency and congressional majorities in both houses, but to achieve two-thirds majorities so that constitutional reforms could be passed. This was his "Plan C", after he had tried passing such reforms in Congress (Plan A) and again, with modifications (Plan B). By March 2024 he made this explicit and repeatedly explained it and emphasised it in his *mañanera* press conferences so that voters would understand its importance.[23] The most crucial element in this Plan C was judicial reform, without which nothing else could be achieved; but resource sovereignty as a constitutional principle was one of the most important practical policies.

NOTES

1. www.sdpnoticias.com/negocios/rocio-nahle-mexico-reunion-de-la-opep-barriles-de-petroleo-que-paso.html abril 09,2020, Accessed 23/09/2024.
2. www.pemex.com/deerpark/en/aboutus/Paginas/default.aspx, Accessed 24/09/24
3. www.nsenergybusiness.com/projects/dos-bocas-refinery-project/?cf-view&cf-closed, Accessed 24/09/24.
4. www.newsmax.com/world/theamericas/mexico-us-energy/2020/10/24/id/993618, and mexiconewsdaily.com/news/us-lawmakers-say-mexico-energy-policy-runs-counter-to-trade-agreement/, Accessed 26/10/2020.
5. www.gob.mx/presidencia/, Morning Press Conference 26/10/2020, Accessed live.
6. www.gob.mx/presidencia/, Morning Press Conference 15/01/21, Accessed live.
7. "CFE: poner fin al saqueo", www.jornada.com.mx/2021/02/03/edito, accessed 09/02/2021.
8. www.gob.mx/presidencia/, Morning Press Conference 09/02/2021, Accessed live.
9. www.gob.mx/presidencia/ Morning Press Conference, 15/03/2021, Accessed live.
10. www.gob.mx/presidencia/ Morning Press Conference, 22/03/2021, Accessed live.
11. www.gob.mx/presidencia/ Morning Press Conference, 26/03/2021, Accessed live.
12. www.gob.mx/presidencia/ Morning Press Conference, 06/05/2021, Accessed live.
13. www.gob.mx/presidencia/ Morning Press Conference, 21/04/2022, Accessed live.
14. https://laopinion.com/2022/04/20/mexico-nacionaliza-el-litio-amlo-publica-en-el-diario-oficial-de-la-federacion-las-reformas-a-la-ley-minera/ Accessed 29/09/2024.
15. www.gob.mx/inecc/articulos/presidente-presenta-decalogo-de-acciones-contra-el-cambio-climatico-en-foro-de-las-principales-economias-sobre-economia-y-clima, 17 de junio de 2022, Accessed 30/09/2024.
16. www.gob.mx/presidencia/, Morning Press Conference 28/07/2022, Accessed live.
17. www.gob.mx/presidencia/ Morning Press Conference, 05/08/2022, Accessed live.
18. www.bloomberglinea.com/english/mexicos-state-owned-lithium-company-is-negotiating-partnerships-with-private-firms/ Februrary

09 2023, Accessed 02/10/2024.
19 https://expansion.mx/empresas/2023/09/11/presupuesto-litio-mx-2024/paquete-economico
20 www.gob.mx/presidencia/ Morning Press Conferences, 17 & 18/02/2023, Accessed live.
21 www.eluniversal.com.mx/nacion/huachicol-por-que-llaman-asi-al-combustible-robado-en-mexico/ 11/01/2019, Accessed 01/10/2024; and www.gob.mx/presidencia/ Morning Press Conference 30/09/2024, Accessed 01/10/2024.
22 www.jornada.com.mx/noticia/2024/02/06/editorial/xochitl-galvez-peligrosa-irresponsabilidad-2415, Accessed 06/02/2024.
23 https://politica.expansion.mx/presidencia/2024/08/28/cual-es-el-plan-c-amlo, Accessed 02/10/2024.

12

Crime, the military and public order

The problem of criminality, in particular drug cartels and related violence, is notorious and has been a major problem in Mexico for decades. Unlike Colombia, the cartels are not related to an internal political and social armed conflict, but criminal penetration of state institutions has been part of the problem.

As we saw in Chapter 2, former president Felipe Calderón of the PAN had made the problem much worse by his demagogic "War on Drugs" which increased the homicide rate from 10,000 a year in 2006 to 27,000 a year in 2011, killing large numbers of innocent civilians through massive and indiscriminate use of the military. Subsequent revelations that his Chief of Security Genaro García Luna was in league with the Sinaloa cartel only confirmed the pernicious implications of this approach (and there are obvious reasons to suspect that Calderón himself may have been directly implicated). Calderón's unconstitutional authorisation of direct intervention by armed US agents in operation *Rápido y Furioso* (Fast and Furious) was another scandalous component of his malign legacy.

From 2012 to 2018 PRI president Peña Nieto continued these policies but with less intensity; and it was on his watch that another grave aspect of the intertwining of corruption and criminal violence was most dramatically illustrated, with the brutal Ayotzinapa massacre of 43 students on 26 September 2014. Implicating municipal, Guerrero State and federal authorities, the police and military and a criminal gang, it remains unsolved to this day despite extensive ongoing investigations and intense political controversy.

From the beginning, AMLO insisted on the need to combat violence and criminality by firm but peaceful authority, investigation and justice, not by force. "Evil cannot be defeated by more evil, violence cannot be combatted by more violence", he declared. A strong military and police presence was necessary wherever serious cases of crime and violence occurred or were expected, but avoiding the use of force unless absolutely necessary; cartel and gang operations should be addressed through intelligence gathering, use of financial sanctions (such as closing bank accounts) and legal prosecutions.

Police and the military

One of the first issues to be addressed was the inefficiency and corruption of the police. Mexico had a multiplicity of police forces, federal, state and municipal, most of them ill-equipped, poorly trained, badly paid and corrupt. The most notorious was the Federal Police which in the years preceding AMLO had at most 40,000 members of whom only about half were operational, a completely inadequate number for Mexico's size and population. The federal force had no regular barracks and was often accommodated in hotels, and it was notoriously corrupt and often brutal in its actions.

AMLO's solution was to dissolve the Federal Police, pensioning off as many of its members as possible and retraining and relocating others. In its place he would create a National Guard, trained by the military and educated in human rights, with well-designed barracks all over the country: there would be nearly 300 such installations throughout the national territory, with a total force (now achieved in 2024) of 140,000, many of them women, well-paid and trained to work with local communities in providing security and helping to implement social services. The law creating the GN (*Guardia Nacional*) was passed with large majorities in Congress and constitutionally ratified in March 2019.

Despite this constitutional status, the GN was officially subject to the Secretary of Public Security; AMLO wanted to place it under the Ministry of Defence because he regarded this as a better guarantee against corruption (after all, García Luna had been Secretary of Public Security). But this would require another constitutional amendment, which the opposition blocked until the 2024 elections gave Morena and its allies the necessary two-thirds majority. The reform placing the GN under the Defence Ministry was passed in September 2024.

The GN is so far a success, very popular with approval ratings around 70%; I have seen them in operation and conversed with some of their members, and at least on an anecdotal basis can confirm that compared to the old Federal Police, they are as day compared to night. But state and municipal police forces are a different matter: the federal authorities cannot directly intervene in them. What they can do, and have been doing where local authorities cooperate, is to offer funds to improve pay and conditions of these forces and to assist with training.

As for the military, their role is a fundamental issue. Many human rights organisations see the Mexican military as responsible for numerous violations over the years, and have an ingrained distrust of military establishments anywhere. But AMLO indicated from the start – and indeed, had already given signs of this long before becoming President – that he regarded the military as an essential instrument of his policy of transformation and an ally in the process of change. He pointed to the army's origins in the epic Revolution of 1910-21, when the old elite army of Porfirio Díaz was destroyed and a new army emerged from the popular insurgents of Villa, Zapata, Felipe Ángeles, Obregón and others, and was formally instituted by Venustiano Carranza as First Chief of the Constitutionalist Army. The military continued to be of popular origin and, unlike the armies of several Latin American countries, was not dominated by an elitist officer corps.

As for the notorious repressive actions implemented on many occasions later in the 20th century and into the 21st, AMLO pointed out that in most cases the ultimate responsibility lay with civilian politicians, above all presidents, who had given the orders. He found that the military, as a disciplined professional force, were less corrupt than the civilians and with their training, often more efficient in executing infrastructure projects and providing services to the population. During his administration military engineers have played a crucial role in construction projects like the new AIFA airport and the Tren Maya railway, delivering these on time, within budget and with high quality, a real novelty in Mexico.

There is no doubt that this position of AMLO´s has had a salutary effect on the current military: by educating them in their popular and revolutionary origins, and using them to assist in public works and welfare programmes, he has imbued them with a sense that they are indeed "the people in uniform". In AMLO's five years and ten months in office there were very few incidents of human rights violations by soldiers, and the few incidents that occurred were investigated and in most cases, those individuals responsible were brought to justice. The Secretary of Defence, General Luis Cresencio Sandoval, and the Secretary of the Navy, Admiral Rafael Ojeda Durán, were chosen by AMLO after carefully studying the human rights records of all qualified candidates, and it has to be said that in words and deeds both of them showed total dedication to principles of democracy and social justice. Those chosen for these positions by President Claudia Sheinbaum, General Ricardo Trevilla and Admiral Raymundo Pedro Morales, also seem to have appropriate training and attitudes.

Not surprisingly, AMLO was accused by the opposition and by human rights groups at home and abroad of "militarising" the country. His response was that the civilian government gives the orders and the military obey; there are no military cabinet ministers other than the Defence and Navy Secretaries, and no military members of Congress or State Governors.

The Cienfuegos case

This however has not prevented repeated criticisms of the military from both the right-wing opposition – who can easily be accused of hypocrisy on this, given their authoritarian views and the frequent abuse of military force by previous establishment presidents – and from the left, who point with some justification to past military abuses. A particularly controversial episode concerned retired General Salvador Cienfuegos who had been Peña Nieto's Defence Secretary and who was arrested on 15 October 2020 at Los Angeles airport on narcotics and money laundering charges.[1] He was not a US resident and had just been on a tourist visit with his family, and apparently had no financial interests there.[2]

The initial reaction of many – including quite a few supporters of AMLO and the Fourth Transformation – was to assume that the General was guilty and that the Mexican Government would accept the situation. They could not have been more mistaken. There was no immediate public comment from the Mexican authorities, but in private they expressed to the US Ambassador their discontent at the lack of prior consultation. Then on 28 October they sent a diplomatic note on the subject, and two days later they received a communication from the US DEA with a 732-page legal file.

Foreign Secretary Ebrard had a further conversation with US Attorney General William Barr, and in mid-November there was a joint declaration reaffirming existing arrangements on judicial cooperation. On 18 November a US judge in New York (where the General had been taken under custody) agreed to drop charges in order for the accused to be transferred to Mexico for further investigation and possible trial in his own country.

There was of course speculation on both sides of the border that AMLO might be giving in to pressure from the Mexican military and abandoning his pledge to end impunity. But both the President and Ebrard were emphatic in saying that no-one, including the General, is above the law, and that criminal investigation of individual officers does not affect civil-military relations as a whole or the importance of the Armed Forces for the Transformation project. The Mexican Attorney-General would now take charge of the investigation.

The ramifications of this are profound. More than ever, Mexico was proclaiming its judicial sovereignty, and it had scored a notable victory in persuading the US to back down. It would be ingenuous to assume that US prosecutions of Mexican officials, even when based on sound legal grounds as in the García Luna case, have an altruistic motivation.

It is remarkable that the 732-page DEA file on Cienfuegos goes all the way back to 2013, yet no action was taken until 2020. As pointed out in a trenchant article by John M Ackerman, "Espionage by US authorities against Cienfuegos since 2013 was never intended to struggle against corruption or combat drug trafficking. These two issues are of no concern to the US so long as foreign governments maintain blind obedience to Washington."[3] Rather such intelligence gathering would be aimed at obtaining compromising information with which to blackmail Mexico. Ackerman points out that the US could have taken action against Cienfuegos during the presidency of Peña Nieto who was his boss, but they had no interest in doing so given the corrupt servility of the PRI president to Washington. The decision to arrest the General in 2020, with no prior warning, was surely aimed at reasserting control over Mexico now that AMLO was taking measures to reclaim sovereignty.

Indeed, the issue of sovereignty was made very explicit in other declarations by Ebrard. In response to a journalist's question about the possible presence of DEA officers in Mexico, the Foreign Secretary declared that any US agent must respect Mexican law and could not therefore bear arms.[4] This was followed up by a legislative proposal in the Mexican Congress to regulate the activities of all foreign agents, which prompted a critical response from US Attorney-General William Barr who said it would "make cooperation more difficult" and favour organised crime.[5] The chequered role of the DEA and other US agencies in favouring organised crime when it suits them, going back at least to the Iran-Contra affair, was not of course considered by Barr.

Justice and corruption

Domestically AMLO was pursuing his quest for justice despite many obstacles. Calderón's former Security Chief García Luna was already detained and under investigation in the US on narcotics-related charges, but late in 2020 Mexican Attorney-General Gertz Maneiro filed a case and requested his extradition, showing Mexico's desire to take responsibility for its own dirty linen. But this would not occur and it would be in New York that García Luna would finally be tried and condemned in February 2023.

Also in early December 2020 a Constitutional Reform of the Federal Justice System, the product of two years' work, was approved by both houses of the Mexican Congress.[6] It owed much to then progressive Chief Justice Arturo Zaldívar (AMLO could not intervene himself because he always respected judicial independence); it created a judicial college to professionalise the system and end political patronage, established gender parity among judges and improved access to justice with legal aid for the poor and excluded. But it did not achieve constitutional status because Morena and its allies lacked the necessary two-thirds majority in Congress; conservative use of injunctions prevented the reform from being fully implemented, and when Zaldívar's term as Chief Justice came to an end on 31 December 2022 he was replaced by right-wing Justice Norma Piña, and the reform was abandoned.

Returning to the issue of political and administrative corruption, in mid-2020 a group of 11 conservative and/or corrupt state governors in the centre-west and north tried to challenge AMLO's authority directly by forming a "Federalist Alliance" based on what in the US would be called States' Rights. In particular they refused to accept AMLO's security strategy and implied that the solution was something like Calderón's violent War on Drugs. But when AMLO decided to face them down directly by touring several of these states with his security team (including the Defence and Navy Secretaries), they could not refuse to feign collaboration since their rights do not extend to rejection of all federal authority.

In each case AMLO would hold his 7 am Morning Press Conference in the respective state capital along with the Governor, but more than this, he would also oblige them to attend the security meeting which he holds every morning at 6 am. Thus in Michoacán Governor Silvano Aureoles of the PRD (originally a left-wing party but now profoundly corrupt) was very nervous given his poor record on crime and security. Then on 15 July came Guanajuato with PAN Governor Diego Sinhué Rodríguez; having previously refused to attend the security meetings, he changed his mind "for the sake of the security of the guanajuatenses";[7] his state had an appalling homicide rate which had risen from 600 in 2015 to 2,261 in 2019 (in a state with six million population) and he and his PAN predecessors were widely suspected of collusion with organised crime and thus of direct responsibility for the violence.

The next day, 16 July, a similar drama was played out in Jalisco, home to Mexico's second city Guadalajara and with another right-wing governor, Enrique Alfaro of the "Citizens' Movement". Alfaro was regarded as the unofficial leader of the opposition governors, and had openly challenged the president some six weeks earlier over problems of popular protests and repression in Jalisco. State police had arrested a young man for a minor breach of Covid quarantine rules, and he subsequently appeared dead. Popular protests over this turned violent, and Alfaro blamed AMLO and Morena for this; AMLO warned him not to make baseless accusations.[8] Independent sources suggested that the violence may well have been caused by provocation on the part of Jalisco State agents who were also accused of arbitrary seizure and temporary disappearance (in effect kidnapping) of several young demonstrators.[9]

At the Jalisco press conference on 16 July the tension was palpable, but it was Alfaro who looked nervous and was visibly sweating; he was confronted not only by the President but by several journalists, including two brave local women who challenged him over repression by state forces. Alfaro was forced to recognise the need for change in the State Attorney-General's office and to accept federal investigations into human rights issues.

The fourth governor to be put on the spot in this remarkable presidential tour was José Ignacio Peralta of Colima, a small Pacific coastal state which is home to Manzanillo, now Mexico's largest port. On 17 July Peralta also expressed some differences with AMLO, but equally had to accept federal security policy. But the biggest blow to Peralta came when the President announced that administration of all of the country's ports was being taken over by the Navy in order to end smuggling and corruption, and that customs administration was being completely overhauled. "Who ran the customs?" asked AMLO rhetorically: "The politicians!", and he explained how running the customs service of a port had been a handy money-spinner for many sleazy operators.[10] Peralta (a member of the PRI) put on a brave face as he tried to hide his discomfort.

Returning to the opposition governors' offensive, their dissent was not limited to security policy but was an attempt to use the Covid crisis to force a complete change of policy, calling on the government to postpone or cancel infrastructure projects like the Mayan Train or the new AIFA airport, and to meet the economic crisis by resorting to debt and international agencies; in other words, a total abandonment of AMLO's Transformation and a return to conventional neoliberal solutions.[11] At the same time, conscious of their political failure hitherto, they were taking a leaf from the manual of similar movements elsewhere in Latin America (Brazil, Bolivia, Venezuela, Nicaragua), and trying to create disorder and chaos which they could then blame on the government, using organised crime for political purposes.

The most spectacular example of this had occurred on the morning of 26 June 2020 when the head of Public Security in the Mexico City administration, Omar García Harfuch, was subject to an attempted assassination in the capital. Shortly after he left home in an armoured vehicle the car was attacked by a gang of heavily-armed men; two of his security guards were killed but he suffered only minor wounds. Authorities declared that the assault was the work of the *Cartel Jalisco Nueva Generación* (CJNG, Jalisco New Generation Cartel), the largest criminal gang at the time. Several of the assailants were captured and over the next few days there were more arrests and vehicles, arms and other goods were seized by authorities.[12] In a special public statement AMLO spoke of his determination to continue the campaign for peace and security, and stressed that intelligence, not force, was central to the government's approach, in contrast to previous administrations.[13]

Further events not long afterwards vindicated AMLO's intelligence-led strategy and demonstrated the vulnerability of corrupt governors. On 2 August 2020 the boss of the Santa Rosa de Lima Cartel, *El Marro*, was captured in Guanajuato along with five associates in a skilful operation headed by a military special forces unit, with scarcely a shot being fired.[14] Although for both legal and political reasons members of the State Attorney's office were involved, the key to the operation was intelligence coordinated by AMLO's security chief Alfonso Durazo. In terms of military force no chances were taken, with 120 Special Forces personnel and another 120 federal troops engaged in the operation, but the decisive action which involved the simultaneous seizure of four of the Cartel's "safe houses" produced only one casualty, one of El Marro's bodyguards who was wounded in the leg. A similar operation under previous administrations would probably have involved troops going in with all guns blazing and dozens of casualties, many of them innocent. El Marro was held at a State Penitentiary for initial interrogation and then transferred four days later, under heavy guard, to a federal jail in Mexico State.

Corruption and international relations

The quest for justice also extended to former officials who had taken up residence abroad to escape retribution and enjoy their ill-gotten gains. AMLO's Solicitor-General (*Fiscal General*) Alejandro Gertz Maneiro, and Foreign Secretary Marcelo Ebrard were engaged in seeking extraditions back to Mexico from the US, Canada and Spain, something which was virtually unheard of previously when the only extraditions were of Mexicans being sought by other countries (usually the US). The forging of a relationship of respect and judicial cooperation was crucial in this.

One of the most important and spectacular cases was that of former PEMEX boss Emilio Lozoya, who spearheaded the privatising "Energy Reform" under PRI President Peña Nieto. He was detained in Málaga, Spain in February 2020 on an Interpol warrant after being on the run for some time; five months later his extradition was approved and he arrived back in Mexico in July.[15] He was subject to serious corruption charges but was given the status of "collaborating witness" subject to reduced penalties in return for spilling the beans on gross corruption at the highest level. His revelations related to the notorious Odebrecht scandal in which the Brazilian engineering firm of that name was shown to have bribed politicians in several Latin American countries.

Mexico was one of the few countries where the Odebrecht affair had not yet caused heads to roll, but Lozoya revealed million-dollar payments which were used to finance Peña Nieto's 2012 election campaign and to bribe Congress members to pass his "Energy Reform" in 2014. His testimony included colourful details about huge amounts of cash being handed over to politicians in wads of dollar bills at a house in the luxury Lomas de Chapultepec district. His revelations also related to purchase by PEMEX of a fertiliser plant at a highly inflated price (some $200 million US above market value).[16]

Other extradition cases included the former Governor of Chihuahua State, César Duarte of the PRI, who was under arrest in Florida on numerous corruption charges and was extradited to Mexico on 2 June 2022; he was sentenced initially to six months' preventive detention. However, as would occur in many cases, on 5 June 2024 he was released on a legal technicality; the case is ongoing.[17] Another high-profile case concerns Tomás Zerón de Lucio, who held a series of important security, judicial and police positions under presidents Calderón and Peña Nieto and was accused of numerous abuses of human rights; most seriously he was in charge of the Criminal Investigation Agency from 2013 to 2016 under Peña's *Procurador General* (Attorney General) Jesús Murillo Karam, who was arrested in August 2022 in relation to the forced disappearance of the 43 Ayotzinapa students in 2014. Zerón was already a fugitive in Canada when in 2020 Foreign Secretary Marcelo Ebrard announced that an Interpol red notice was being issued for his arrest, but Zerón fled to Israel which has no extradition treaty with Mexico. Formal requests to Israel have been made on more than one occasion since, but with no result.

Another crucial case was that of Genaro García Luna, Calderón's Chief of Security who was accused of several narcotics-related charges; as already mentioned, he was arrested in the US on 10 December 2019, and although Mexico pursued its own investigation, he would be held in New York and eventually tried there and condemned on five charges on 21 February 2023. This case had multiple ramifications which continue to reverberate in both countries. First of all, evidence at the trial confirmed what everyone believed, that García Luna had been in league with the Sinaloa Cartel while waging war on its rivals and in effect, on many innocent people in Mexico. Secondly, there was strong reason to suspect that his boss, President Calderón (and Calderón's predecessor Vicente Fox), knew what was going on and may well have ordered it himself. Thirdly, it was difficult to believe that the DEA and other US agencies were not aware of this.

Questioned on the subject in January 2023, AMLO said he was considering three hypotheses: 1) that there was no hard evidence against García Luna (but this would reflect very badly on US authorities); 2) that there was such evidence, but García Luna was acting on his own and deceiving Calderón, Fox and the US; or 3) that García Luna was guilty and Fox and Calderón also.[18] Clearly AMLO was implying that his real hypothesis was number 3. As for the US, AMLO pointed out that the then US Ambassador celebrated the death of cartel dissident Arturo Beltrán Leyva in December 2009 and declared that Washington had more faith in the Mexican Navy than the Army, in a blatant confession of interference.[19]

AMLO also made it clear that apart from exposing the corruption of previous governments, Mexico's main practical interest was in recovering the ill-gotten gains of corrupt officials which were in fact stolen from the Mexican people. He brought Pablo Gómez, Director of the Financial Intelligence Unit, to explain at a morning press conference that they were pursuing a legal case in Florida against García Luna and several of his associates for 30 corrupt contracts by which they had embezzled Mexican public funds and transferred them via tax havens to buy properties and luxury cars in Florida. The total value thus far identified was $745 million. There were also related cases in Mexico itself, and the Financial Intelligence Unit had blocked bank accounts (or to be more accurate, had blocked the guilty individuals from access to the banking system). But in some cases these individuals had obtained injunctions allowing them to evade sanctions; these were typical examples of corrupt judges favouring criminal activities, showing the need for judicial reform.[20]

García Luna was condemned on 21 February 2023, found guilty of drug smuggling and distribution, criminal association, money laundering and false testimony; sentencing was delayed but he would be subject to at least 20 years in jail.[21] The Florida case continues as does speculation about Calderón's responsibility (the former president remains in Madrid); there have also been fierce debates in both the US and Mexico about the involvement of US officials, including politicians. For AMLO it confirmed the importance of his campaign against corruption, the need for judicial reform and the principle of defending Mexican sovereignty.

The Ayotzinapa case

The most notorious case of repression, corruption and impunity in recent years was the forced disappearance (and presumably murder) of 43 students from the Rural Teacher Training College (*Escuela Normal Rural*) of Ayotzinapa in Guerrero on 26-27 September 2014. There was a long history of militancy among students of the Rural Teacher Colleges and of arbitrary repression against them, not just in Guerrero; but northern and central Guerrero was also an area where corruption, repression, armed insurgency, and criminality including cartels, went back decades.

Local municipal politicians and police were notoriously corrupt and violent. The students had a tradition of protest including taking buses and using them to travel to protest events in the state capital Chilpancingo and in Mexico City. On 26 September (and in the days preceding) they seized some buses, apparently intending to travel to Mexico City to participate in the national protests of 2 October, anniversary of the 1968 Tlatelolco massacre. Where this might usually have led to some conflict with police and some violence and arrests, what happened on this occasion was much worse: it became apparent over the next few days that as many as 57 students were missing, a number reduced to 43 when 14 were found to be safe.

There were immediate accusations and suspicion of the involvement of the municipal police of Iguala, Cocula, Huitzuco and Tepecoacuilco, of the Guerrero state police, the Iguala mayor and his wife, a local cartel called *Guerreros Unidos* (United Warriors) and the military of the 27th Infantry Battalion in Iguala. Further suspicion related to the Federal Police, the National Intelligence Agency CISEN. and the Navy. But suspicion also extended to higher authorities, and this was confirmed with meetings held on 7 and 8 October 2014 in the official presidential residence of Los Pinos, the office of the Attorney-General (*Procurador General de la República*) and the HQ of the 27th Infantry Battalion. At these meetings those present included President Peña Nieto, his Home Secretary (*Secretario de Gobernación*), the Defence and Navy Secretaries, the Attorney General, the Director of CISEN and the head of the Criminal Investigation Agency Tomás Zerón de Lucio.[22] It was they who decided on an official (false) version of the events in order to end speculation and manipulate public opinion, which was confirmed in a press conference on 7 November given by Attorney General Murillo Karam. In what he described as the "Historic Truth" he alleged that the 43 students had been handed over by the Iguala and Cocula municipal police to the *Guerreros Unidos* gang who shot them, burnt the bodies and threw them in a Cocula rubbish dump (and supposedly later put the remains in bags and threw them in a river).

All of this was bad enough for the national and international image of Mexico, but the advantage for Peña Nieto and his government was that it put the blame entirely on local authorities and criminals and absolved higher officials. Not surprisingly, it was rejected by the families of the students, much of the media and opposition politicians including AMLO, who demanded further investigations. The families insisted that the evidence was inadequate and that the 43 disappeared must be considered alive until proof of death were presented.

In his election campaign AMLO promised to implement a complete new investigation and to seek justice for the families. Within days of taking office he announced that a new investigative body would be created, and on 15 January 2019 the Commission for Truth and Access to Justice in the Ayotzinapa Case (COVAJ by its Spanish initials) was installed by the Interior Ministry (*Gobernación*).

On 7 July 2020 the Mexican Solicitor General, Alejandro Gertz Maneiro, announced in a press conference the official annulment of the "Historic Truth" invented by the previous government, and the issuance of arrest warrants including one via Interpol for Tomás Zerón de Lucio. On 26 September 2020 AMLO held a meeting with the relatives of the 43, informing them about the work of COVAJ so far and offering a formal apology on behalf of the Mexican State, recognising that what had occurred was a State Crime for which their must be a full explanation and justice. From this time onwards there were regular reports in press conferences by Alejandro Encinas, Under-Secretary for Human Rights in *Gobernación* and President of COVAJ, about the ongoing investigations. There were also regular meetings of Encinas and of AMLO with the relatives of the 43.

In August 2022 Encinas presented a detailed report on behalf of COVAJ of its work up to that point. To a large extent as a result of this work, there were important arrests, including those of former Attorney General Jesús Murillo Karam and General José Rodríguez Pérez, former commander of the 27th Infantry Battalion. A number of lower-ranking military personnel were also arrested, and police and local politicians.

By the end of July 2023 AMLO was able to declare that there were 115 individuals under arrest including the Attorney General and two Army Generals, something which would have been inconceivable under previous governments or in many other countries.[23]

The investigation was (and still is) extremely complicated, not only because of the confusing sequence of events and the large number of individuals and institutions involved, but due to a few specific and crucial circumstances. First, there is the distinction between responsibility for the actual disappearance and killings and the subsequent cover-up and invention of the "Historic Truth". Second, it was revealed quite early in the investigation that many participants in the creation of the "Historic Truth" had been tortured to oblige them to collaborate.

Testimony obtained through torture is quite rightly considered invalid in Mexico as in other countries. However, there is an internationally established procedure for evaluating the validity of an individual's claim to have been tortured, the Istanbul Protocol, which is regularly applied in Mexico. The problem that arose was that many of those detained for presumed guilt in the Ayotzinapa case claimed to have been tortured; after one of them obtained an injunction authorising his release for this reason, a corrupt judge immediately authorised the release on similar grounds of some 80 accused individuals. This was a blatant abuse of procedure since the Istanbul Protocol has to be applied individually and takes time. AMLO pointed out that many of those released on this basis may very well have been directly involved in the original disappearances and killings.

This brings us to the fundamental problem with the entire investigation: it has been politicised, indeed it was always a political matter but in the past couple of years the politicisation has reached an extreme which makes any rational legal solution virtually impossible. Frustrated by slow progress, many of the relatives of the 43 came to have more confidence in investigations carried out by international bodies and human rights organisations than in the COVAJ. An organisation called the Inter-Disciplinary Group of Independent Experts (GIEI by its Spanish initials) was set up in October 2014 by agreement between the Inter-American Human Rights Commission, the Mexican Government and the relatives of the 43. It did good work but more recently has been repudiated by COVAJ and the Mexican authorities as having been manipulated. Similarly, the *Centro de los Derechos Humanos Miguel Agustín Pro Juárez* (generally known as ProDH), a prestigious NGO which AMLO, among others, had often worked with, has been taking very critical positions against the federal authorities and COVAJ.

The problem is not simply that such organisations have critical positions, or that the families of the disappeared are frustrated (they have every right to express their discontent and to continue their search for justice), but that certain groups and individuals have been using the Ayotzinapa case as an instrument for uncompromising and violent attacks on AMLO's (and now Claudia's) government. At the beginning of March 2024 one group of relatives of the 43 (they had split into two tendencies) protested in Mexico City, throwing stones at the offices of the Interior Ministry, the Senate and the Solicitor General's office, and then camped in tents in the Zócalo. Then on the morning of 6 March they (or others associated with them), masked and armed with sticks and metal bars, broke down the barriers to Calle Moneda on the north side of the National Palace and used a pickup truck to break down the door on that side of the Palace during AMLO´s press conference. It is impossible to be sure of their real identity since they were wearing balaclavas. The police and military personnel used minimal force (foam from fire extinguishers) to control them, on orders from the President himself who said he would not respond to provocations.[24]

AMLO declared that they were being manipulated by Senator Alvarez Icaza (a maverick politician allied with right-wing parties), the Inter-American Human Rights Commission and the OAS, all of whom were trying to sabotage his government. Also involved (indeed by some reports directly involved in the violent assault) was Vidulfo Rosales, a lawyer from Guerrero representing the relatives but who by this time had adopted openly provocative positions, even claiming responsibility for the violence (a very strange position for a lawyer).[25] Rosales and several of these "human rights defenders" had shown their displeasure when Murillo Karam was arrested, and celebrated when the detained "tortured" suspects were released. There had also recently been assaults on Morena party members in the mountains of Guerrero, confirming the political and provocative nature of these activities. It was all part of a dirty war and had nothing to do with the just demands of the Ayotzinapa relatives who were being manipulated.[26] Further acts of provocation would occur subsequently, and Vidulfo Rosales and his group threatened to disrupt Claudia Sheinbaum's election campaign (but not the campaign of the right-wing opposition).

It should be pointed out that one of the main arguments of these provocateurs is that responsibility for the Ayotzinapa disappearances and killings lies with the military: "It was the Army". AMLO insists that the military have cooperated throughout the investigation, that two Generals and about 20 military personnel in total have been arrested, and that the top brass recognise that weeding out corrupt or repressive individuals will only strengthen the Army and Navy in the long run. Given the invaluable contribution of the military to AMLO's Transformation with assistance in infrastructure and welfare, condemning "militarisation" has become one of the right wing's main campaign issues, and it is no accident that they have seized on the Ayotzinapa case for their own ends.

As for judicial corruption, it became more and more blatant and political as the election campaign progressed, and we shall examine this further in due course. We shall also see that, with the overwhelming electoral victory of Claudia Sheinbaum, Morena and its allies, this became the main cause of political confrontation during the transition of power from June to October 2024, and that the security team introduced by the new president would take decisive action to combat corruption and crime.

NOTES

1. www.lajornada.com.mx/2020/10/17/politica/002n1pol, Accessed 03/10/2024.
2. Much of what follows comes from my article of 02/02/2021, https://prruk.org/justice-in-mexico-does-not-depend-on-the-united-states/
3. John M Ackerman, "El Retorno de Cienfuegos", *La Jornada*, 23 de noviembre 2020, www.jornada.com.mx/ultimas/politica/2020/11/23/el-retorno-de-cienfuegos-john-m-ackerman-2236.html, Accessed 17/12/2020.
4. www.gob.mx/presidencia/ Morning Press Conference, 18/11/2020, Accessed live.
5. www.jornada.com.mx/notas/2020/12/11/mundo/procurador-de-eu-alerta-que-regular-agentes-en-mexico-beneficia-al-crimen/ Accessed 17/12/2020.
6. Arturo Zaldívar, "La Reforma Constitucional a la Justicia Federal", *Milenio*, 08/12/2020, www.milenio.com/opinion/arturo-zaldivar/los-derechos-hoy/la-reforma-constitucional-a-la-justicia-federal, Accessed 17/12/2020.
7. 15/07/2020, www.hansdigital.mx/lasmananeras/diego-sinhue-reconoce-que-fue-un-error-no-haber-asistido-a-reuniones-de-seguridad-ira-inclusive-sabados-y-domingos/ Accessed 13/08/2020.
8. www.gob.mx/presidencia/ Morning Press Conference, 05/06/2020; Accessed live.
9. polemon.mx/no-seas-cinico-alfaro-tu-eres-culpable-de-la-represion-en-jalisco, Accessed 23/06/2020.
10. www.gob.mx/presidencia/ Morning Press Conference, 17/07/2020, Accessed live.
11. noticiaszmg.com/zmg34395.htm, Accessed 21/06/2020.
12. www.jornada.com.mx/ultimas/capital/2020/06/27/aseguran-20-autos-de-lujo-en-cateos-por-ataque-a-omar-garcia-harfuch, Accessed 28/06/2020.
13. twitter.com/lopezobrador_/status/1276982961280372736, Accessed 28/06/2020.
14. www.jornada.com.mx/ultimas/politica/2020/08/03/la-captura-de-el-marro-por-grupo-de-elite-del-ejercito-2046.html, Accessed 04/08/2020.
15. *El Universal*, 30/06/2020, "Emilio Lozoya acepta extradición de España a México", www.you-tube.com/watch?v=uqUCPOhXbuA, Accessed 13/08/2020.
16. www.gob.mx/presidencia/ Morning Press Conferences, 21, 24 &

CRIME, THE MILITARY AND PUBLIC ORDER

31/07/2020, Accessed live.
17 www.infobae.com/mexico/2024/06/06/que-hizo-cesar-duarte-estas-son-las-acusaciones-que-recaen-en-el-ex-gobernador-de-chihuahua-que-podria-librar-la-carcel/ Accessed 07/10/2024.
18 www.gob.mx/presidencia/ Morning Press Conference, 24/01/2023, Accessed live.
19 www.gob.mx/presidencia/ Morning Press Conference, 31/01/2023, Accessed live.
20 www.gob.mx/presidencia/ Morning Press Conference, 09/02/2023, Accessed live.
21 www.justice.gov/usao-edny/pr/ex-mexican-secretary-public-security-genaro-garcia-luna-convicted-engaging-continuing, Tuesday February 21, 2023, Accessed 08/10/2024.
22 es.wikipedia.org/wiki/Desaparicion-forzada-de-Iguala-de-2014, Accessed 09/10/2024.
23 www.gob.mx/presidencia/ Morning Press Conference, 27/07/2023, Accessed live.
24 www.milenio.com/politica/videos-normalistas-entrando-a-palacio-nacional-hoy 06/03/2024, Accessed 10/10/2024.
25 www.jornada.com.mx/noticia/2024/03/07/editorial/ayotzinapa-restaurar-la-confianza-278 Accessed 07/03/2024.
26 www.gob.mx/presidencia/ Morning Press Conferences, 06/03/2024 & 07/03/2024, Accessed live.

Author (pictured centre in hat) with staff of the muncipal health centre in Lerma

13

Labour, women and Mexican humanism

A transformation based on social justice, with priority for the poor and excluded, must necessarily include benefits for labour, both organised and unorganised, and for women, engaging with women's rights and feminist movements. This would also involve issues of human rights, although as we have already seen, the quest for justice and ending impunity would face its biggest obstacle in the profound corruption of the judiciary.

Labour from the time of Díaz to the present
Labour struggles had played a major part in the movements against the Porfirio Díaz dictatorship, with the strikes at Cananea and Río Blanco and their brutal repression, and the Mexican Liberal Party (really anarcho-syndicalist) of the Flores Magón brothers. During the actual armed conflicts labour contingents played a significant role, and contributed to Constitutionalist success and to the crucial declaration of workers' rights in Article 123 of the 1917 Constitution (still reflected in the existence in many towns of streets named "Article 123").

Organised labour was a political mainstay of the 1920s governments of the Sonoran presidents Álvaro Obregón and Plutarco Elías Calles, and contributed to their fierce anti-clericalism (although the main union federation of the time, the CROM or *Confederación Regional Obrera Mexicana*, Regional Confederation of Mexican Workers, was plagued by serious corruption). Independent unions with influence from anarcho-syndicalists and from the nascent Communist Party emerged in the following years, and would form part of the political base of progressive president Lázaro

Cárdenas. Under Cárdenas a new union federation, the CTM (*Confederación de Trabajadores Mexicanos*, Confederation of Mexican Workers), would become dominant and would continue to predominate for decades afterwards. There was significant Communist Party influence in the CTM, but its leader for many years, Vicente Lombardo Toledano, was above all close to the governing party (PRM, then PRI), and would use Marxist and anti-imperialist rhetoric to justify critical support for the ruling party for years afterwards.

Independent unions, particularly of railway and electrical workers and teachers, would have Communist leadership and suffered serious repression on several occasions from the 1950s onwards. The CTM and other "official" unions did make significant gains for their members (this was one of the foundations of PRI rule), but they were notoriously corrupt; Fidel Velázquez, CTM leader after Lombardo Toledano left in 1946, retained control until shortly before his death in 1997 at the age of 97. Velázquez led the CTM to adopt thoroughly right-wing and repressive policies.

By the time of the emergence of the democratic tendency and then the PRD as the left independent movement in Mexico from 1987 onwards, the labour movement was profoundly divided. Even some of the independent unions, while politically progressive, were corrupt and undemocratic in their internal functioning. At the time of AMLO's victory in 2018 one of his priorities was a law to democratise unions, intended to ensure workers the right to choose a union of their choice (existing unions often ran closed shops backed by management) and providing for union elections to be supervised by the Federal Labour Department.

One of the few really independent and democratic unions was the Mining and Metallurgical Workers,[1] led by Napoleón Gómez Urrutia, who returned from 11 years exile in Canada after the Morena victory and ran for the Senate for AMLO's party; as a senator he would pioneer progressive labour legislation of all kinds. Gómez Urrutia had been forced to leave after threats against him and his family when he refused to abandon the struggle for justice in the 2006 Pasta de Conchos coal mine disaster in Coahuila state, where 65 workers had been killed in the mine run by Grupo México, a very powerful company owned by one of the country's richest men, Germán Larrea. Grupo México, backed by local and national political authorities, abandoned rescue efforts after only four days, and after months of protests and demands for investigation, Gómez Urrutia and his family accepted the solidarity of the United Steelworkers in the US and Canada. With their help he continued to run the union from exile until his return in 2018. When AMLO was elected, he promised to support the campaign for justice for the families of the Pasta de Conchos workers.[2]

AMLO was in any case committed to pro-worker reforms. The minimum wage was one of the lowest in Latin America in 2018, there had been no increase in more than 30 years and it had lost 70% of its purchasing power. It was immediately increased, on 1 January 2019, by 15%; then in 2020 by 20%, 2021 by 15%, 2022 by 22%, 2023 by 20% and 2024 by 20%, for a total increase from 88.36 pesos a day to 248.93 pesos a day.[3] This was well above the rate of inflation, amounting to a real terms increase of over 90%, so almost double in terms of purchasing power, making it now the sixth highest in Latin America.

The basic reform of Mexican Federal Labour Law was passed early in AMLO's term and took effect on 1 May 2019.[4] It declared that workers could decide to join a union, change unions or not join one, without discrimination or reprisals; they can participate in fundamental union decisions by personal, free, direct and secret vote, in elections and to ratify collective agreements. Voting by raising hands or by delegates is forbidden; slates of candidates must have gender equality; federal authority can verify electoral processes at any time, including at the request of 30% of union members. A Federal Centre of Conciliation and Labour Registry, with members selected by public examination, would provide supervision on behalf of the Labour Department. This certainly made union elections and procedures much more democratic, although entrenched resistance in some unions still occurs; the most notorious is the PEMEX Oil Workers' Union in which reports of threats, bribery and other forms of malpractice continue.

In October-November 2020, following pressure from Senator Gómez Urrutia (but also in keeping with his overall policy), AMLO announced the intention to halt fraudulent outsourcing or subcontracting, which was used in Mexico (as in the UK and elsewhere) to deprive workers of legitimate rights and benefits. He pointed out that many workers were dismissed from regular jobs in November and transferred for a couple of months to subcontracting firms as temporary employees, then re-hired in January by their real employers. In this manner they were deprived of the Christmas bonus and also lost seniority and accompanying benefits.

One such company had more than 200,000 workers on its books. This also amounted to false accounting, and was under investigation by the Public Administration Secretary and the Tax Collection Office.[5] Secretary of Labour Luisa María Alcalde explained that the new law will ban outsourcing of the principal activity of any enterprise; outsourcing of ancillary activities (e.g. cleaning for a manufacturing company) will be permitted but under controlled conditions; and there will be greater sanctions for companies breaking the law.

She declared "We start from the principle that labour is a right and not a commodity".[6] Of course it was not easy to implement the policy and there were protracted negotiations, but after some six months, on 23 April 2021, Luisa Alcalde and employers' representative Carlos Salazar were able to announce agreement on the issue. Subcontracting was completely banned in the public sector, and in the private sector any subcontractors in permitted activities must be registered with the Ministries of Labour and

Finance within 90 days;[7] it would take effect in September 2021. Senator Gómez Urrutia subsequently declared that he regarded this as the most important reform of all for Mexican workers. Implementation would be a constant battle, but within another six months the number of workers registered with the Social Security Institute (in other words, with permanent formal benefits) increased by 3.5 million, and Gómez Urrutia told me in an interview in August 2023 that approximately 5 million workers (of the 10 million previously affected by outsourcing) had now gained formal contractual status.[8]

Labour rights were an area where the Biden administration in the US was generally in agreement with AMLO and Morena, although it was remarkable that free collective bargaining and union rights were included in the USMCA Trade Agreement signed with the Trump administration in July 2020. The legal requirement of democratic union elections introduced by AMLO and backed by Biden led to an independent union gaining recognition for the first time at a big General Motors plant in Guanajuato state.

AMLO also achieved success in a major legacy conflict: in 2009 the public electricity utility *Luz y Fuerza del Centro* (Central Light and Power), supplying most of central Mexico, was shut down under president Calderón and thousands of workers were dismissed and denied compensation. AMLO succeeded in negotiating a deal with the private successor company to provide benefits for surviving workers and their families.

Another very significant advance in labour law, and for women, was the recognition of domestic workers as having full labour rights, registered with the Social Security Institute and entitled to contractual working conditions and the minimum wage.[9] This covered 2.3 million workers, 95% of them women. This included ratification of the International Labour Organisation's Convention 189 which formalises domestic workers' rights.

A small but important gain was the recognition of workers' right to paid holidays, starting at twelve days a year and increasing by two days each year to a maximum of 30. That such a basic right had to be spelled out was an indication of how far the achievements of the revolution and of Cárdenas had been undermined; under the neoliberals Mexico had a very low-wage economy. What has happened with AMLO, and now Claudia Sheinbaum, is that recognition of labour rights has strengthened workers' bargaining position, the social wage has increased very substantially with benefits in pensions, scholarships, free education and health care and many other direct transfers, and massive investment in public works (especially in previously deprived areas) has provided many thousands of well-paid jobs and increased overall demand for labour. It is no accident that in the last six years 9.5 million people have been lifted out of poverty, as recognised by the World Bank, something which AMLO said was his greatest source of satisfaction.

Women, feminism and manipulation

If the labour movement has had to struggle constantly against political manipulation, the same is true of the women's movement. From the beginning several feminist groups in Mexico and internationally criticised AMLO, accusing him of *machismo* and his government of ignoring women's demands. His repeated statements to the effect that the family was the most important institution of welfare and social security were taken as a defence of conservative views, and the absence of a strong explicit position on the right to abortion was seen as confirmation of this.

There is no doubt that women's discontent was fully justified: the prominence of *machismo* in Mexican traditional culture is notorious, and the country registered the highest figures of femicide in Latin America. Whether the figures were accurate was very difficult to ascertain; what is important is that femicide, and more generally violence against women, is now officially recognised and recorded by the INEGI (*Instituto Nacional de Estadística y Geografía,* National Institute of Statistics and Geography). Protests regularly take place (as in many countries) on 8 March (International Women's Day) and 25 November (International Day for the Elimination of Violence Against Women).

But both as Head of Government of Mexico City and then as President, AMLO had gender parity in his cabinets. His insistence that in the local school committees of "The School Is Ours", and more recently also in health committees of "The Clinic Is Ours", the treasurers must be women, must be seen as significant. On abortion, it is clear that he personally believes in a woman's right to choose, but regards the law as a matter for the legislature and the judiciary, not the executive; he also wanted to avoid "culture wars" on such issues. Women's right to choose was quickly established in Mexico City and several states, and then, somewhat surprisingly, by the Supreme Court. AMLO has also been quite clear on his support for LGBTIQ+ rights, taking flack for his invitation to activists to appear on stage with him in one of his *mañanera* press conferences in June 2019. His sympathies were clearly with working-class and peasant feminism, not with strident elite activists.

On 25 November 2020 AMLO gave a formal report in his *mañanera* on violence against women,[10] and the Home Secretary (*Gobernación*) Olga Sánchez Cordero said they were beginning 16 days of activities on the matter: "Machismo kills! Enough is enough!"; the government was committed to equality. She quoted INEGI figures of about 3,800 women and girls murdered per year, and explained that they now had an Inter-institutional Group for the Elimination of Violence, many women's refuges, programmes to deal with violent men and training in the subject in the National Guard and police and in the Departments of Education and Culture, among others. It was a systemic problem, and many feminist demands were legitimate. Patriarchal attitudes must change, she declared to applause. AMLO argued that violence in general had increased because of the social decomposition caused by neoliberalism, but he also recognised the need for legal changes and measures to guarantee protection and combat violence against women.

Then on 8 March 2021 AMLO again spoke of women's struggle for equality, for women of all social classes, cultures and regions.[11] The struggle was against violence and femicide, but also in favour of women's participation in government which was being promoted as never before, for example with women as Home Secretary and Public Security Secretary; and also in favour of all the welfare programmes which benefited women. The conservative opposition were now pretending to be feminists, just as they were pretending to campaign for the environment.

Again Olga Sánchez Cordero declared that much inequality remained, but she was proud to be part of a government which was doing so much for women. Mexico had a historical debt to indigenous, migrant and trans women, among others. There must be an open and frank dialogue. Then there was a statement by Dina, a young woman from an indigenous community in Sonora who was benefiting from a "Young People Building the Future" apprenticeship, who said that women were at the centre of the Transformation. Another woman explained how there were now official Alert Mechanisms for Gender Violence in 18 states, plus 52 Centres of Justice for Women and 61 refuges. Finally a woman from *Inmujeres*, the official Women's Institute, explained how they were working with all 73 federal government departments and agencies.

At this point it it necessary to point out that the opposition (or sectors of it) were not only pretending to be feminist, but also using the feminist cause as a means of provocation. On 9 March 2021 there was much concern about they way in which the previous day's huge women's march from the Angel of Independence monument to the Zócalo had been hijacked by violent protesters. They vandalised shops, breaking windows and stealing goods, and on reaching the central square masked rioters broke down the protective barriers in front of the Cathedral and the National Palace and attacked the police (women officers of the Mexico City force), throwing petrol bombs and setting fires. There were even men among those creating mayhem. The police acted with extraordinary restraint, and it was fortunate that they had very effective shields and protective clothing. The police were prepared because the same had happened the previous year, and indeed it would be repeated in subsequent years.[12] Clearly the aim was to provoke violent repression so they could allege that the government was repressive and anti-feminist, and indeed they did post very misleading reports and photos in international media.

As was to be expected, the reaction of the general public was to repudiate the provocateurs, and if there was any discontent against the authorities it was for not acting more firmly. But in the long run it was the opposition which was discredited, and indeed in more recent years many politicians of the PRIAN (PRI and PAN) have once again revealed their true colours, openly opposing women's rights and making misogynistic statements.

Much remains to be done for women in Mexico, but it cannot be denied that there has been a remarkable transformation in both attitudes and practice. With Claudia Sheinbaum in office as President, and with an unprecedented number of women in official positions of all kinds, Mexico is in some respects in advance of many European countries, the US or Canada. As Claudia declared, it is not just that she as a woman is now President, but "with me, women have arrived".

One of the examples which merits attention is that of Clara Brugada, the working-class woman who was a very successful mayor of Iztapalapa (Mexico City's largest borough with 1.8 million people) and who has now become Metro Mayor of the capital.[13] Having been active as a community organiser in a deprived neighbourhood from an early age, she pioneered social programmes in Iztapalapa, becoming an elected representative at both city and federal levels before playing a leading role in the Mexico City Constituent Congress of 2016 which brought a fully democratic structure to the mega-city for the first time. She was elected mayor of the borough in 2018 and re-elected for another three years in 2021, and led the burgeoning population of migrants from all over southern and central Mexico in pioneering participatory projects and massive investments in community infrastructure. She told me about her difficult career in interviews in December 2021 and January 2022.

The most notable infrastructure projects are "Utopias" which are a combination of park, community centre, sports and cultural hub. The term is officially the Spanish acronym for Units of Transformation and Organisation for Inclusion and Social Harmony, and she succeeded in building 12 of these in her borough, and is now promoting them across the entire city. They are remarkably well-equipped installations which are transforming prospects for local people; each Utopia has a semi-Olympic swimming pool and one has a full Olympic pool. They have football and baseball pitches, boxing rings, outdoor gyms and running tracks; buildings include auditoriums, women's centres with health facilities, childcare and craft equipment, a senior citizens' room and either musical, theatre or audiovisual studios. Professional guidance and instruction is available and everything is free of charge; all of this was financed by an economy drive (in line with AMLO's "civic austerity") and financial support from then Metro Mayor Claudia Sheinbaum. I was able to visit three of these Utopias – Meyehualco, Papalotl and Teotongo – and can testify to their quality; they resemble the best such facilities in the UK which are usually only available on a commercial basis.

As explained to me by Aurora Corona, the young woman in charge of Teotongo Utopia, all of this is the result of 40 years' struggle. Aurora's mother founded the Squatters' Association of San Miguel Teotongo, a neighbourhood named after a town of the same name in Oaxaca state from where some of the migrants had arrived. In the 1970s and 1980s they squatted on barren lands to build their own community, guarding it day and night against repressive local and national governments. They built their own houses and defended a public green space which has now become their Utopia, and among those at the heart of this struggle was Brugada who conceived the Utopias project and led the community's move into formal politics through the Morena party.

Brugada has also placed women at the heart of these projects and each Utopia has a "Siempreviva" (forever flower) unit for those affected by domestic violence. She has also promoted "routes for free and secure women" with special lighting and security features through hazardous areas of Iztapalapa. Women work in groups to learn new skills and take their knowledge out into the community.

When I visited Meyehualco Utopia it had only just been inaugurated and in three days more than 36,000 people had visited. Hundreds of people were queuing to register for access to the Olympic swimming pool and the velodrome (they were free, but such was the demand that registration was necessary). Papolotl ("Butterfly" in the Nahuatl language of the Aztecs) Utopia has a school for cinematic and video journalism; it has hothouses for orchids and butterflies, supplying the previously neglected local environment. Teotongo has among other things a disused airliner which has been fitted with computers to provide free IT access and instruction.

The Utopias have security staff provided by the municipality, but access is free to all and it is striking that many local people were at first reluctant to enter, not believing that such installations were available to them, and certainly not for free. Now they realise that all kinds of professional, cultural and sporting careers are open to them, and young people especially have aspirations of which they never dreamed before. All of this helps to rebuild social networks and combat criminality.

Other activities promoted by Brugada in Iztapalapa, often in collaboration with neighbouring boroughs, include urban agriculture, commercial exchange based on local production and self-sufficiency, water conservation and restoration of Mexico City's aquatic heritage, participatory budgeting and public art, especially murals by local artists depicting native traditions, cultures and collective struggles. Brugada was working closely with Claudia Sheinbaum as Metro Mayor, and now that Claudia is President and Brugada is Metro Mayor, such inspiring programmes will spread to other boroughs and regions of the country.

Mexican Humanism

From the beginning AMLO talked about his "Fourth Transformation", and as it progressed many people – especially sympathisers – began to ask how it should be defined and what was its philosophy: socialism? participatory democracy? or something entirely new?

A significant indication was given in the *mañanera* on 26 November

2020: AMLO declared that Mexico's crisis was one of values, and so they were going to prepare an Ethical Guide for distribution to millions of senior citizens who could then explain it to their children and grandchildren.[14] Media Secretary Jesús Ramírez Cuevas explained that there was a Moral Constitution Committee composed of himself and six or seven other members; they had already held many meetings and open workshops on the subject. The Ethical Guide would not be a law, it was entirely voluntary, but it would include 20 principles such as respect for difference, for life, for dignity, fraternity, work, family, keeping agreements, etc. Another member of the Committee said they were inviting Mexicans to give their opinions, diversity and respect were essential. They believed in freedom, the only limit being the rights of others. Another member stressed knowledge of the past and the future, it was important to know where we came from and where we were going. A woman spoke about wealth, it was legitimate when obtained without deceit, corruption or harm to others. The family should be respected, but it could take different forms. Nature should be respected to restore environmental balance.

Subsequent references to Mexican Humanism by AMLO would become more frequent, and while they may seem like elementary moral statements, closer examination shows that they are incompatible with neoliberalism and in some respects anti-capitalist. AMLO would often reinforce them with references to leading Mexican historical figures such as Hidalgo, Morelos, Juárez, Madero, Cárdenas and others, and above all to deep roots in the country's indigenous cultures.

In his latest book *¡Gracias!* AMLO dedicates a long chapter to *El Humanismo Mexicano*. He declares that while it is nourished by universal ideas, "the essence of our project comes from our millenarian cultures, infused with nobility, and from our exceptional and fertile political history".[15] It is this which gives Mexicans their identity as an honest, hard-working and fraternal society. It is a great lie to say that the European invaders brought civilisation to a region where civilisation had existed for many centuries. The Mexica (Aztecs) who founded Tenochtitlan (now Mexico City) in 1325 achieved impressive political and cultural development in just 200 years, but other cultures such as the Maya had founded great and beautiful cities like Calakmul 2,300 years ago, and the "mother culture", the Olmecs, created massive sculptured figures 3,000 years ago.

In terms of values, the indigenous cultures did not favour individualism, but community and specifically, collective tenure and cultivation of land. Secondly they practised mutual help, solidarity within communities, manifested in communal labour when required as in the *tequio*. Thirdly, AMLO maintains that they had a libertarian spirit and did not practice chattel slavery as introduced by the Spaniards. Furthermore there was a culture of honesty; theft and corruption arrived with the Conquest and the quest for gold of the conquistadors.

As for the country's modern history, Mexico was one of the countries (along with Venezuela) where the initial revolt against Spanish rule in 1810 rapidly developed into a mass insurgency of the "lower castes", peasants and labourers of indigenous, black or *mestizo* (mixed-race) background, seeking not just formal independence but land and freedom from slavery or peonage (serfdom). Father Miguel Hidalgo who proclaimed the initial *grito* (shout) of rebellion was a creole (white) parish priest, but he identified with the common people and was soon leading a spontaneous horde of insurgents threatening to overwhelm Mexico City. It can be argued that his decision to halt outside the capital so as to avoid a massacre (which led to his defeat) was a manifestation of humanism, avoiding bloodshed; he showed his sympathies with a decree to abolish slavery. His successor as insurgent leader, José María Morelos, was another priest but of mixed race, a former mule-driver who showed no hesitation in waging guerrilla war in the mountains of the south until also captured and executed by the Spanish. Morelos called for "moderation of indigence and opulence", in other words, greater social equality; for children of peasants and labourers to be educated just like the child of the wealthiest landowner; for equality before the law (ending the legal privileges of the military and the clergy); and that "sovereignty derives directly from the people".[16] All of this in 1813.

Most of these principles would not be realised for many years, but they show that a vigorous revolutionary spirit was thriving in Mexico from the beginning of its movement for independence, and this is the foundation of "Mexican Humanism". AMLO also quoted the indigenous Liberal Benito Juárez, whom he regarded as the greatest president the country ever had: "The triumph of reaction is morally impossible", and "The rich and powerful do not feel, and even less do they try to rectify the sufferings of the poor". Finally there is the most famous of Juárez' sayings: "Between nations as between individuals, respect for the rights of others is peace".

AMLO continues his chapter on Mexican Humanism with detailed assessments of Ricardo Flores Magón, Francisco I Madero, Emiliano Zapata and Francisco Villa. In all cases, whatever their faults, he shows admiration for their revolutionary commitment and identification with the common people. He mentions others such as Francisco J Múgica and Felipe Carrillo Puerto, but he concludes with the greatest president of the 20th century, Lázaro Cárdenas. It was Cárdenas who did far more than any other president to satisfy the land hunger of peasants and rural workers by legal means, to complete what had been done by force of arms in limited areas by Zapata and others. He also supported workers' rights and organisation more effectively than ever before, and reclaimed Mexico's economic sovereignty with the 1938 oil expropriation and railway nationalisation. But Cárdenas could not prevent a resurgence of the right after he left office in 1940; AMLO is determined to ensure that this does not happen with the Fourth Transformation, and it seems clear that with the succession of

Claudia Sheinbaum, he has been successful.

The essence of Mexican Humanism is summed up by AMLO in two parallel phrases, one from Ricardo Flores Magón: "Only the people can save the people", and the other from Benito Juárez: "With the people, everything; without the people, nothing".[17] This is what AMLO means when he refers, to the surprise of many, to "the noble art of politics": authentic politics is profoundly human and must give priority to the poor. Mexico's first woman president has already shown that she is more than capable of continuing to work with the people to ensure the advance of the Fourth Transformation.

NOTES

1. Full name *Sindicato Nacional de Trabajadores Mineros, Metalúrgicos, Siderúrgicos y Similares de la República Mexicana*, National Union of Mining, Metallurgical, Steel and Similar Workers of the Mexican Republic.
2. Napoleón Gómez, *Collapse of Dignity: The Story of a Mining Tragedy and the Fight Against Greed and Corruption in Mexico*, Dallas, TX, 2013, BenBella Books; and Napoleón Gómez Urrutia, *El Triunfo de la Dignidad: Una Historia Extraordinaria de Convicciones, Lucha y Esperanza*, México, 2021, La Jornada/MAPorrúa.
3. www.eleconomista.com.mx/economia/Salario-minio-en-Mexico-Cuanto-ha-crecido-entre-2018-y-2024-20240109-0047.html, Accessed 01/11/2024.
4. https://reformalaboral.stps.gob.mx/ejes-reforma#eje_libertad_democracia_sindical Accessed 01/11/2024.
5. www.gob.mx/presidencia/ Morning Press Conferences 27/10, 28/10 & 12/11/2020, Accessed 14/11/2020.
6. www.gob.mx/presidencia/ Morning Press Conference, 12/11/2020, Accessed 14/11/2020.
7. www.gob.mx/presidencia/ Morning Press Conference, 23/04/2021, Accessed 15/05/2021.
8. e-voice.org.uk/mexicosolidarity-2/the-4T/ "Labour, sovereignty & dignity in Mexico's Transformation: a conversation with Senator Napoleón Gómez, David Raby, 02/08/2023.
9. http://www.gob.mx/stps/prensa/el-gobierno-de-mexico-dignifica-las-condiciones-laborales-de-las-trabajadores-del-hogar?idiom=es, 28 de febrero de 2023 Accessed 01/11/2021.
10. www.gob.mx/presidencia/ Morning Press Conference, 25/11/2020
11. www.gob.mx/presidencia/ Morning Press Conference, 08/03/2021, Accessed live.
12. www.gob.mx/presidencia/ Morning Press Conference, 09/03/2021, Accessed live.
13. Much of what follows is an edited version of my article in the *Morning Star*, https://morningstaronline.co.uk/article/f/socialist-borough-leads-way-mexico, 15/02/2022.
14. www.gob.mx/presidencia/ Morning Press Conference, 26/11/2020, Accessed live.
15. Andrés Manuel López Obrador, *¡Gracias!*, México 2024, Planeta, p. 447 (translation mine).
16. López Obrador, *¡Gracias!*, p. 468.
17. López Obrador, *¡Gracias!*, p. 503.

14

Campeche: transformation despite problems

Campeche is a fascinating state, small in population (928,000) but medium-sized in territory (57,000 square km), thoroughly tropical in climate and very much part of the Mayan culture of the Yucatán peninsula. The only cities of any size are the capital, with the same name, an almost perfectly preserved Spanish colonial fortified port with walls to protect against the pirates (English, French and Dutch) of earlier centuries, and Ciudad del Carmen, a port and resort town on an island enclosing a maritime lagoon (the *Laguna de Términos*) in the southwest of the state.

Apart from the glories of the ancient Mayan cultures, most visibly represented in the state by the pyramid and other remains at Edzná, Campeche features in Mexican history for the naval battle of Chakan-putún (now Champotón) where the first Spaniards to arrive on the coast, three ships commanded by Francisco Hernández de Córdoba in late March 1517, were attacked by about 1,000 Mayan warriors in canoes and put to flight leaving about 20 dead. This victory is rightly celebrated in Campeche and Mexico as a whole.

In colonial times Campeche was exploited mainly for its tropical hardwoods, in particular a tree known as *palo de tinte* (dye wood) used for that purpose and as timber. The city and the entire coast was subject to regular pirate attacks by British, French and Dutch marauders from the mid-16th to the early 18th centuries, indeed a few hundred of them settled for long periods around the *Laguna de Términos*.

Dye wood continued to be the mainstay of the export economy until the early 20th century when it was replaced by chicle, the raw material for chewing gum. This would last until the late 1940s when a synthetic substitute was invented in the US, and what followed for Campeche was shrimp fishing on an industrial scale, which continued until about 1994. By this time it was being replaced by oil, with the discovery in 1977 of the Cantarell field, offshore from Ciudad del Carmen; this would be the main activity into the 21st century, peaking in 2004 and then steadily declining.[1]

From this brief summary it is clear that the state has had a typical boom-and-bust primary product export economy, with no sustained or balanced development. Only now are there signs that this may be beginning to change. There was significant development of rice production for the national market from the 1950s to the 1990s, but this was then largely abandoned. In 1940 Mexico contributed 80% of the world's chicle exports to the US, and 50% of this came from Campeche; in 1945 8,000 families in the state relied on chicle production. Then shrimp production boomed to reach 13,887 tons in 1980 with a fleet of 600 boats; this began to decline through over-fishing and then the rise of petroleum. This in turn boomed through uncontrolled extraction promoted by the neoliberal governments which simply exported crude oil (mainly from Cantarell), with Mexican production peaking at 3.4 million tons under President Fox, as we have seen undermining PEMEX and its industrial capacity.

In political terms the Mexican Revolution entered Campeche, like neighbouring Yucatán, when the Constitutionalist military arrived and imposed their will on the local oligarchy: what General Salvador Alvarado did in Yucatán was done in Campeche by General Joaquín Mucel. As interim governors of the two states they decreed the end of debt peonage and the beginnings of agrarian reform, popular education and women's emancipation, opening the way to the remarkable rise of the Socialist Party of the Southeast under Felipe Carrillo Puerto. After setbacks in the 1920s there would be a tense situation with more progressive reforms in both states in the 1930s at the time of the national government of Lázaro Cárdenas, followed by the corporatist and capitalist rule of the PRI from the 1940s until the neoliberal turn of the 1980s onwards. In the late 1930s the rise of a militant left-wing movement centred around the teachers of the Rural Normal School of Hecelchakán was reinforced by Cárdenas' agrarian reforms and the initiation of the construction of the Southeastern Railway, supervised by his close associate and Secretary of Public Works General Francisco J Múgica, a very committed revolutionary. My own research in the late 1960s confirmed that Múgica's abortive left candidacy for the 1940 presidential elections had a strong base in Campeche, particularly among the teachers.[2]

Layda Sansores and the democratic movement

Political corruption, with PRI domination and some participation by the Citizens' Movement, PAN and PVEM (Greens) would prevail until the rise of Morena and its victory in Campeche in 2021 with Layda Sansores San

Román. But it is important to realise that the popular discontent which had manifested itself nationally from the late 1980s onwards, leading to the rise of the PRD, was also present in Campeche. Layda Sansores was already a leading figure in the democratic movement: her father, Carlos Sansores Pérez, was governor of the state from 1967 to 1973 and was one of the better governors of the PRI era, founding several educational institutions. Like many democratic leaders, Layda participated in the PRI until 1996 when she joined the PRD and ran as an opposition candidate in the 1997 elections for governor; she was declared defeated by the official PRI candidate, but claimed that the result was fraudulent. In this she was supported by thousands of *campechanos* who joined her in protests of the "Civil Resistance Movement" for months afterwards; but on 19 October 1997 state police unleashed brutal repression with teargas, beatings and gunfire. A number of people were killed and many injured, and 19 October came to be seen as a turning point in the state's politics. In 2016 a Morena city councillor in Campeche, Bertha Pérez Herrera, declared that in the 1997 elections "civil society, the left, the opposition and Layda Sansores won, making it clear that the people had chosen a new path", and that the democratic opening which later emerged would not have been possible without the figure of Layda Sansores.[3] Also in 2018, celebrating AMLO's victory, an independent Campeche journalist, Eudaldo Chávez Molina, who had participated in the resistance, recalled how Layda led the protest marches and her leadership inspired thousands of *campechanos*.[4]

Before discussing the remarkable transformation achieved by the Morena Governor and her team, it is worth looking at the sordid record of PRI governor "Alito" Moreno (Alejandro Moreno Cárdenas) from 2015 to 2019. Alito, who is relatively young (b. 1975), had been federal deputy and senator before becoming governor of his home state, and from 2019, National President of the PRI (he resigned as governor in order to run for this position).

Alito has been accused by Layda Sansores, but also by many others not linked to Morena or the left, such as *Reforma* newspaper, of numerous acts of gross corruption.[5] In 2019 he was accused of possessing a luxury residence worth $2.3 million US, built in two years, when he declared an annual income of $250,000, and 19 other buildings, 10 of them in a luxury suburb of Campeche city. Most of these were acquired when he was a federal deputy earning little more than $50,000 a year. Governor Sansores has accused him of fraud and selling favours (influence peddling): fixing the price of certain public lands or buildings at a nominal level and gifting them to his mother, they would then be sold at as much as 100 times the price. She has also accused him of bribing local assembly members to support his legislative initiatives. He was also denounced in 2021 to the Tax Collection Service for using fraudulent contracts with "ghost companies" to avoid tax. Alito has been recorded threatening other politicians or civil servants, saying he would "screw their mothers" and using other colourful phrases.

All of this simply illustrates not only Alito's corruption but also his utter contempt for the people of Campeche: he owned a number of local media enterprises, and sacked more than 300 workers without any compensation. Alito is merely the most prominent of a mafia of corrupt and venal operators who helped to ruin a state which was already in dire straits, in a local reflection of what the PRI and PAN were doing nationally. What Morena and Layda Sansores have done, with great difficulty, is to turn this situation around and to give hope to Campeche for the first time in generations.

2021: Layda and Morena take office

When the new government took office on 16 September 2021, Layda's team immediately took stock of the situation. The Public Security Secretary, a determined young woman by the name of Marcela Muñoz, reported that of 1,076 state police supposedly on duty, they could only locate 88; the others had gone AWOL and were enjoying a life of luxury, or if not so lucky were performing menial tasks as janitors. Quite a number were working as bodyguards for politicians or civil servants who should not need such services. Those who were on duty were crowded into run-down stations, many police cars were broken down while several quite new vehicles already had thousands of kilometres on their odometers, raising suspicions that they had been tampered with to make false expenses claims. On closer inspection it was concluded that there were only 300 operational state police, a totally inadequate number, plus municipal forces. All of them were very poorly trained and paid, with a culture of ingrained corruption.[6] Another remarkable point (not a discovery as it was common knowledge) was the existence of a Campeche State Air Force with quite a number of pilots and support staff, clearly unnecessary and a waste of public funds. They would be pensioned off immediately.

As for the civilian bureaucracy, it included 700 employees in positions "of confidence", political appointees hired without formal procedures or exams. They claimed to be career civil servants, but the new Solicitor General said each case would be examined and those who were not qualified would be dismissed. In many government offices computers and other equipment had been stolen by politicians or others who had left. In one case it was reported that a departing employee had been observed passing office equipment through the window to his mates.

The gross neglect of public services and property extended to health and education. The Ciudad del Carmen Maternity & Paediatric Hospital, built in 2014-15, was largely abandoned and left to decay, some departments had broken doors and no electricity supply; high technology equipment was left in unopened boxes and there was a serious lack of personnel. In general there was a serious lack of medicines, supplies covered only about 40% of needs and this was particularly pronounced for cancer medications. The one area of health care that was functioning well was Covid vaccinations, because it was implemented directly by federal agencies (including the military). The new national health service being implemented by AMLO's government was beginning to make a difference, but opposition-governed states had not signed up to it and still ran their own health systems, so the benefits of the INSABI (Institute of Health for Welfare) were only just being provided by agreement with the new state government. The Carmen Maternity & Paediatric Hospital needed 30 million pesos for repairs and renovations, and INSABI (later *IMSS-Bienestar*) immediately pledged to provide the state with 102 million pesos for improvements at that hospital and elsewhere.[7]

In education many schools were neglected and vandalised. The Campeche Technological University had a serious debt and could not pay its staff; the Champotón Higher Technological Institute was also unable to pay its staff and lacked computers, having only a few which dated from 2002 or 2004, and the same applied to other such institutions.

The state had a new central administrative building which was nearing completion, but there were a number of design faults which were already apparent, including inadequate accessibility for the disabled. In virtually all respects the state administration was falling apart, and Layda Sansores' government had to start from scratch or at the very least, repair abandoned, damaged or vandalised installations so as to re-establish basic services. Fortunately the majority of the new cabinet and administrative team were well qualified, enthusiastic and hard working, and they had full support from AMLO's federal government. Within months dramatic improvements could be seen in most areas.

Starting immediately on assuming office, Layda Sansores launched her own version of AMLO's *mañanera* morning press conferences, not every day but once a week, and in the evening rather than the morning: her *Martes del Jaguar* (Jaguar Tuesdays) press conferences, held in the largest room in the governor's suite of the *Palacio de Gobierno* (State Capitol or in UK terms, County Hall). A couple of hundred people would be squeezed into this room, between government officials, reporters and ordinary citizens. The sessions typically last a couple of hours, with the governor reporting on the week's events, inviting ministers or secretaries to explain their policy areas, and fielding questions. The sessions are very participatory and often include music or poetry; these and other activities are very well organised by her executive assistant Elvira Nájera and publicised by the Media and Communications Secretary, Walther Patrón.

Layda is a very colourful woman, literally and figuratively, and emotional, wearing her heart on her sleeve. With the force of her personality she dominates the scene, but if she imposes anything it is her personal charisma being used to promote positive change, the local version of the 4T Transformation, and she does so through participation. She does not sit in the impressive governor's seat but sits to one side and invites an ordinary citizen to take the seat of authority and act as "governor" for a few minutes, presenting their own priorities. She also invites guests to speak, and I was privileged to do this in June 2024 during my visit, being interviewed by Layda about my interest in Campeche, in Mexico and its Transformation.[8]

Reporting back to the people

The same colourful, even theatrical, approach was on display in Layda's first annual report to the state in August 2022. In a large public assembly with several hundred, possibly a thousand people, the event began with music and dancing, and very symbolic music: the Italian anti-fascist resistance tune *Bella Ciao*, but with words referring to Campeche and its democratic transformation. Layda made reference to the Resistance of 1997 and its connection with the national movement led by AMLO, and thanked the national leaders of Morena, Mario Delgado and Citlalli Hernández, for their presence.

The actual report was presented with the various cabinet ministers or secretaries going up one by one to talk about their policy areas in conversation with Layda.[9] The government secretary emphasised the importance of participation, how the team had maintained dialogue with all people who had questions or grievances and had systematically visited small towns and neighbourhoods. The governor always attended the public security meetings, just as AMLO did nationally. Title deeds had been given to more than 4,000 peasant smallholders who had been demanding this for years so as to have security of tenure; public housing was being delivered; water supplies and irrigation works were being provided with the help of Conagua, the National Water Commission; and the long overdue dredging of the River Palizada in the south of the state had begun.

Bureaucratic procedures were being modernised and simplified, and internet access was being extended to the whole population with help from the Mexico City administration of Claudia Sheinbaum; 559 internet access points had been installed and more were coming. As with AMLO's "Civic Austerity" drive, the state government was reducing waste, avoiding debt and improving tax collection.

The State Welfare Secretary reported on a welfare programme for indigenous women and the appointment of 208 women as Welfare Promotion Officers. Diversity and inclusion of all minorities, ethnic, the disabled, gender etc were being promoted. In Public Health progress was being made in the repair of equipment (631 items so far) and vandalised or deteriorated hospitals and clinics, 900 medical staff had been given permanent appointments and medicine supplies now satisfied 80% of demand.

With regard to Public Security the woefully inadequate pay of municipal police was doubled, from 6,000 or 7,000 pesos to 13,000 pesos a month; 250 more officers had been trained and new cars, radios, uniforms and weapons supplied. This, together with the Solicitor General's work to ensure that crimes were investigated and suspects prosecuted (tasks previously routinely neglected) had led to reduction by 50% in homicides and significant reductions in other crimes. Also, the governor had revived a priority of her mother many years previously, of working seriously to rehabilitate offenders: she regularly visited jails and instituted a programme to make them live up to their name of CERESOS (*Centros de Rehabilitación Social*, Centres of Social Rehabilitation).

In education, progress was being made in the repair of neglected and vandalised schools, 390 of which had benefited from improvements, and the post-Covid return to classes was going well. The Culture Secretary reported that Mayan language and culture was being promoted as never before; he spoke in Mayan (with translation), and indeed it should be pointed out that in her "Jaguar Tuesday" sessions Layda often uses Mayan phrases, and the sessions begin with a Mayan language teacher giving a brief class in the language for all present. Also (as I was able to observe myself through discussions with Culture Secretary Esteban Hinojosa) cultural activities included more support for orchestras and music in general, and renovation of theatres.

Development policies included transport infrastructure (of course the Tren Maya which is a federal undertaking), but also improvement of roads, plans to purchase new buses from China, a light rail link from the city centre to the Tren Maya station, and modernisation of ports. A solar power project, the second largest in the country, was being planned. In agriculture more than $12 million US was being invested in fertilisers and maize seeds supplied directly to small producers, and more than 100 agrarian technicians were providing assistance, particularly in the Sembrando Vida programme which is big in Campeche. The fishing sector, which had been abandoned, was revived with a new Fishing Institute, more than 5,000 men and women had registered and an existing subsidy for sustainable fishing was increased from 1,800 to 3,000 pesos per person. Environmental protection was being increased with assistance from federal authorities, with special attention to preventing illegal tree felling and logging.

The session ended after more than three hours with music by the State Youth Orchestra, and a final passionate declaration by Layda, "Another World Is Possible! I am the red woman warrior! *¡Es un Honor estar con Obrador!* (It's an Honour to be with Obrador!)"

The second annual report on 1 August 2023 followed the same format,[10] as did the third report on 1 August 2024.[11] The third report was even more participatory, each departmental secretary gave a brief report with both live and video contributions by ordinary citizens explaining the benefits they had received. Progress was outstanding in many areas and it was clear that the term "Transformation" was indeed appropriate for what was being achieved in Campeche.

In terms of power supplies, negotiation with the federal authorities and specifically the CFE had led to the state being favoured with the lowest consumer electricity tariff of all. A major gas pipeline, Cuxtal II, built by the French public enterprise Engie, was being completed to supply Campeche along with other Gulf of Mexico states. The La Pimienta Solar power installation in Ciudad del Carmen municipality had begun operation, with over a million photovoltaic panels covering 625 ha and supplying electricity to 300,000 families throughout the Yucatán peninsula, and work had begun to install solar panels on the roofs of all public buildings.

In agriculture support for small producers was being extended to dairy farmers with guaranteed prices for milk, and a project was under way to revive rice production which had been important in Campeche in the 1980s but had been abandoned. The fishing industry now had 7,020 men and women registered with support for sustainable fishing.

Planned improvements in public transport were reaching fruition, not just the major federal contribution of the Tren Maya but the Digital Rail Link, 20.7 km from the city centre to the airport and the Tren Maya station and a total of 14 stations, now almost complete with five trains of four coaches each, Chinese-built.[12] The state legislature had also passed a new Transport Act which facilitated public planning, overcoming entrenched opposition from private bus companies. 22 Yutong electric buses would soon be providing much improved service in the capital, and the old diesel buses would provide services in smaller towns.

All of this public investment was finally producing results in the overall economy; in marked contrast to previous years, Campeche in 2023 was the fourth-ranked state in economic growth at over 5%. In the previous administration the state had lost 10,000 jobs, 91% of that number had now been recovered. Industrial investment, both foreign and Mexican, was rapidly increasing; among others the semi-public Mexican cement company Cruz Azul, with four major plants elsewhere, was building a fifth plant in Campeche.

In terms of welfare, in addition to all the federal programmes there was a state scheme for "Communities in Transformation" where neighbourhood committees were given 100,000 pesos for their own use, and in almost all cases they would raise more funds themselves. Civil Protection, previously much neglected, had been greatly improved, with Fire Brigades given much improved equipment and much more efficient communications technology. This had already produced results in the early-season hurricane which caused flooding in late June 2024.

In health care, the restoration and improvement of hospitals and clinics had now reached 90%, new personnel were being hired including 50 Cuban doctors, there were 29 new ambulances and integration with the new free federal system *IMSS-Bienestar* was advancing rapidly. A remarkable event took place on 11 February 2023 when the President of

Cuba, Miguel Díaz-Canel, visited Campeche to celebrate the new Mexico-Cuba medical agreement; both the Cuban romantic poet José María Heredia and the country's national hero José Martí had spent time in Campeche, and Governor Layda Sansores declared that in no other corner of Mexico was Cuba loved so much as in Campeche. A Cuban doctor who was working in the *IMSS-Bienestar* hospital of Ciudad del Carmen spoke of their commitment to the state. Then in the Mayan site of Edzná AMLO presented Díaz-Canel with the Mexican Order of the Aztec Eagle, the country's highest honour for foreigners.[13]

In education there was also impressive progress; among many interesting developments mention should be made of the Campeche Intercultural University inaugurated in July 2024 in Dzitbalché with a secondary campus in El Juncal, Palizada.[14] One of a number of such universities across the country, it was developed with participatory community workshops and began with courses in Mayan Language and Culture, Agroecology and Food Sovereignty, and Sustainable Tourism. Cultural and environmental improvement along with tourism have benefited enormously with the restoration of the great Mayan site of Calakmul and the adjacent urban development linked to Tren Maya, in the deep southern interior of the state close to Guatemala; around it is the huge pristine jungle area, the Calakmul Biosphere Reserve of 728,000 hectares.[15] Indeed, the nucleus of the reserve, with the greatest protection, has been increased from 200,000 to 519,000 hectares, and with two more adjacent natural reserves in Campeche and Tabasco, they comprise the Great Calakmul Region of 1.5 million hectares, the biggest such area north of the Amazon.

In many ways Campeche can be seen as a fine example of what the Fourth Transformation means for Mexico. But there was recently a controversial issue which arose when early in December 2024 Governor Layda Sansores appointed as Secretary of Economic Development an ex-PAN politician, Jorge Luis Lavalle, who was accused of corruption in relation to the Odebrecht scandal and former President Peña Nieto's privatising Energy Reform, and was in fact condemned and spent 18 months in jail for this. Many pro-4T progressive journalists condemned this decision,[16] but closer examination suggests that Lavalle may be innocent and has changed his political alignment;[17] indeed, a recent report made available by the Campeche Communications Secretary indicates that he was victim of a frame-up by PRIAN politicians angry at his change of allegiance.[18] However, on 10 December when the matter was raised in the *mañanera* press conference, President Claudia Sheinbaum declared "It's a decision of Governor Layda Sansores. I would not have invited him [Lavalle] to my cabinet".[19] Later the same day in Acapulco Claudia Sheinbaum presided over the National Public Security Conference, with her entire security team and all state governors, and Layda Sansores was there and embraced the President.[20] It would seem very unjust to assume that Layda Sansores has betrayed all her principles and political commitment; her government continues to implement all of the 4T programmes and seems fully committed to the project of President Claudia Sheinbaum.

In her "Jaguar Tuesdays" press conference of 17 December Layda Sansores, with her legal officer, gave a detailed defence of the decision with evidence to suggest Lavalle's innocence,[21] but there remains room for doubt because other testimonies implicating him in the Odebrecht bribery scandal have never been legally resolved.[22] Many progressive journalists continue to make serious criticisms of Layda's decision; some have made quite vitriolic accusations of betrayal against her which are completely unjustified. There may be grounds for questioning her judgement in the matter, but intemperate accusations only cause unnecessary polarisation. It is very regrettable that this scandal has cast a shadow over the positive Transformation of Campeche in which Layda Sansores has been central, and it has to be viewed as an example of the unresolved contradictions of the process.

NOTES

1. www.scielo.org.mx/scielo.php?script=sci_arttext&pid =S1870-57662008000200003, Accessed 11/10/2024.
2. David L Raby, *Educación y Revolución Social en México (1921-1940)*, México, 1974, Editorial SepSetentas, capítulo VII, "Los maestros y la política local en Campeche". My work was based on interviews with local teachers and others, local newspapers and the personal archive of General Múgica in Pátzcuaro, Michoacán, consulted by permission of his widow Carolina Escudero viuda de Múgica.
3. paginabierta.mx/2016/10/20/resistencia-civil-de-1997-parteaguas-de-la-democracia-campechana/ Accessed 27/10/2024.
4. www.poresto.net/campeche/2018/10/18/19-de-octubre-layda-el-despertar-del-pueblo-campechano.html Accessed 27/10/2024.
5. es.wikipedia.org/wiki/Alejandro_Moreno_Cardenas, Accessed 12/10/2024.
6. layda.com.mx/martes-del-jaguar/ 21 & 26/09/2021, Accessed 24/10/2024.
7. layda.com.mx/martes-del-jaguar/ 26/10/2021, accessed 25/10/2024.
8. layda.com.mx/martes-del-jaguar/ 11/06/2024.
9. layda.com.mx/primer-informe-de-gobierno/2022/08/01 also available on radiobufalo.mx www.youtube.com/watch?v=mS0X0uH-4E, accessed 27/10/2024.
10. Segundo Informe de Gobierno del Estado de Campeche, 2022-2023/ Layda Sansores San Roman www.youtube.com/watch?v=NarWcwku9as Accessed 30/10/2024.
11. Tercer Informe de Gobierno del Estado de Campeche, 2023-2024/ Layda Sansores San Román, en TRC Televisión: www.youtube.com/watch?v=xdKTf_tF3Dc Accessed 30/10/2024.
12. es.wikipedia.org/wiki/Tren_Ligero_de_Campeche Accessed 29/10/2024.
13. https://heraldodemexico.com.mx/nacional/2023/2/11/amlo-recibe-miguel-diaz-canel-presidente-de-cuba-en-el-aeropuerto-de-campeche-480751.html Accessed 09/11/2024
14. www.comie.org.mx/congreso/memoriaelectronica/v17/doc/0330.pdf Accessed 29/10/2024.
15. http://gatopardo.com/noticias-actuales/legado-amlo-en-mexico/, "Fin de sexenio: una mirada desde el sur", 17.9.24, Étienne von Bertrab.
16. https://tribunacampeche.com/05/periodistas-de-la-4t-arremeten-contra-layda-por-nombramiento-de-lavalle-maury-si-su-problema-es-la-lana-que-invitan-a-alito-ironizan/701042/ 5 de diciembre de 2024 citando a Alvaro Delgado y Alejandro Páez. Accessed

07/12/2024.
17. www.msn.com/es-mx/noticias/mexico/él-es-jorge-luis-lavalle-nuevo-secretario-de-campeche-involucrado-en-odebrecht-AA1vh6yw 05/12/2024. Accessed 07/12/2024.
18. Caso Lavalle dic24 v1, report available from Campeche Government. Accessed 07/12/2024.
19. www.gob.mx/presidencia Morning Press Conference, 10/12/2024. Accessed live.
20. www.gob.mx/presidencia/prensa/presidenta-claudia-sheinbaum-hace-llamado-a-gobernadores-y-gobernadoras-a-trabajar-en-coordinacion-a-favor-de-la-seguridad-del-pais 10/12/2024. Accessed 11/12/2024. Also x.com/LaydaSansores/status/1866669276897186196 11 Dec 2024. Accessed 11/12/2024.
21. layda.com.mx/martes-dl-jaguar 17/12/2024. Accessed 18/12/2024.
22. ¡Al Chile! con Meme Yamel, https://www.youtube.com> watch?v=2F6XQW0HfCE 18/12/2024 "Layda defiende con uñas y dientes a Lavalle Maury, estalla contra Los Periodistas". Accessed 18/12/2024.

15

Acapulco: much more than disaster relief

The Pacific beach resort of Acapulco used to be Mexico's number one tourist destination: a stunningly beautiful bay overlooked by mountains, it was the favourite destination of sun-seeking *gringos* from the 1930s to the 1960s. Now a disorderly city of over a million inhabitants and the largest urban centre in the state of Guerrero, it suffers from widespread poverty and a reputation for crime, although its natural beauty remains and US and Canadian visitors are rivalled by domestic Mexican holiday-makers.

On 25 October 2023 Acapulco was hit by Hurricane Otis; such storms were a regular problem for the resort and the entire Pacific coast, but this one was exceptional, unprecedented for the speed with which it developed from a tropical storm to a category 5 hurricane (the highest level) in about 12 hours. AMLO immediately mobilised several thousand members of the army, navy and national guard to begin relief and clean-up efforts.

With local airports out of action, he and members of his cabinet tried to travel there by road the very next day, and there are moving images of him trudging through the mud when the motorway also proved to be impassable. In the next few days communications were restored and AMLO himself visited four times in a fortnight. More important, he mobilised the ministries of the interior, defence, navy, security, welfare, environment, public works, housing and others on a large scale, implementing an enormous relief operation.

But media critics and opposition politicians immediately launched a barrage of criticisms and attacks alleging neglect, failure, indifference and corruption. They pointed to the FONDEN, a disaster relief fund of the old regime which AMLO had abolished as a den of corruption. They claimed its absence led to a lack of assistance, ignoring evidence that 65 percent of its funds went to pork-barrel arrangements for local bosses to line their pockets with poorly implemented road repair and similar schemes. The opposition also claimed that the military were preventing distribution of aid packages provided by private enterprise, but the one piece of evidence they produced for this was shown to be completely false.

Critics subsequently alleged that AMLO had failed to warn in advance of the hurricane, when international meteorological authorities declared that it was no more than a tropical storm until shortly before impact and had grown to category 5 with unprecedented speed. Hostile media also repeated ad nauseam a claim that the real death toll was over 350, but this was based on one unsubstantiated report. AMLO was clear that all deaths were to be lamented, but nothing was to be gained by alarmist reports; official records were checked and re-checked and showed 48 dead and 26 other missing persons; the final figure was 68 dead.

International media also tried to discredit the relief effort. Insight Crime, a British-based agency operating worldwide, alleged that those who would benefit most from the disaster, "in the absence [of assistance from] the Mexican state" were the drug cartels (and it named four of the most notorious).

Nothing could be further from the truth: as we shall see, the Mexican authorities' relief and reconstruction effort was massive and unparalleled, providing immediate assistance on an enormous scale and then restoration of essential services, followed by gainful employment and support to rebuild legitimate businesses as never before. But this was typical of British establishment journalism on Mexico, which seizes on the bad news (or invents it) and completely ignores AMLO's transformative programmes.

A brief summary of the assistance provided will give some idea. The military distributed 50,000 hot meals and 40,000 emergency food hampers, with bottled water, every day. The Public Welfare Department carried out a house-by-house survey of 300,000 dwellings to determine individual needs, and in the second week of November, in a quite unprecedented form of assistance, the government began distributing domestic appliances, beds and other furniture to those who had lost such goods in the hurricane. Emergency health brigades began circulating, particularly in deprived areas, within days, and everything possible was done to restore basic services like water and electricity. It's worth examining the case of electricity to see just what was achieved.

Around 90% of the area was without electricity, and the public CFE immediately swung into action. In 48 hours they had completed a survey of the damage, and after three days they had restored about 50% of the service. Some 10,000 pylons and posts were down, and to replace them quickly glass fibre posts were used. After a week 75% of service was restored, with a work force of 2,900 operating full time. By 4 November, ten days after the hurricane, service was virtually complete at 99%.

This contrasts favourably with hurricane Katrina in New Orleans, where it took several weeks to fully restore service, or the south Texas snowstorm in 2022, where it took some three weeks. It has been pointed out that CFE could only mount such a huge and efficient operation because it is a fully public enterprise, rescued from privatisation over the previous three years by AMLO's restoration of public control in the face of tenacious opposition.

On 1 November AMLO announced a 20-point Plan for Relief and Reconstruction which included all the points already mentioned, plus bringing forward by two months all benefit payments to local inhabitants, incorporating 10,000 more young people into the government's very successful apprenticeship scheme and paying them to work in relief and reconstruction, cancelling electricity bills for three months, a four-month tax holiday for all businesses and individuals in the area, interest-free credits to small businesses, major infrastructure investments, and more. The total value of the package was about $3.5 billion, making it one of the biggest relief and reconstruction efforts in the world.

More than this, AMLO's government recognised that this was the opportunity to adopt a completely new development model for the Acapulco region. This was one of the poorest areas of Mexico, and for decades unplanned speculative development had produced massive inequality and social and environmental degradation. What was being undertaken was a comprehensive plan to revitalise tourism, with public subsidies for commercial loans to restore hotels and the tourist economy, but also environmental projects to recover and extend parks, reforestation and sustainable agriculture, and promotion of new productive enterprises. There would be a greatly increased presence of the National Guard, recognising that insecurity had left the population at the mercy of organised crime and had also caused the decline of Acapulco as a tourist destination.

In December 2023 *La Jornada* newspaper declared that the reconstruction of Acapulco was "unprecedented".[1] In addition to other services, the Director of the national water board Conagua reported that drinking water supplies in the city were now much better than before the hurricane. State Governor Evelyn Salgado said that by the end of December (ten days after her report) 127 hotels would have reopened, with 4,534 rooms available; 162 shops were open along with most bank branches. Operation of the city's port was also recovering. The return to something resembling normality in little more than two months after such a disaster was a record.

Then on 10 January 2024 Román Meyer Falcón, the brilliant young architect who heads SEDATU, the Regional Planning Agency, announced that in the municipalities of Acapulco and Coyuca de Benítez they were investing in the reconstruction of 138 public spaces or facilities damaged by the hurricane.[2] Their Urban Improvement Programme would provide an initial investment equivalent to about $20 million US. These projects were being planned, designed and implemented with local communities; so far 85 community committees had been organised and accounts were being opened with *Banjército* (the Armed Forces Bank) to ensure that work could begin in late January or early February, with completion early in July. This would include 59 sports grounds, 33 markets, 27 Community Development Centres, 18 parks and the corridor of the historic centre of Acapulco, including restoration of beaches, and would restore roofs, fences, lighting, furniture, painting and planting vegetation, as appropriate.

Sadly only about a year later Acapulco and the surrounding region were hit by another similar phenomenon, Hurricane John, which was not as severe in terms of wind damage but worse for rainfall and flooding. It caused damage in Oaxaca and Michoacán and in much of the Guerrero coast, but from 23 to 27 September 2024 it overwhelmed Acapulco with the equivalent of a year's rain in four days. There were at least ten deaths in Acapulco and 22 in total.

Once again AMLO's government (in its last week in charge) carried out a big relief operation, which was continued under Claudia Sheinbaum in October and November. After her inauguration on 1 October, the very next day, following her first morning press conference, she travelled to Acapulco with several cabinet members to see the damage and show her intent to take action. Her positive reputation was apparent in the declaration of a local woman who had lost her small business in the hurricane, "You are awesome, President, you will solve our problems!"[3] The President said the most urgent issues were to supply drinking water and reopen roads. The state administration of governor Evelyn Salgado also took swift action with its *Fuerza Operativa Guerrero* (Guerrero Operational Force) to rescue families, distribute bottled water and food, electric generators and other equipment.[4] Efforts were not limited to Acapulco, as there was severe damage along much of the coast to the southeast and in neighbouring mountainous areas. On 8-9 October the governor and her team were in Cuajinicuilapa, a centre of Afro-Mexican culture, delivering galvanised roofs, cleaning supplies, mattresses, blankets, clothes and food parcels.[5]

As in the previous year, several government agencies took urgent action in the following days and weeks to restore water supplies, electricity and roads, to provide food and other necessities and clean up the city and neighbouring coastal areas. Then on 27 October the President visited Acapulco for the third time since Hurricane John to announce a plan of reconstruction for the city and 50 more municipalities of the region. In a formal meeting at the local Naval Base, with several cabinet members and the governors of Guerrero and Oaxaca, Claudia declared that the emergency phase was over but assistance would continue as "Acapulco is being transformed with you".[6] Federal assistance for Guerrero so far amounted to $333 million US for Guerrero and $50 million for Oaxaca.[7]

Once again the relief and reconstruction effort was exceptional and both Acapulco and the surrounding areas are back to normal, with tourism and other activities. It is worth pointing out that in the last three years, as part of a plan for administrative decentralisation, the Federal Health Department with *IMSS-Bienestar* has moved from Mexico City to Acapulco, so attention to emergency health demands was rapidly available. But there is a realisation that the vulnerability of Acapulco and the Pacific coast to hurricane damage must be addressed in long-term planning for the region, it cannot rely on emergency salvage operations every year.

Tourism is a major factor in the economy of Guerrero state, as well as Acapulco there are other beach resorts such as Zihuatanejo, and in the northern interior lies the picturesque colonial silver mining town of Taxco. But poverty is widespread throughout the state, as are local corruption and criminality. The state's historic revolutionary roots going back to the insurgents of Independence, José María Morelos and Vicente Guerrero (who gave the state its name) were reflected in the 20th-century guerrilla movements of Genaro Vázquez and Lucio Cabañas; political repression and corruption were the response of the local elite, supported by the federal authorities of PRI and PAN, and intertwined with criminality. It is therefore not surprising that the worst violent repression of recent times, the Ayotzinapa massacre, should have occurred in Guerrero, and it remains an unresolved human rights investigation and a political headache for the governments of the Fourth Transformation which have nothing to do with it. The massive reconstruction effort in Acapulco and the coast, together with the federal authorities' welfare programmes, are the best hope for the future of this key state. On 13 November 2024 there was a high-level meeting at the National Palace between Claudia Sheinbaum, Economy Minister Marcelo Ebrard, several other cabinet members, Governor Evelyn Salgado, Carlos Slim of Grupo Carso and several other business leaders to discuss plans for Acapulco;[8] they declared that the insurance companies were providing $2 billion US, the government was investing large amounts in infrastructure and business groups would provide more to ensure that the area would not be overwhelmed every time there was a major hurricane.

NOTES

1. www.jornada.com.mx/2023/12/21/editorial/acapulco-reconstruccion-sin-precedente-981, Accessed 21/12/2023.
2. www.gob.mx/sedatu/prensa/anuncia-sedatu-reconstruccion-de-138-espacios-publicos-en-acapulco-y-coyuca-de-benitez, 10/01/2024. Accessed 06/11/2024.
3. elpais.com/mexico/2024-10-03/sheinbaum-llega-a-acapulco-tras-los-estragos-de-john-en-su-primer-viaje-oficial-los-vamos-a-atender.html Accessed 06/11/2024
4. www.acapulcorevista.com/2024/09/fuerza-operativa-guerrero-al-rescate-de.html Accessed 07/11/2024
5. @EvelynSalgadoP post on "X", 09/10/2024. Accessed 07/11/2024.
6. www.elsoldeacapulco.com.mx/local/anuncia-claudia-sheinbaum-inicio-de-reconstruccion-de-acapulco-12777687.html Accessed 07/11/2024
7. https://losreporteros.mx/la-presidenta-claudia-sheinbaum-visita-por-tercera-vez-acapulco-para-supervisar-avances-de-reconstruccion/ Accessed 07/11/2024
8. www.jornada.com.mx/noticia/2024/11/14/politica/evalua-sheinbaum-con-empresarios-avances-de-reconstruccion-en-acapulco-1210 Accessed 25/11/2024.

16

The 2024 elections

Everyone knew that the 2024 elections (to be held on 2 June) would be crucial: the presidential succession and renewal of both Houses of Congress, plus several state governorships and many local positions. Although the official campaign did not begin until the end of March 2024 (with a rather strange "pre-campaign" from December 2023 to February 2024), unofficial campaigning was in full swing from early 2023.

The long campaign from early 2023

In a sense the starting point of the political positioning was the formal annual ceremony of the anniversary of the 1917 Constitution which still, with many amendments and counter-amendments, governs Mexico. On 5 February, the date of its promulgation, a ceremony is held in Querétaro, the colonial city just two hours' drive north of the capital where the Constitutional Congress had been held. Members of Congress, the Supreme Court and other judicial dignitaries, and the Executive crowded into the historic theatre to make formal speeches on the subject. But it was already clear that the judiciary, and its power to interpret the Constitution, was becoming a key political issue. The Supreme Court had a conservative majority which had to an extent been neutralised while the progressive Arturo Zaldívar was Chief Justice, but his term had just ended and the new Chief Justice was Norma Piña of the PRI.[1] She made much of the fact that she was the first woman to hold this position, and also insisted on the importance of judicial independence and the need to respect the existing constitutional text. This was a barely disguised conservative declaration, since several of AMLO's proposed reforms, passed by congressional majorities, were being blocked by judicial decisions.

AMLO's speech at the event, and that of Senate chair Alejandro Armenta (Morena), emphasised the crucial clauses on land, mineral rights, labour, education and welfare in the original Constitution and how they, like Morena's current proposals, had reflected popular rights and demands. The constituent power represented in the 1916-17 assembly was not dead, the people were sovereign and had the right to reform the Constitution to meet their needs.

Another focus of opposition activity was to defend the corrupt electoral commission INE (*Instituto Nacional Electoral*), whose long-serving Chair, Lorenzo Córdova, insisted on paying himself and his colleagues a highly inflated salary (considerably more than AMLO's) and abused its authority for conservative political ends. AMLO had tried and failed to reform INE, and now had a "Plan B" for its reform, but the right now made this a major campaigning issue and organised a mass demonstration with the slogan "*¡El INE No Se Toca!*" (The INE Must Not Be Touched!) on Sunday 26 February 2023.[2] They claimed democracy was under threat, and Córdova along with several right-wing politicians addressed the crowd. It was a large demonstration, around 90,000 people, although the organisers said there were 500,000 which was greatly exaggerated. But this showed the terrain on which the opposition was choosing to fight in view of its continuing (and growing) weakness in Congress: using its strength in corrupt establishment institutions like the Supreme Court and INE.

AMLO declared that it was good to have the establishment showing its true colours, and that what their slogan really meant was that their privileges, and the narco-state they benefited from, should not be touched. Little more than three weeks later AMLO held a mass rally for the 18 March anniversary of the oil expropriation, mobilising probably four times as many people as at the opposition rally. More and more the right was relying on lawfare: on 28 March a judge ordered a halt to work on the Tren Maya, supposedly to prevent tree felling, and injunctions were also being issued against the new free school textbooks. Such manoeuvres had limited impact since the government had a well organised judicial team and was able to get such injunctions annulled fairly quickly.

It should be pointed out that the hard core of the opposition was not just the political parties but an extensive network of conservative media barons, financiers and intellectuals. AMLO constantly denounced them and ridiculed them in his *mañaneras*, although always recognising their freedom of speech and repeating that there would be no censorship: "they can criticise me, attack me, insult me as they do every day, but I will exercise my right of reply".

Foremost among the intellectual critics were two well-known historians, Enrique . Krauze and Héctor Aguilar Camín. Both had emerged in the 1970s at the prestigious *Colegio de México*, indeed I remember briefly meeting both of them at that time. They were prolific authors, writing many academic studies on modern Mexican history. But as time went on both of them became intellectual entrepreneurs with political connections; Krauze runs the magazine *Letras Libres* and writes regularly for the New York Times, El País of Spain and *Reforma* newspaper in Mexico, and is a board member of the huge Televisa TV network and of Santander Bank (Mexico). As for Aguilar Camín, he ran his own magazine *Nexos* and from 1989 to 1993 received significant financing directly from President Carlos Salinas de Gortari; AMLO has denounced him more than once, with photographic evidence, showing begging letters from Aguilar Camín to Salinas and payment confirmation. Aguilar Camín is also close to both Televisa and TV Azteca, the other dominant TV network.

Along with these two intellectual mercenaries there are many more journalists and commentators (or "commentocrats" as Claudia Sheinbaum calls them) who make a living from political journalism and are widely regarded as authorities or experts, as occurs in most countries. Whether they deserve such a reputation is questionable, and AMLO did a brilliant job of discrediting most of them. They include Leo Zuckermann, Denise Dresser, Ciro Gómez Leyva, Carmen Arístegui, Carlos Alazraki, Carlos Loret de Mola, Jorge Castañeda and others, all of whom write or appear regularly for prominent Mexican and US media. Some like Castañeda have also held political office, and some of them were previously on the left, but parted company with AMLO and the Fourth Transformation early in the process.

While the term intellectual or journalistic mercenaries could apply to many of these (others may simply be opportunists), it is important to realise that behind them are the real magnates of the opposition, those who call the shots through wealth or political power. Among them are Claudio X González Laporte of Kimberly-Clark Mexico, and more particularly his son Claudio X González Guajardo, who in 2015 founded *Mexicanos Contra la Corrupción y la Impunidad* (MCCI, Mexicans Against Corruption and Impunity) which AMLO maintains is a complete fiction and should be called Mexicans *For* Corruption and Impunity. The younger Claudio X González is connected with Televisa among other interests, and campaigned actively against AMLO from the beginning. In 2020 he founded *Sí Por México* (Yes for Mexico) as a political movement to promote political organisation, and in 2022 he was the main organiser of the marches to defend the INE.[3]

Questioned about this by one of the best independent investigative journalists, Nancy Flores, AMLO declared on 3 July 2023 that "We are observing a new phenomenon, that in all the opposition's work it is not the political parties that have influence, but an informal power: the 'Supreme Conservative Power' has as its leader Claudio X González Junior, [they are] oligarchs, collaborative intellectuals and newspapers."[4] He said they received funds from the US Government (and indeed, MCCI does receive significant funding from the National Endowment for Democracy, among other sources), they were not democrats but used the term as propaganda, and used figures like Krauze, Aguilar Camín and Castañeda. They were promoting Xóchitl Gálvez as their possible presidential candidate (in this of course he was absolutely right, as we shall see).

There were of course other wealthy magnates in the *Consejo Mexicano de Negocios* (Mexican Business Council) and the *Consejo Coordinador Empresarial* (Entrepreneurial Coordinating Council), but few of them were so politically active promoting opposition to AMLO and the Fourth Transformation, indeed one of the wealthiest, Carlos Slim, has collaborated with AMLO and invested in several of his public works such as the *Tren Maya*.

Another hostile magnate who should be mentioned is Ricardo Salinas Pliego whose Grupo Salinas controls TV Azteca among other things; not only is he an outspoken opponent, he refuses to pay taxes: his business group has been legally challenged by the Tax Collection Agency as owing more than $3 billion US, and this was confirmed by none other than the (frequently corrupt) Supreme Court SCJN.[5]

Preparations for the elections were moving ahead: early in June 2023 Marcelo Ebrard, the Foreign Secretary, resigned from his position in order to participate in Morena's internal contest to select a presidential candidate.[6] It was expected that Claudia Sheinbaum (Metro Mayor), Adán Augusto López (Home Secretary), Ricardo Monreal (Morena leader in the Senate), Gerardo Fernández Noroña (leader of the allied PT) and Manuel Velasco (PVEM, also an ally) would soon do the same. To those who questioned whether such jockeying for position was desirable, AMLO pointed out that it was open and legitimate, and far preferable to the behind-the-scenes cloak-and-dagger infighting which used to occur in the PRI until the incumbent president gave his *dedazo*, undemocratically pointing his finger to reveal the *tapado* (the hidden one) chosen to succeed him.

The opposition alliance of PRI, PAN and PRD formed its *Frente Amplio por México* (Broad Front for Mexico) and in August 2023 announced that its pre-candidates were Santiago Creel (PAN, Speaker of the Chamber of Deputies), Enrique de la Madrid (PRI), Xóchitl Gálvez (PAN Senator) and Beatriz Paredes (PRI Senator).[7]

Internal campaigning in Morena continued for almost three months; the result was decided not by primaries, but by a series of opinion polls agreed among the candidates and supervised by the party leadership. The results were announced on 6 September and showed Claudia Sheinbaum as the clear winner with between 36 and 41% and Marcelo Ebrard second with between 25 and 26%.[8] Ebrard questioned the result and for some time afterwards showed considerable hostility towards Claudia Sheinbaum; there were rumours, which he seemed to encourage, that he might leave Morena and form his own party, or stand for the Citizens' Movement opposition party. AMLO always maintained that Marcelo Ebrard was his friend, and eventually Ebrard made his peace with Morena and with Claudia Sheinbaum.

Claudia becomes leader of the Fourth Transformation

With Claudia's victory, AMLO declared right away on 7 September 2023 that he was no longer leader of the Fourth Transformation; the political leadership and the staff of command (*Bastón de Mando*) now passed to Claudia, although with AMLO still President of Mexico for another year. Claudia was also Coordinator of the Committees for the Defence of the Fourth Transformation, which were an important component of the movement;[9] this meant in effect that she was their presidential candidate. In the following months she travelled the country tirelessly to promote these committees and create a personal bond with the people as AMLO had done.

In an interview with Chamuco TV (*Los Chamucos* are a trio of progressive satirists who do outstanding work on social media)[10] Claudia said that AMLO was of course irreplaceable, but it was necessary to begin building the next phase of the Transformation, its "Second Floor". There must be continuity with change, defending the principles of the movement: "For the good of all, women and men, but first, the poor", the ideals of Mexican Humanism. Energy transition had to be promoted and accelerated along with sovereignty. Women's rights were fundamental.

Some people alleged that Claudia was upper-class, but one of the *Chamucos*, Pepe Hernández, said he had first met her in the thick of popular struggles, and she replied that at 15 years of age she had participated in the *Rechazados* (rejected, excluded) movement. She had been an activist all her life.

The government, she said, must have a project, a programme, which would begin by consolidating the welfare system and the public works left by AMLO: universal healthcare with *IMSS-Bienestar*, access to housing, and education, public works to benefit all, honesty and responsibility.

Asked about her work in Mexico City on the issue of public security (there had been a very significant reduction in criminality), she said she had improved working conditions for the city police, including a 54% salary increase, and had developed the work of the metropolitan solicitor-general's office, particularly in terms of intelligence; all agencies had to work together. She had also improved conditions for young people, not only with the federal "Young People Building the Future" apprenticeships, but also her own programmes of scholarships and *Pilares* (*Puntos de Innovación, Libertad, Arte, Educación y Saberes*, Centres of Innovation, Freedom, Art, Education and Knowledge), which were similar to the *Utopías* of Clara Brugada in Iztapalapa but on a smaller scale. Another of her initiatives was called "Reconnect with Peace" which provided retraining for delinquents. Serious crimes in the metropolitan area had declined by 59%.

Claudia would also maintain the direct communication with the people as in AMLO's *mañaneras*; she would not do it in exactly the same way but would always be close to the people, and would also continue visiting all regions of the country.

Asked about the problem of the judiciary, she insisted that they could not engage in politics, there must be effective justice; it remained to be seen exactly what AMLO was going to propose in his latest project for judicial reform, and it must be discussed throughout the country. As for labour and working conditions, Mexico must end the idea of cheap labour; the minimum wage must continue to increase and workers must have good conditions. As for corruption, the drive to eradicate it must continue.

The Fourth Transformation movement must be united; questions were asked about new arrivals joining from the PAN or the PRI, her view was that the movement must be open to all, but only if it was clear that they had really changed their attitudes. The opposition had no real answer to this: sometimes they called for reconciliation, but their behaviour and discourse showed that this was not serious. They claimed that Claudia was just AMLO's puppet, but her strength of character belied any such suggestion.

As for the opposition Broad Front for Mexico, at the beginning of September 2023 they officially declared the winner of their internal selection process to be Xóchitl Gálvez, who spoke at a public rally on 3 September. Although they had said the decision would be made by a democratic vote, in practice it was a small group of politicians and media barons who announced the result, and it was immediately questioned by another pre-candidate, Beatriz Paredes.

There was little doubt that among conservative sectors of the electorate Xóchitl was the favourite to represent them. To choose a woman, and one of indigenous background, showed that they were at least minimally in tune with the transformation the country was going through. She had been Director of the National Commission for the Development of Indigenous Peoples, and claimed that as a child she had sold jellies on the street in her home town in Hidalgo. She also had a degree in computer science and business experience, so could be presented as having a number of favourable points as a candidate. Interestingly, AMLO had been predicting for nearly a year that she would be the opposition candidate.

However, Xóchitl had her weaknesses, beginning with the fact that her entire political career had been in the right-wing PAN, and nothing suggested that she had really abandoned its conservative policies. She claimed (but not consistently) that she now supported AMLO's social programmes, but the obvious objection was that she had voted against them in the first place and there were good reasons to doubt her word on the subject. As for her humble origins, some of those who knew the area said her family, while indigenous, was the wealthiest in the town.

Treason and dirty tricks

Much worse would come when the initial campaigning period was under way: on 5 February 2024 she gave a speech at the Wilson Center in Washington DC, she alleged that Mexico's "populist" government was "flirting with Russia and China" and was soft on organised crime or even in league with it. She also alleged that AMLO (and Claudia Sheinbaum) would "end judicial independence in Mexico", implying that the US should interfere in the electoral process, and hinting that if elected, she would open up energy, health, education, infrastructure and security to foreign interests.[11] *La Jornada* declared that this amounted to treason.

With these declarations Xóchitl obviously alienated a great many people in Mexico, while gaining support among Mexican conservatives and powerful interests in the US. But it was swiftly apparent that she was not acting alone: on 30 January an article was published in *ProPublica* (a US website that claims to provide "Investigative Journalism in the Public Interest") by Tim Golden, who has won the Pulitzer Prize twice, dredging up discredited old allegations that AMLO's 2006 presidential campaign had received funding from narco cartels.[12] The same allegations were also reproduced by the German website *Deutsche Welle* and by Insight Crime. AMLO pointed out that this was based on DEA (US Drug Enforcement Agency) reports which were derived largely from hearsay, and these investigations were officially closed in 2011 for lack of evidence. It was very interesting that these old allegations were suddenly revived at this time.

Despite confirmation from Biden administration officials that these investigations had long been closed, a massive social media campaign began disseminating hashtags like #*NarcoPresidente*.[13] Trolling by bots of this and similar hashtags soon reached 200 million hits; it was clear that large amounts of money were being invested in this, but fortunately it became apparent that such tactics had no success in Mexico, indeed they backfired and surveys showed that both AMLO's and Claudia's poll ratings had risen.

On 18 February the opposition returned to conventional tactics with a mass rally in the Zócalo; as on the previous occasion, they were able to mobilise 90,000 to 100,000 people, which was impressive but only about a quarter of the number who would turn out for Claudia's official campaign launch on 1 March.

Then on 21 February came another twist in the dirty tricks saga: none other than the *New York Times* bureau in Mexico sent a letter to AMLO's press officer Jesús Ramírez Cuevas, declaring that there was a new US investigation into possible narco links to AMLO and his associates, relating not to 2006 but to the current administration.[14] The letter quoted three informants with totally unsubstantiated allegations of meetings between the president, members of his family or associates and drug traffickers, and monetary transactions. The letter (authored by a female journalist with long experience) then had the effrontery to demand a reply by 5pm the same day.

AMLO quite rightly replied that the *NYT*, a supposed "newspaper of record", had shredded whatever remained of its reputation and had become a "filthy rag" (*pasquín inmundo*) of professional slanderers. At least AMLO was able to reaffirm that Mexico had good relations with the Biden administration, and a couple of days later none other than US ambassador Ken Salazar made a public statement declaring that "as far as we are concerned, there is no investigation of President López Obrador". He added that relations with Mexico had never been closer.

But this was far from the end of the matter: it reflected a rift in the US establishment in which Republicans, but also many Democrats and institutions like the DEA and the CIA, with backing from powerful financial and media interests, wanted to discredit Mexico's Transformation.

Early in March opposition circles in Mexico began to resort to new dirty tricks involving direct action and manipulation of popular protest. As we saw in chapter 12 the complex issue of truth and justice for the families of the 43 Ayotzinapa students, which AMLO had vowed to resolve and to which he had devoted enormous efforts, was now being exploited by NGOs, lawyers and foreign agencies sympathetic to the opposition. As previously explained, on 6 March a faction of the Ayotzinapa relatives, led by an opportunistic lawyer, Vidulfo Rosales, and others, protested outside the National Palace and then used a truck to break down a door and burst into part of the palace complex during AMLO's morning press conference; with incredible restraint, AMLO insisted that no violent repression be used against them. However, AMLO pointed out the dubious record of Vidulfo Rosales and of one of the key instigators of the unrest, Emilio Alvarez Icaza, a PRD Senator.[15] Rosales actually claimed responsibility for the attack – a very strange position for a lawyer.

Then on 7 March two students currently enrolled in the Ayotzinapa college were involved in a confrontation with Guerrero state police, and one of them was shot dead by an officer. It is well known that the state police are still riddled with corruption, and protests immediately erupted. But again, AMLO insisted on a full investigation by federal authorities, and the two police officers involved were arrested. It seems clear that the opposition was involved in such provocations, and only complete honesty, calm and a firm hand by AMLO and his government would thwart such dirty tricks.

Then on 13 March Claudia Sheinbaum, campaigning in the southeast, denounced what was becoming increasingly clear for all to see: that the opposition, recognising the inevitability of its crushing defeat at the polls on 2 June, was using dirty tricks and its control of the judicial system to discredit the elections, and its ultimate goal was to annul the vote. But, she declared, the Mexican people were more and more determined to achieve victory, and massive popular participation could and would defeat these attempts at a judicial coup. Indeed, this was the only way forward, and the reactionary establishment's fear of losing power for good – of a peaceful revolution – would only bring to fruition what they most feared.

What the opposition clearly lacked was a viable programme, a credible proposal for the future of Mexico. It had been apparent from early in AMLO's term that they had little to offer except rejection of the Fourth

Transformation, defence at all costs of the status quo, and distorted, exaggerated or simply false criticisms of the president and his government. As time went on and AMLO's achievements became more and more impressive, they resorted to a combination of mendacious propaganda and use of the judiciary and other establishment institutions like INE to prevent change. Fortunately their control of the judiciary was not always effective in preventing implementation of the government's reforms, and while the INE could interfere in political procedures, it was no longer capable of imposing completely fraudulent elections. The result was that their reactionary manoeuvres only increased popular indignation and made the likelihood of electoral victory for Morena and its allies (and of Claudia as presidential candidate) greater than ever.

This scenario also enabled AMLO and the partisans of the Fourth Transformation to focus on the really decisive issue: the need for them not only to win a clear victory at the polls but to achieve a two-thirds super majority in both houses of Congress. This was the benchmark for passing constitutional reforms, without which the entrenched right wing could continue to block fundamental change. AMLO had been talking about this for over a year, and as the elections approached he emphasised it constantly: if people believed in the Transformation they should not just vote for Claudia as president but for Morena (or allied) candidates at all levels. Indeed, AMLO had prepared a package of 20 constitutional reforms which he would like to see adopted by the new Congress if the two-thirds majority could be achieved: he presented this package on 5 February (the anniversary of the Constitution), it was immediately backed by Claudia Sheinbaum and Morena and became a central plank of the election campaign. The proposed reforms began with reform of the judicial system (without this none of the other measures could be enforced), plus electoral reform, inclusion in the Constitution of all the welfare programmes, national energy sovereignty and other measures which had already been passed into law but lacked constitutional status.

The official campaign period began on 1 March, although as we have seen electioneering had been under way for months previously. The alliance backing Xóchitl was now officially called *Fuerza y Corazón por México* (Strength and Heart for Mexico) and the Morena/PT/PVEM coalition was *Sigamos Haciendo Historia* (Let's Keep Making History). There was also a slate of candidates for the Citizens' Movement party headed by Jorge Álvarez Maynez. Xóchitl began her campaign in Zacatecas, focusing her message on combatting crime: the opposition had decided that this was AMLO's and Morena's weakest point, and she promised to "bring peace back to Mexico".[16] Although organised crime was an ongoing problem, most people recognised that this was something inherited from previous neoliberal governments, and homicide rates were beginning to decline while some offences like kidnapping had fallen dramatically.

As the campaign continued and polls showed her trailing by 20 or even 30%, Xóchitl tried arguing that Claudia was taking orders from AMLO and that she was cold and remote. Claudia simply focused on policy and her commitment to continue the Transformation, and pointed to her opponent's lack of credibility and association with corrupt interests. As for Alvarez Maynez, he tried with difficulty to propose a third alternative, although towards the end of the campaign there were signs he was eating into Xóchitl's support.

Claudia began her official campaign with the mass rally in the Zócalo, and concluded her speech with 100 promises, just as AMLO had done six years earlier. Her campaign showed confidence and clarity, building on the mass support she inherited from AMLO, her own outstanding record as Metro Mayor of the capital, and the popular following she had consolidated as leader of the Fourth Transformation over the previous six months.

The moment of truth

As election day approached the right-wing media tried to promote a highly unlikely last minute surge for Xóchitl, but the polls continued to show a massive advantage for Claudia and the "Let's Keep Making History" coalition. My own impression, having arrived just a few days before the vote, was that the only question was the size of the majority, and this would be confirmed as results came in on the night of 2 to 3 June. Talking to people queuing to vote in the central working-class district of Tlatelolco, I found a quiet confidence among most of them (who were overwhelmingly Fourth Transformation supporters) that they would win. There was a massive turnout, with a sense of enthusiasm, patience and unity. Many people were willing to talk and allow photography and video recording; they were pleased to know there was interest in Britain in learning the truth about Mexico. "This process has to continue", said one man; we cannot let the corrupt old guard return". Several voters, male and female, mentioned the importance of having a woman as president, especially one with scientific training in environmental sciences and a long record of participation in popular struggles.

Preliminary figures in the presidential race gave 59% to Claudia Sheinbaum, 28% to Xóchitl Gálvez and 10% to Jorge Álvarez Maynez. Xóchitl and her coalition at first seemed determined to deny reality and mount a judicial challenge to the results, but after midnight she conceded defeat and congratulated the winner. Claudia Sheinbaum and thousands of supporters held a victory rally in the Zócalo; she declared that this was "the triumph of the Mexican people, of the peaceful revolution of consciousness, and the recognition by our people that there is a clear mandate to continue with the Fourth Transformation of Mexico's public life". She proclaimed her admiration for outgoing president AMLO, and the crowd chanted "It's an honour that she's with Obrador!". Clouds of uncertainty and fears of judicial coups and civil strife were dispelled, at least for the time being (although subsequent events would show that the matter was not quite so simple).

Morena and its allies also won six of the eight state governorships being contested, plus the Metro Mayor (Head of Government) of the capital, which went to Clara Brugada, the very progressive former mayor of Iztapalapa borough. As for Congress, early results indicated that the "Let's Keep Making History" coalition had won between 370 and 380 seats out of 500 in the Chamber of Deputies (well over two thirds) and at least 84 out of 128 Senate seats. For two thirds in the Senate they would need 86 or 87 (there was some disagreement on how to interpret the two thirds rule in the Senate). As we shall see, they would eventually win two thirds, but only after complex disputes and manoeuvres.

Opinion polls had in fact been predicting this for months, but few dared believe it. Incessant and vitriolic hostile propaganda from the right created a tense atmosphere although it failed completely to win over Mexican voters, in fact it had a boomerang effect. It is worth briefly examining the reasons for this overwhelming victory, especially in view of the rise of the right elsewhere in Latin America (and across the world). What AMLO and Morena had achieved over the previous five and a half years had no parallel in the region. Honesty and modesty in government, a serious attack on corruption which he denounced as the root of Mexico's problems, creation for the first time of a true welfare state, protection of Mexican sovereignty while maintaining cordial relations with the US: all of this was accompanied by constant communication and dialogue with the people.

Also he achieved economic growth and financial stability, financing programmes by reinforcing tax collection without raising tax rates and without borrowing. His bold progressive foreign policy favouring Latin American independence, sovereignty and unity and actively opposing the blockade of Cuba, restored Mexico's prestige in the region.

Despite his enormous popularity AMLO always insisted that he would not seek re-election, in fact he declared again and again that on leaving office he would retire to his small farm in Palenque and would abandon politics altogether: he would not seek or accept any public office, would not give interviews and would not comment on political events. Many refused to believe this and tried to persuade him to change his mind, but this is precisely what he has done since attending Claudia Sheinbaum's inauguration on 1 October 2024. One effect of his steadfast adherence to this position was to oblige Morena to organise more effectively as a mass party and to address the question of the succession in good time; we shall now see how the transition occurred over the next four months.

NOTES

1. *La Jornada*, lunes 6 de febrero de 2023, "La disputa por la Constitución" (Editorial), Accessed 06/02/2023.
2. www.gob.mx/presidencia/ Morning Press Conference, 27/02/2023, Accessed live; and https://politica.expansion.mx/mexico/2023/02/26/marcha-ine-2023-minuto-a-minuto#uuid0000186-908e-d7a7-a7fe-fdbeeb860000 Accessed 09/11/2024
3. politica.expansion.mx/mexico/2023/07/04/quien-es-claudio-x-gonzalez-hijo. Accessed 15/11/2024.
4. www.gob.mx/presidencia Morning Press Conference, 03/07/2023. Accessed live.
5. es.wikipedia.org/wiki/Ricardo_Salinas_Pliego. Accessed 15/11/2024.
6. www.gob.mx/presidencia/ Morning Press Conference, 07/06/2023. Accessed live.
7. https://edition.cnn.com/videos/spanish/2023/08/10/mexico-oposicion-precandidatos-presidenciales-elecciones-2024-panorama-mundial.cnn Accessed 09/11/2024.
8. www.gob.mx/presidencia/ Morning Press Conference, 07/09/2023. Accessed live.
9. www.elfinanciero.com.mx/nacional/2023/09/07/amlo-entrega-baston-de-mando-morena-a-claudia-sheinbaum-en-vivo-hoy-7-septiembre/ Accessed 09/11/2024.
10. Chamuco TV, retransmisión You Tube, Chamuco TV con Claudia Sheinbaum (24/09/2023). Accessed 10/11/2024.
11. www.jornada.com.mx/noticia/2024/02/06/editorial/xochitl-galvez-peligrosa-irresponsabilidad-2415, Accessed 06/02/2024; and m-x.com.mx/al-dia/xochitl-galvez-denuncia-en-eu-debilidad-de-amlo-contra-el-crimen-organizado/ Accessed 10/11/2024.
12. www.proceso.com.mx/nacional/2024/2/9/tim-golden-ira-la-mananera-esto-respondio-propublica-los-reclamos-de-amlo-323681.html
13. www.gob.mx/presidencia/ Morning Press Conferences, 09/02/2024 & 14/02/2024. Accessed live.
14. www.gob.mx/presidencia/ Morning Press Conference, 22/02/2024. Accessed live.
15. www.jornada.com.mx/noticia/2024/03/07/editorial/ayotzinapa-restaurar-la-confianza-278. Accessed 07/03/2024.
16. www.elfinanciero.com.mx/elecciones-mexico-2024/2024/02/29/inicio-de-campana-xochitl-galvez-en-zacatecas-en-vivo-sigue-minuto-a-minuto/ Accessed 11/11/2024.

17

The Transition: Claudia Presidenta

Claudia Sheinbaum would take office on 1 October, so there were almost four months to prepare the way. Some of it was straightforward, but there were still obstacles to overcome: the opposition would not take its defeat lying down. Xóchitl Gálvez retracted her acceptance of the election results and tried to contest them, and with her supporters she called for a recount. No-one except hard-core conservatives took this seriously: when you're trounced two to one the only rational reaction is to examine the reasons for your failure. But the right tried to dispute the Congressional results, using procedural arguments which led to protracted debate.

In the lower house there were 300 directly elected seats and another 200 "plurinominal" seats apportioned by lists. Also in the Senate, each of the 32 states had four senators, three elected directly and one proportionately by a similar procedure. This was the constitutional procedure, originally introduced by the PRI and PAN when they were in control. But as this mechanism reinforced the majority of the leading party or coalition, it contributed significantly to the "Let's Keep Making History" coalition's two-thirds control, so the opposition suddenly tried to change it. Legally they didn't have a leg to stand on, the rule could only be changed by constitutional amendment and of course they were clearly in a minority in both houses so could not even begin such a procedure. But this did not stop them from claiming that the rule was unjust and should be changed. However, after prolonged debate the majority of the INE declared that this could not be done, and confirmed the election of the "plurinominal" list members.

Judicial reform

More contentious was the issue of judicial reform, which everyone knew was crucial for the Transformation to continue. In June AMLO, with his usual tactical astuteness, sought dialogue and inclusion, and arranged for the Chamber of Deputies to host a public discussion of the matter to which more than 60 leading judges, magistrates and Supreme Court justices – including Chief Justice Norma Piña, ringleader of the opposition – were invited. Merely to attend such an event was a humiliation for many of these judicial bigwigs, especially since Norma Piña had called only a few days earlier for an illegal boycott of the reform. Nothing was achieved, but it probably strengthened AMLO's hand for the approaching confrontation.

Although the presidential handover of power – Claudia's inauguration – was not due until 1 October, the new Congress would take over on 1 September, meaning that judicial and other constitutional reforms could then be passed by the two-thirds majorities which had been elected. Knowing this, Chief Justice Piña had led the judiciary in going on strike,1 an unprecedented action which was purely political since they had no salary or work-related demands, and was almost certainly illegal since they were not covered by labour law and were breaching their obligation to provide administration of justice. Moreover, to further underline their contempt for the law they were supposed to administer, they continued to claim their inflated salaries and benefits, something ordinary workers on strike would not be able to do. To cap it all, they engaged in street demonstrations and highway barricades, led by none other than Piña herself.

It is worth explaining just what was proposed in the judicial reform. It provided for judges, magistrates and justices to be elected by popular vote from lists of candidates; these candidates must have legal training and could not represent political parties; existing members of the judiciary could stand; once elected, they would be regularly evaluated to ensure their prompt and impartial application of the law; the existing judicial council (completely ineffective as it is dominated by high-ranking justices) would be replaced by a truly independent body which would evaluate judges and act on citizens' complaints; and their salaries and benefits must conform to constitutional limitations.[2]

The proposal was duly debated and passed in the Chamber of Deputies on 3 September; this was easy since Morena and its allies had more than enough votes. But in the Senate it would be more difficult since the governing coalition appeared to have only 85 seats out of 128. The plenary debate in the Senate was scheduled for 10 September, and tensions were reaching boiling point.

The media were overwhelmingly against the reform, and the US Ambassador, who a few weeks earlier had indicated agreement with it, had (clearly on instructions from the State Department) condemned it. AMLO, Claudia and Morena rejected this as an unacceptable infringement on

Mexican sovereignty, and also pointed out that in the US judges are elected in 43 out of the 50 states. Some judges issued injunctions trying to prevent the Senate from debating it, but it was obvious they had no power to do this.

Some right-wing politicians openly called for violence: a female senator of the PAN party from the state of Aguascalientes declared that those who voted for the reform should be lynched. When the Senate debate began, the opposition minority senators allowed the protesting judges and judicial employees into the chamber where they began a violent assault on the majority senators. There was total mayhem and several people were injured. The Senate leader, Gerardo Fernández Noroña of the PT, showed remarkable composure and managed to evacuate the chamber and lead the senators to another building where they resumed the debate.[3]

The protesting members of the judiciary tried to assault the alternative venue, but were prevented by the Mexico City police (who showed commendable restraint). The debate continued into the early hours of September 11; two opposition senators declared their support for the reform, and it was finally passed by 86 votes to 41 (one member was unable to attend).

Ratification of the reform requires approval by 17 of Mexico's 32 state assemblies, and within three days 20 had already done this. Some violent protests continued, but demonstrations and declarations of popular support were much greater. The opposition knew they were defeated; Chief Justice Piña's surname means "pineapple", and there was now a very sour pineapple.

As for the US, despite its displeasure, it did not take any serious hostile action. President Joe Biden had a judicial reform proposal of his own, so was not in a strong position to object. But negative comment in the international media, combined with completely distorted reporting, would continue.

AMLO and Claudia prepare the way

In the meantime both AMLO and Claudia and their teams continued apace with preparations for the formal handover of power. Claudia had already announced many appointments to her cabinet, and continued to do so. "It is the time of women", she proclaimed; her own election was symbolic of a much broader change. Of a total of 52 nominations including cabinet but also directors of many public agencies like the CFE, public radio and TV stations and other cultural institutions, 25 were women. The formidable Rosa Icela Rodríguez, AMLO's security chief, would be Home Secretary; a new Ministry for Women would be headed by Citlalli Hernández, formerly Secretary General of Morena; Emilia Esther Calleja headed the Federal Electricity Commission; Claudia Curiel, Culture; Ariadna Montiel would continue as Welfare Secretary; Edna Elena Vega would take charge of SEDATU, the Agricultural, Urban and Regional Planning Ministry which had become such a crucial instrument of development under Ramón Meyer

Falcón; Luz Elena González would be Minister of Energy; Alicia Bárcena, AMLO's Foreign Secretary, would move to Environment; Rosaura Ruiz would take the new ministry of Science, Humanities, Technology and Innovation; and Luisa María Alcalde, the brilliant young outgoing Home Secretary, became leader of the Morena party.

Together with Clara Brugada as Metro Mayor and several state governors, the advance of women was clear for all to see. There were of course also several very capable men in the new cabinet, including the Finance Minister (Hacienda) Rogelio Ramírez de la O who continued in post, Marcelo Ebrard (who had previously opposed Claudia) as Economy Minister, Jesús Ramírez Cuevas (AMLO's media officer) as Coordinator of presidential advisors, Mario Delgado (much criticised by the left) in Education, Octavio Romero Oropeza in Housing (Infonavit), Alejandro Svarch in Health (IMSS-Bienestar), the young Marath Baruch who continues at Labour, Omar García Harfuch (a controversial figure, but one who is very capable and loyal) as head of Security and former Chief Justice Arturo Zaldívar as general coordinator, among others. The all-important Secretaries of Defence and the Navy would only be named when the new president took office: General Ricardo Trevilla and Admiral Raymundo Morales. What Claudia has achieved here is to combine professional ability with political balance and unity.

Throughout the transition period AMLO continued to tour the country incessantly, inaugurating public works he wanted completed before leaving office, and Claudia Sheinbaum accompanied him in order to improve her knowledge of all states and regions and promote her public image and relationship with the people. During the election campaign and afterwards it was interesting to see how Claudia gained in confidence and speaking ability, assuming presidential stature in her own right. While she had a distinguished record as Metro Mayor, and in political activism for more than two decades previously, to address hundreds of thousands and to deal with politics at the highest level is very demanding, but she has demonstrated remarkable ability, strength and conviction; as AMLO declared, *"Yo soy fresa comparado con ella"*, "I am weak compared to her", and while no-one would surely accept such a view of the pioneer of the Transformation, it is true that Claudia has shown impressive strength of character.

On 1 September AMLO gave his final address to the nation before a vast crowd in the Zócalo, declaring that he was "more convinced than ever that the best of Mexico is its people, heir to civilisations which flourished long before the arrival of the European invaders". He spoke of his programmes in education, health and welfare; of the reduction in poverty, the importance of emigrants' remittances, the constitutional reforms that had been implemented reversing the damage done during the pernicious neoliberal period and others that were still pending, above all judicial reform. Universal free health care was a reality in 23 of the 32 states; for the first time in more than 50 years the peso had not been devalued, in fact it was second in the world among currencies to have appreciated against the US dollar; 173 useless trust funds had been eliminated, saving some $7 billion US; where under Calderón the richest sector of the population earned 35 times as much as the poorest, now it was only 15 times; the minimum wage had increased by more than 100% in real terms; all public school students received grants, and over a million university students from poor families were receiving scholarships; and the public Electricity Commission had been restored. Finally, he was satisfied because he would be handing over the presidential sash to an exceptional, honest and experienced woman committed to the principles of their movement.[4]

The next ten days saw the drama of the congressional approval of the judicial reform, but this was far from being the end of urgent business for the new legislature which moved on quickly to consider further constitutional reforms which AMLO had proposed and which Morena and its allies wanted to enact. The first was to place the National Guard (GN) under the authority of the Ministry of Defence, as a police force with civilian duties but with military training and discipline; AMLO had long advocated this as a guarantee against the kind of corruption which had prevailed with the former Federal Police under García Luna, Calderón's notorious security chief. Then there was the reform to guarantee the rights of Indigenous and Afro-Mexican Communities, with their own territories, jurisdiction, language and educational rights, traditional medicine, agricultural practices and developmental consultations. Several other reforms would follow in October after Claudia's inauguration.[5]

There was one more big public event on AMLO's schedule, the annual independence celebrations of 15-16 September. Beginning on the evening of the 15th it was, as usual, a huge popular fiesta in the Zócalo and surrounding streets, with similar events in towns and cities across the country. AMLO gave the ceremonial proclamation specific characteristics, including women independence heroes: Josefa Ortiz and Leona Vicario as well as Miguel Hidalgo, Ignacio de Allende, José María Morelos, Vicente Guerrero and the anonymous heroines and heroes; and the concepts of Liberty, Equality, Justice, Democracy, Sovereignty and Universal Fraternity. Then also Death to Corruption, Greed, Racism and Discrimination; and more Vivas! to Love, to Mexican Workers, Migrants, the Indigenous Peoples, Mexico's Cultural Greatness and to the Fourth Transformation. The following day there was the usual military parade, but with participation by large costumed contingents representing historical revolutionary movements, the Maderistas, Zapatistas, Villistas, Constitutionalists and so on, with theatrical representations of the great moments of national history. The message was clear: Mexico was reclaiming its past as the foundation for present and future achievements, with Mexican Humanism.

AMLO also made it clear that his final mañanera on 30 September would be more like a farewell party, and so it was, but with a surprise for him prepared by his media team: there was music by the Veracruz band Mono Blanco, a video presenting his history of struggle and leadership, and a song written and performed by his wife Beatriz Gutiérrez Mueller, the singer Eugenia León and others. AMLO himself, and many others, were moved to tears.

Claudia Sheinbaum's Inauguration

Then on 1 October came the climactic moment of Claudia Sheinbaum's inauguration as Presidenta, the first woman to hold the office and the one who would ensure continuation of the Fourth Transformation. As preparations were being made at the San Lázaro Legislative Palace east of the city centre, a few diehard right-wing judicial protestors tried to block the entrance, but they were easily moved away and preparations went ahead as planned. A joint session of the two houses of Congress began at 9 am with formal statements by the various political parties, followed by a recess while special guests arrived, including Jill Biden, the US First Lady, and Presidents Gustavo Petro of Colombia, Lula da Silva of Brazil, Xiomara Castro of Honduras, Bernardo Arévalo of Guatemala, Miguel Díaz-Canel of Cuba, Gabriel Boric of Chile, Luis Alberto Arce of Bolivia and Santiago Peña Palacios of Paraguay; also Prime Minister John Briceño of Belize and four other Caribbean leaders, and the presidents of Ghana, Libya and the Saharawi Democratic Republic.6 Other guests included none other than our own Jeremy Corbyn, whose presence (and the absence of Prime Minister Keir Starmer) could hardly go unnoticed.

AMLO, surrounded by wellwishers, left his house in Tlalpan shortly after 10 am and arrived about half an hour later, followed by Claudia Sheinbaum shortly afterwards. They both paid their respects to the presiding officer, Ifigenia Martínez, an extraordinary woman who had a lifetime career as an economist and public figure, being a federal deputy and also senator on various occasions, she had left the PRI in 1987 and was one of the founders of the Democratic Current and then the PRD, and later joined Morena to support AMLO. She became president of the Chamber of Deputies on 1 September 2024 and in that capacity, at the age of 99, she presided over this historic session; she would die a few days later, on 5 September.7

At 11:30am Claudia Sheinbaum Pardo was sworn in, to shouts of "Presidenta! Presidenta!" and "Long Live the Fourth Transformation!" She acknowledged the presence of representatives of 105 countries, and in particular the presidential guests and Jill Biden for the US; she also made special mention of a group of Spanish MPs who had arrived despite their government's disrespect to Mexico, and of others including Jeremy Corbyn. In her speech she recalled the 2006 desafuero or impeachment attempt against AMLO, whom she described as Mexico's best president for his work with the Fourth Transformation. She defended the judicial reform which was essential; this statement was met with applause by the majority of those present, including the three progressive Supreme Court justices, but Chief Justice Norma Piña and her seven conservative colleagues looked on in silence. Claudia declared that with her, women had arrived in power, and the Transformation would continue; the government would never repress the people, and those who talked about authoritarianism were lying. She recounted her list of 100 promises, and declared that her government would be inspired by Mexican Humanism: "With the People, Everything; Without the People, Nothing!" "I will not disappoint you, I invite you to Keep Making History!"

Her speech was greeted with delirious applause by the great majority of those present, and there were emotional scenes as she was embraced by many of her colleagues. Further emotional gestures followed as AMLO took his leave.

The new president then went to the National Palace for a formal reception for all the diplomatic guests, and at 4pm she took the stage in the Zócalo for the formal ceremony in which representatives of the indigenous and Afro-Mexican peoples gave her the Bastón de Mando, the Staff of Office which has great symbolic significance. She then gave a final speech to the assembled crowd, repeating her 100 promises and pledging to offer "my knowledge, my soul, my life and the best of myself for the welfare of the people of Mexico". Like AMLO before her, she promised never to lie, to steal or to betray the people.[8] If anything the inauguration had exceeded expectations; few countries in the world today could hold such an enthusiastic, hopeful and inspiring ceremony.

NOTES

1. www.infobae.com/mexico/2024/08/21/es-oficial-el-paro-nacional-del-poder-judicial-esta-es-la-declaratoria/ Accessed 14/11/2024
2. www.gob.mx/cms/uploads/attachment/file/892010/REFORMA_AL_PODER_JUDICIAL__2_CS.pdf Accessed 14/11/2024
3. www.jornada.com.mx/2024/09/11/politica/003n1pol Accessed 14/11/2024.
4. cnnespanol.cnn.com/2024/09/01/frases-ultimo-informe-gobierno-presidente-mexico-amlo-orix/ Accessed 14/11/2024.
5. www.diputados.gob.mx/LeyesBiblio/sumario/CPEIJM_sumario_crono.pdf Accessed 17/11/2024.
6. mexiconewsdaily.com/politics/world-leaders-sheinbaum-inauguration/ Accessed 17/11/2024.
7. es.wikipedia.org/wiki/Ifigenia_Martinez Accessed 17/11/2024.
8. www.razon.com.mx/mexico/2024/10/01/asi-se-vivio-la-toma-de-protesta-de-claudia-sheinbaum-como-presidenta-de-mexico-video/ Accessed 17/11/2024

18

Claudia in office: the transformation continues

As president Claudia Sheinbaum lost no time in showing her priorities: on 2 October, her first working day, she began with a *mañanera* which demonstrated her commitment to maintaining this vital instrument of communication, and in the afternoon travelled to Acapulco to continue relief work following hurricane John.

The morning press conference would begin at 7:30 rather than 7:00am, and it would be renamed *mañanera del pueblo*, "the people's mañanera". There was also a change of style: she was more succinct and direct than AMLO, less given to long dissertations and showing less patience with irrelevant or inappropriate questions or comments.

New programmes and reforms

Claudia had promised to introduce a new welfare programme, a Pension for Women Aged 60 to 64, in recognition of women's lifetime work in family care. She confirmed this right away on 2 October, it is a bi-monthly payment of 3,000 pesos which will benefit over a million women; registration would begin in the following weeks.

Other major reforms would follow: she had pledged that she would continue AMLO's railway building programme, indeed that she would create double the amount of new passenger lines compared to AMLO, over 3,000 km of new services, above all in the centre and north of the country. Sure enough, this was passed as a constitutional reform later in October, establishing that railways are a priority for national development and that the executive can create public passenger rail services or grant concessions to private operators. Plans included creating (or in reality restoring what had existed 30 years previously) routes via Monterrey to Nuevo Laredo on the Tamaulipas-Texas border; via Guadalajara and the northwest to Nogales on the Sonora-Arizona border; and from Mexico City to Veracruz. On 13 October work began to build the line from Mexico City to Querétaro, 225 km north, an attractive colonial city which has become a major commuting hub for the capital, to be completed in four years.[1]

A further crucial constitutional reform related to energy sovereignty, it decreed that in relation to power generation (CFE and PEMEX) the term "productive state enterprise" would be replaced by "public state enterprise"; this means that these essential enterprises will no longer be required to obey market forces but rather their priority will be security and self-sufficiency. It also confirmed that there would be no concessions for lithium exploitation. There followed another decree which reinforced the judicial reform already passed: it declared that constitutional clauses or reforms cannot be subject to legal objections or controversies, and the right of *amparo* (injunction) does not apply to constitutional measures; this is yet another blow to Chief Justice Piña and her pals.

Then in November came a reform confirming advances in women's and gender rights: it modifies several constitutional articles relating to substantive (effective) equality, gender perspectives, the right of women to a life free from violence, and eradication of the gender salary gap.[2] Senator Martha Micher Camarena said the secondary laws which ensure the reform is put into practice are already being debated in Congress, and this is unprecedented in Latin America.

Tensions and difficulties

An issue which would very quickly demand the president's attention was that of violence and security, with a series of sensational incidents in Sinaloa and Guerrero. In Sinaloa confrontation between rival cartel factions once again became very serious, while in Guerrero the mysterious murder of the mayor of Chilpancingo was followed by a major confrontation in Tecpan de Galeana between rival gangs which ended in an assault on the military, leading to 17 deaths (all among the criminals except for two local police officers).

Claudia insisted that under no circumstances would they return to the "war on drugs" strategy of former president Calderón, and in the *mañaneras* questions were answered mainly by her Security Secretary Omar García Harfuch who was very direct, specific and calm in explaining each incident and the official response. It was clear that the security team of García Harfuch, Home Secretary Rosa Icela Rodríguez and the Defence and Navy Secretaries, and the president herself, was efficient and competent. All casualties are immediately reported for investigation by the military authorities, and also to the state and/or national Solicitor-General's offices; there is no impunity. The efficiency and determination of the team led by García Harfuch was confirmed when on 22 November a major move called Operation *Enjambre* (Swarm), involving 1,500 members of the State of Mexico Solicitor-General's office, the National Guard, the army and navy and the federal and state security departments, seven mayors or security officials of municipalities in that state were arrested and charged with homicide, extortion and kidnapping; it was said they were involved with criminal gangs like the Michoacán Family, the Jalisco New Generation Cartel, Tepito Union, New Empire and Tepito Anti-Union, and the operation was ongoing.[3] In a separate development on the same date federal authorities in Mexico State arrested Alejandro Benítez Palacios, "El Cholo Palacios", said to be head of the "United Warriors" (*Guerreros Unidos*) gang in Guerrero and alleged to be a key figure in the disappearance of the 43 Ayotzinapa students; Alejandro Encinas, a leading investigator of the case, declared that this man may reveal a great deal about the responsibility of public authorities at different levels in the case, and the location of the students' remains.[4]

Of course there are differences within Morena and not all of those who hold public office are really committed to the party's, or the movement's, high ideals. Claudia, like AMLO before her, is well aware that politics requires compromises, and winning two-thirds majorities in the congressional elections required not only massive popular support - which they genuinely achieved - but accepting some candidates who were by no means the most desirable. One such who has a distinctly chequered record is Ricardo Monreal, now leader of Morena in the Chamber of Deputies; as a senator during AMLO's period he at times flirted with the opposition, and had public disagreements with Governor Layda Sansores of Campeche and at one point with the president himself. Just recently he was criticised for using a private helicopter for personal travel; questioned on the matter, Claudia Sheinbaum said this was not in keeping with the principle of civic austerity. Monreal's brother David who is Morena Governor of Zacatecas has also been the object of much criticism.

Another prominent figure who has been much criticised and is seen by many as untrustworthy is Marcelo Ebrard, who was AMLO's Foreign Secretary for a long time and is now Economy Minister; he is undoubtedly very capable, but as we have seen, competed with Claudia for the presidential candidacy and publicly opposed her for a while afterwards. Almost certainly Claudia sees it as preferable to have such powerful figures close to her and accepting the need to collaborate, rather than being in competition or in dispute. Another figure who has aroused criticism is Javier Corral, former Governor of Chihuahua (2016-2021) for the PAN, who in December 2023 declared his support for Morena and was selected as a candidate for the Senate. He was duly elected and has explained his admiration for the achievements of AMLO and belief in public integrity and social justice, and support for Claudia Sheinbaum. However in November 2024 there was a fierce political confrontation over the appointment of a new Chair of the

National Human Rights Commission (CNDH, *Comisión Nacional de Derechos Humanos*); the Senate has to vote on a slate of three candidates, and the winner must have a two-thirds majority.[5] Morena and its allies favoured re-election of the outgoing Chair, Rosario Piedra Ibarra, who was vigorously opposed by the opposition. After a long and difficult debate Rosario Piedra Ibarra was re-elected with 87 of 128 votes; among those who opposed her was Javier Corral. Although the CNDH is not supposed to be political, the view of many commentators is that human rights have been used by the opposition as a tool to attack AMLO and the Fourth Transformation, and especially now they are losing control of the judiciary, the right wing want to use this all-important institution to discredit Claudia Sheinbaum and the continuing transformation process.[6] Claudia herself studiously avoided taking a public position, but there is no doubt she is aware of the issue's importance.

Claudia's triumph at the G20

While dealing with such difficult issues Claudia is moving ahead decisively with the agenda of change. She made it clear that she would travel to Brazil for the G20 summit of leading industrial countries in order to reassert Mexico's international standing. Following AMLO's example she took an ordinary commercial flight, with a stopover in Panama for a brief meeting with that country's president. In Rio de Janeiro on 18 November in the first session on "The Struggle Against Hunger and Poverty", she gave a speech which put most of her colleagues to shame, proposing that they should devote 1% of their military spending to finance the biggest reforestation programme in history, replicating Mexico's *Sembrando Vida* project internationally. This would provide $24 billion US a year (12 times what Mexico was already spending itself) to support six million cultivators in reforesting 15 million hectares, equivalent to four times the territory of Denmark, or Guatemala, Belize and El Salvador together. This would mitigate global warming and restore the social fabric by removing families from poverty. "What is happening in our world that in just two years spending on arms grew almost three times as much as the global economy?" she asked. "How is it that the economy of destruction grew by more than 2.4 billion dollars? How is it that more than 700 million people in the world still live below the poverty line? It is absurd, senseless that there is more spending on arms than in dealing with poverty or climate change. We could reduce migration and hunger if only we raised the word love above hate, the generosity of the humble and dispossessed above greed and the desire for domination...the proposal is that instead of sowing wars we should sow peace and sow life".[7]

She explained how since 2018 Mexico had been building a new project thanks to Mexican Humanism, with the model of a Moral Economy and shared prosperity expressed in the principle "for the good of all, first the poor", leaving behind the neoliberal dogma with its idea that the market would solve all problems. Among the OECD countries Mexico was one of the least indebted, with least unemployment and where the minimum wage had more than doubled in six years; where public education and health are rights, and 80% of families receive support directly from the state. At the same time there are record levels of foreign investment and reserves in the Bank of Mexico. "Railways, roads, ports and airports are being built, poverty has been reduced by more than 9 million people and inequality is declining. Democracy, freedom, pluralism and the right to dissent exist, the institutions of security and justice are being strengthened and peace is being constructed". She had the honour of being the first woman president of the country, and "I did not arrive alone, women peasants, migrants, workers and professionals, our grandmothers, our daughters and granddaughters, all Mexican women have arrived".

In Rio Claudia had several meetings with other world leaders, and returning home on the evening of 19 November she immediately resumed a hectic domestic schedule. The next day, 20 November, was the anniversary of the outbreak of the great 1910 revolution, and she presided over the customary parade followed by a dramatic theatrical representation of all aspects of the epic struggle. Then with the environment and agriculture secretaries, the director of the National Water Commission Conagua, and other relevant officials she presented a comprehensive National Water Plan to improve water supplies across the country, for human consumption, irrigation and industrial use in the difficult situation caused by climate change; indeed, a few days later this was formalised with the signing by the President, the director of Conagua, several other officials and governors (or their representatives) of all 32 states, of the National Agreement on Water for Human Consumption and Sustainability.[8] She also announced greater funding and expansion for free public higher education with the Benito Juárez Welfare Universities (created by AMLO and providing access to students from deprived communities), the new Health Universities and the Rosario Castellanos University which she had founded in Mexico City when she was Metro Mayor (now with 13 campuses and 60,000 students from deprived backgrounds in the capital), which would now become a nation-wide institution with new campuses opening in Chiapas and Baja California.[9]

It should also be pointed out that the 4T is not only advancing through governmental initiatives; Morena is being reinforced as a mass party through tireless and systematic work led by its new president Luisa María Alcalde, who travels the length and breadth of the country for public meetings. Political consciousness is also being raised with intensive debate and discussions, both live and on social media, promoted by *INFP Morena*, the party's National Institute of Political Training, which invites outstanding intellectuals both young and old, Mexican and international.

The threat of a new Trump administration

The confidence and determination of Claudia Sheinbaum, but also of Morena and its allies and of the Mexican people, are remarkable. This is all the more important as they now have to face the prospect of Donald Trump as US President, with an extreme right administration displaying a hostile agenda in a very unpredictable scenario. It includes as Secretary of State none other than Marco Rubio, ringleader of the most extreme Cuban-American mafia who has revived the wet dreams of the most aggressive Republicans. Anti-communist declarations and threats against Cuba, Venezuela and Nicaragua are combined with condemnation of Lula in Brazil, Gustavo Petro in Colombia and Mexico with its Fourth Transformation and its "apology for the Cuban dictatorship". Trump's promise to deport millions of illegal immigrants "starting on day one" are a direct threat to many Mexicans as well as other Latin Americans and people of diverse origins. There have been threats to classify cartels as "terrorists" in order to justify sending in US special forces on armed raids into Mexico. As for trade, swingeing new tariffs on Chinese goods could be accompanied by similar barriers against Mexican exports. Moreover the prominence in the new administration of Elon Musk ("We will coup whoever we want") is another reason for alarm.

How much of this delirious agenda Trump would actually implement is another matter. Mexicans remember the threats he made when AMLO was elected, and how a combination of firmness, diplomacy and astuteness by the Mexican president succeeded in averting disaster, and indeed led to surprisingly good relations between the two ideologically-opposed presidents. Claudia's reaction so far has shown a calm, resolute and confident attitude which can only be admired. When Trump's victory was confirmed and Kamala Harris conceded on 7 November, Claudia sent official congratulations, and soon afterwards she had a phone conversation with the president-elect which she said went very well, and that among other things Trump had expressed his nostalgia for his good relationship with AMLO.

Moreover Claudia Sheinbaum's forceful and dignified position was dramatically reaffirmed on 26 November 2024 with a public letter she sent to President-Elect Trump, spelling out to him in no uncertain terms the reality of Mexican-US relations in trade, migration and narcotics control.[10] "You are probably not aware that Mexico has developed an integral policy with regard to migrants from different parts of the world who cross our territory and have as their goal the southern border of the USA"; your own figures show a 75% reduction in this from December 2023 to November 2024, and half of those who arrive do so with a legal appointment granted by your CBP One programme. But "it is clear that we must achieve together a different model of labour mobility …[with] attention to the causes leading families to leave their places of origin…If a percentage of what the United States spends on war were dedicated to building peace and development", the root of the problem would be addressed. As for the epidemic of fentanyl in the US, "which is a problem of consumption and public health of your society", Mexico has always shown a willingness to help. "So far this year Mexican armed forces and legal agencies have confiscated tons of drugs of different kinds and 10,340 weapons and arrested 15,640 individuals for violence related to drug trafficking", and we are debating a constitutional reform to make the production and distribution of fentanyl and other synthetic drugs a serious offence with no right of bail. "You must also be aware of the illegal arms traffic which arrives in my country from the US. 70% of the illegal weapons seized from criminals in Mexico come from your country"; we don't produce the arms or drugs, but unfortunately those killed by criminals to supply demand in your country are Mexicans. "President Trump, it is not with threats or tariffs that the migration phenomenon or the consumption of drugs in the US will be resolved"; we need cooperation and understanding. A tariff will provoke another one in response and will endanger common enterprises like General Motors, Stellantis and Ford; it will only lead to inflation and loss of jobs for both countries.

Almost certainly Trump was not expecting such a dignified and unflinching response; no Mexican president for decades has taken such a firm position. This produced immediate and unexpected results with Trump's declaration on the evening of 27 November, saying he had had an excellent conversation with President Claudia Sheinbaum and that she had resolved his concerns about migration, narcotics and trade. In other words, his bark was much worse than his bite, and Claudia's firmness had produced a much more positive outcome than anyone expected. The Mexican President has also made her position clear to Canada, where right-wing Ontario Premier Doug Ford made offensive remarks about Mexico and Prime Minister Justin Trudeau has been equivocal in his declarations. Diplomacy is passing strange, but if it works, so much the better. With the unpredictability of the senile Biden in his final two months, never mind what the Republicans may actually bring as time goes on, there is every reason to be concerned, but panic should also be avoided. For those of us who admire and identify with Mexico's Fourth Transformation, redoubled solidarity and vigilance are the order of the day.

NOTES

1 www.gob.mx/presidencia/es/articulos/version-estenografica-inicio-de-trabajos-preliminares-para-la-construccion-del-tren-mexico-queretaro?idiom=es Accessed 18/11/2024.
2 www.diputados.gob.mx/LeyesBiblio/ref/cpeum_crono.htm Accessed 18/11/2024; this covers all the reforms discussed in these paragraphs.
3 www.jornada.com.mx/noticia/2024/11/24/estados/edomex-publicas-las-audiencias-de-los-7-funcionarios-detenidos-6335. Accessed 24/11/2024.
4 www.milenio.com/policia/detienen-a-presunto-jefe-de-plaza-de-guerreros-unidos-en-edomex, 22/11/2024. Accessed 24/11/2024. Also @A_Encinas_R on "X", 23/11/2024. Accessed 24/11/2024.
5 www.sdpnoticias.com/mexico/cndh-camara-de-senadores-elige-hoy-12-de-noviembre-a-nuevo-titular-rosario-piedra-ibarra-se-podria-quedar-fuera/ Accessed 19/11/2024.
6 www.youtube.com/live/Pc5_8iAXRDw Luis Guillermo Hernández, "La guerra contra Rosario Piedra", Accessed 18/11/2024.
7 www.gob.mx/presidencia/prensa/en-g20-presidenta-claudia-sheinbaum-propone-destinar-1-del-gasto-militar-a-programa-de-reforestacion-mas-grande-de-la-historia Accessed 18/11/2024
8 www.gob.mx/presidencia/ Morning Press Conference, 25/11/2024. Accessed live.
9 www.gob.mx/presidencia/ Morning Press Conference, 21/11/2024. Accessed live.
10 http://www.gob.mx/presidencia/blog Versión estenográfica. Conferencia de prensa de la presidenta Claudia Sheinbaum Pardo del 26 de noviembre de 2024. Accessed 27/11/2024.

Conclusion

If there is one fundamental message to be drawn from the analysis presented in this volume, it is that since 2018 Mexico has undergone a process of change which no-one anticipated and which is nothing short of revolutionary. Those who fail to recognise this are stuck in outdated and often dogmatic paradigms, or else they are not paying sufficient attention to the reality of events in Mexico.

One point needs to be stated right away: if AMLO and Morena had not triumphed in 2018, Mexico today would be a disaster area on an unprecedented scale, totally dominated by the most reactionary interests, no doubt with US military bases in several areas and with massive social unrest and despair. The 2018 victory changed everything, which is why the right is so furious. At first they probably believed AMLO would fail, but by 2020 or so when they realised that the Fourth Transformation was for real and was steadily advancing, they embarked on systematic sabotage, only to find that their tactics were less and less successful.

Central to AMLO's (and now Claudia's) success is "Civic Austerity" and the fight against corruption, including the war on tax evasion. Leftist critics repeatedly draw attention to the fact that taxes on the rich have not been increased, implying that in this the 4T governments are conforming to neoliberal and conservative dogma. What they fail to appreciate is the enormous increase in tax receipts and public resources resulting from effective taxation and austerity, not for the poor but for the rich and powerful. A Portuguese Communist friend understood this perfectly when I explained to him that AMLO was not increasing tax rates but making tax collection really effective: "But that" – he exclaimed – "is an increase in taxes!" The rich in Mexico understand this full well, which is why some of them like Ricardo Salinas Pliego go to enormous lengths to defy the law and avoid payment. Some tax increase may not be ruled out in the longer term: in response to a question Claudia recently said that before considering tax reform, there was still a need for greater enforcement of tax collection.[1]

Mexico's restoration of energy sovereignty is also a crucial move which is greatly underrated by most commentators. Insisting on national control of oil, gas, electric power and lithium has fundamentally transformed the country's prospects, and the 4T presidents have not been shy about using the term "nationalisation" and quoting Lázaro Cárdenas and Adolfo López Mateos in describing those who oppose it as traitors to the nation.

This goes along with the general restoration of the public sector as having economic primacy: not only PEMEX and the CFE, but public ownership of many of the railways starting with the Tren Maya, and of new airports like the AIFA and the "Felipe Carrillo Puerto" Tulum airport, and of ports and other key infrastructure.

The welfare programmes also – public universal pensions, incapacity benefit, restoration of free public education at all levels, free universal healthcare, and so many other free benefits which need not be repeated here – are not only progressive, but in effect increase the economic scope of the public sphere on a scale which has few if any parallels in the "Western world". Moreover the fact that these benefits are delivered direct to citizens without intermediaries via a public Welfare Bank is of great significance. Commercial banks have lost an important share of the market.

While seeking collaboration with important sectors of private capital and welcoming foreign investment on Mexico's terms, the 4T is not only anti-neoliberal but in some respects anti-capitalist, if by capitalism we understand a system in which private profit has primacy. Also in its unwavering solidarity with Cuba and its defence of sovereignty and self-determination of all nations, it is anti-imperialist.

Participatory democracy is also advancing in very important ways: such programmes as "The School Is Ours" and "The Clinic Is Ours" are outstanding in this respect. The constitutional recognition of Indigenous and Afro-Mexican rights including a large measure of self-government and territorial autonomy is another aspect of this. The right of presidential recall, being extended to other public officials, and rights of consultation and legislative initiative, point in the same direction.

Labour rights have also advanced in fundamental respects: free union elections and greater enforcement of the right to organise have been accompanied by effective equal pay legislation, rights for domestic workers and the end of outsourcing and fire-and-rehire.

Finally there is perhaps the most controversial aspect of AMLO's (and now Claudia's) policy: the role of the military as a guarantee of public security, sovereignty, infrastructure development and welfare. The insistence on the military as the people in uniform and on their revolutionary and patriotic roots has been crucial in ensuring the success of the Fourth Transformation, and the development of the National Guard as the federal police force, with human rights training but under military supervision, has been very popular; in my view this is one of the most important aspects of the whole process. For those who express concern about human rights, it must be said that the 4T governments have ensured that the military, the National Guard, police and other officials respect human rights, any violations that occur are immediately reported and investigated and there is no impunity. Such violations as still occur are overwhelmingly due to actions of opposition-controlled states or municipalities, and federal authorities are doing all they can to prevent this. As for the quest for justice for previous abuses (like Ayotzinapa), this is extremely difficult and the 4T authorities are making a great effort to resolve such issues in the face of ongoing obstruction and corruption by the judiciary, which should be much reduced by the current reforms.

Another fundamental aspect of the Fourth Transformation is communication: the *mañanera* press conferences have an impact which has no parallel elsewhere, and public support for independent media is bearing fruit. The concept of Mexican Humanism has taken root, with ideals of social justice, democracy and equality, and the conviction – which President Claudia Sheinbaum never tires of repeating – that Mexico is a free, independent and sovereign country. In this respect also the role of the military is crucial, and it will not have escaped the attention of the most reactionary and interventionist interests that a coup is inconceivable and that if it were ever to be necessary, the military would not hesitate to defend national sovereignty.

Claudia Sheinbaum's clarity and firmness paid off in remarkable fashion with Trump's totally unexpected acceptance of her position, as expressed in their conversation on 27 November. His bark has once again (as occurred with AMLO) proved to be much worse than his bite, but this is undoubtedly a result of Claudia's assertion of dignity and independence which is an example to the world. This of course does not mean all has been resolved: Trump continues to make declarations about mass deportations, and his "Border Czar" Thomas Homan is on record as favouring use of the Armed Forces to round up and deport illegal immigrants; talk continues in the Trump camp about armed raids against "terrorist" cartels. Furthermore, showing that such hysteria is not limited to right-wing Republicans, even the supposedly liberal *New York Times* recently published a very dubious article claiming to show a fentanyl lab its reporters had visited in Sinaloa. But Trump and his associates are well aware of the economic chaos that would result from any such disruption of the lucrative trans-border trade.

US imperialism's fury against progressive Latin America is clearly bipartisan, as shown by the Biden administration's recent decisions to establish a base in Ecuador's ecologically sensitive Galapagos islands and to send 600 troops to bolster the extremely unpopular Boluarte dictatorship in Peru. What they will achieve other than to increase their already overwhelming unpopularity in the region is a moot question, but it shows US desperation to retain access to the region's resources. The incoming Republican administration in the US may still pose a threat to Mexico due to actions of right-wing state governors and foreign policy issues such as Cuba, and there is still reason to anticipate difficult times for Mexico.

Mexico's unflinching stand, repeated in recent days by Claudia Sheinbaum, has earned praise from across Latin America and the world, and its strong economic and political bargaining position may yet enable cooler heads to prevail. It has an unrivalled network of 52 consulates in the US prepared to take all possible legal and diplomatic steps to protect its citizens; they may even persuade irate Republicans to negotiate. There is reason to believe that Mexico may resist US hostility successfully, but the threat remains very serious and has to be denounced in no uncertain terms. Solidarity, above all from those of us in the UK and the US, could not be more important.

NOTES

1   www.gob.mx/presidencia/ Morning Press Conference, 25/11/2024. Accessed live.

THIS PAGE INTENTIONALLY BLANK

Bibliographical Note

This is not a regular bibliography because, as explained in the Introduction, the English-language literature on the Fourth Transformation is very deficient. Journalistic articles abound, a great many of very poor quality in the mainstream media, and many in alternative media, some of good quality; I will list the most useful and well-informed authors and websites. These include above all the US-based Mexico Solidarity Project, https://mexicosolidarityproject.org, with its Mexico Solidarity Media including its English-language podcast Soberania https://mexicosolidarity.com/soberania/ and on social media https://www.facebook.com/MexicoSolidarityProject/ and https://twitter.com/MexSolidarity.

Then here in the UK there is our own Mexico Solidarity Forum with its website https://e-voice.org.uk/mexicosolidarity-2/. Well-informed authors who write regularly on social media include Kurt Hackbarth, José Luis Granados Ceja, Bruce Hobson, Meizhu Lui, Agatha Hinman, Pedro Gellert, Jay Watts, Jesús Hermosillo, Étienne Von Bertrab, William A Booth, John M Ackerman, Edwin Ackerman (no relation), María Pérez Ramos, Andrew Paxman and Ioan Grillo. Progressive journals and websites that are worth following for occasional Mexican-themed articles include the *Morning Star, Tribune, New Left Review, Jacobin, The Nation, Monthly Review, Latin American Perspectives, NACLA Report on the Americas*, alborada.net and Latin America Bureau.

What follows is a listing of the books in both English and Spanish which were most useful in the preparation of this volume.

BOOKS

Benítez, Fernando, *Lázaro Cárdenas y la Revolución mexicana, III. El cardenismo*, 3a ed., México, 2023: Fondo de Cultura Económica.

Cano, Arturo, *Claudia Sheinbaum: Presidenta*, México, 2023: Grijalbo.

Cárdenas, Lázaro, *Obras: I - Apuntes 1913-1940*, México, 1972: UNAM.

Gómez Bruera, Hernán, *Traición en Palacio: El negocio de la justicia en la 4T*, México, 2023: Grijalbo.

Gómez Urrutia, Napoleón, *Collapse of Dignity: The Story of a Mining Tragedy and the Fight Against Greed and Corruption in Mexico*, Dallas, TX, 2013: BenBella Books.

Gómez Urrutia, Napoleón, *El Triunfo de la Dignidad: Una Historia Extraordinaria de Convicciones, Lucha y Esperanza*, México, 2021: La Jornada/MAPorrúa.

Johnson, William Weber, *Heroic Mexico: The Narrative History of a Twentieth-Century Revolution*, Garden City, New York, 1968: Doubleday.

López Obrador, Andrés Manuel, *¡Oye, Trump!* México, 2017: Planeta

López Obrador, Andrés Manuel, *A New Hope for Mexico: Saying No to Corruption, Violence and Trump's Wall*, London, 2018: Pluto, translated by Natascha Uhlmann.

López Obrador, Andrés Manuel, *A la Mitad del Camino*, México, 2021: Planeta.

López Obrador, Andrés Manuel, *Hacia una Economía Moral*, México, 2019: Planeta.

López Obrador, Andrés Manuel, *¡Gracias!* México, 2024: Planeta.

Maria y Campos, Armando de, *Múgica: Crónica Biográfica*, México, 1939: Compañía de Ediciones Populares.

Meyer, Lorenzo, *El Poder Vacío: El agotamiento de un régimen sin legitimidad en México*, México, 2019: Debate.

Muhr, Thomas (ed), *Counter-Globalization and Socialism in the 21st Century: The Bolivarian Alliance for the Peoples of Our America*, London & New York, 2013: Routledge.

Paoli, Francisco J, y Enrique Montalvo, *El Socialismo Olvidado de Yucatán*, México, 1977, Siglo XXI Editores.

Raby, David L, *Educación y Revolución Social en México (1921-1940)*, México, 1974, SepSetentas.

Sader, Emir, *The New Mole: Paths of the Latin American Left*, London, 2011, Verso.

Salmerón, Pedro, *La División del Norte: La tierra, los hombres y la historia de un ejército del pueblo*, México, 2006: Planeta.

Salmerón, Pedro, *1918: México en guerra*, Booket/Ediciones Culturales Paidós.

Scherer, Julio y Carlos Monsiváis, *Parte de Guerra: Tlatelolco 1968*, México, 1999: Nuevo Siglo - Aguilar.

NEW FROM PRAXIS PRESS

Languages of Class Struggle is an account of five significant episodes in the history of the working-class movements in Britain and Ireland which, to various degrees, challenged the power of the capitalist state.

JOHN FOSTER uses these case studies to stress the importance of language, of how arguments are constructed to mobilise for change but also how social barriers obstruct revolutionary transformations.

The author discusses Marxist theories of language, especially those developed in the early Soviet Union, which integrated the processes of thought, language and action. If properly applied, he argues, these can create the conditions for the effective communication of class consciousness and thereby mass mobilisation.

Languages of Class Struggle recovers and re-emphasises the arguments advanced by Marx and Lenin, namely that it is capitalism's own contradictions, economic and political, that can – once actively exposed – be used to challenge ruling-class power. It is these moments of crisis and the contradictions they lay bare that are critical for our understanding of social change.

redlettetterspp.com/collections/john-foster

RECENT TITLES

Robert Griffiths is general secretary of the Communist Party and a prolific author on Marxism and labour history. Two of his latest works, published by Praxis Press, are *A Voice for Freedom*, about the life of Welsh internationalist David Ivon Jones and *'The Gleam of Socialism'* a collection of writings on the Communist Party in Britain.

redlettetterspp.com/collections/robert-griffiths

ESSENTIAL READING ON CHINA

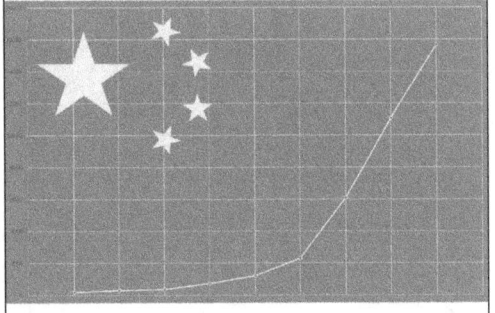

China has undergone a stunning transformation since the 1949 revolution and in particular since the economic reform period begun in 1978.

But how do Marxists explain this astonishing change? Should socialists support or oppose today's People's Republic of China?

These books from Praxis Press set out to provide answers both by analysing the underlying principles of 'socialism with Chinese characteristics' and its application.

redlettetterspp.com/collections/china

MARXIST THEORY

MAKING OUR OWN HISTORY by Jonathan White
A brilliant introduction to the Marxist approach to understanding and participating in social change.

MARX200
Leading scholars and activists from different countries – including Cuba, India and the UK – show that Marx's ideas continue to provide us with the analysis we need to understand our world today.

A PROMETHEAN VISION by Eric Rahim
"This small book is a very useful account of how Marx came to develop his materialist conception of history." Michael Löwy, *New Politics*

SOCIALIST HISTORY

LINE OF MARCH by Max Adereth
A new edition of Max Adereth's historical analysis of British communism, focusing on the development of the party's various programmes. First published 1994.

1000 DAYS OF REVOLUTION
A fascinating account of the Allende Presidency, the dilemmas of peaceful and armed struggles for socialism, the role of US imperialism and domestic right-wing forces, and a self critical evaluation of the role of Chilean communists.

HARDBOILED ACTIVIST by Ken Fuller
A critical review of the work and politics of writer Dashiell Hammett, crime fiction legend, communist and staunch opponent of McCarthyism.

MANIFESTO PRESS

MANIFESTO PRESS publishes working-class history, socialist theory and the politics of class struggle. It is republican and anti-imperialist; secular and feminist; anti-fascist and anti-racist; committed to working class political power, popular sovereignty and progressive culture.

You can browse and order Manifesto Press titles online at
www.redletterspp.com/collection/manifesto-press or
www.manifestopress.coop/

www.ingramcontent.com/pod-product-compliance
Lightning Source LLC
Chambersburg PA
CBHW070317230426
43663CB00011B/2169